LITERATURES OF EXILE IN
REVOLUTION AND ITS AFTEF

Original and thought-provoking, this collection sheds new light on an important yet understudied feature of seventeenth-century England's political and cultural landscape: exile. Through an essentially literary lens, exile is examined both as physical departure from England – to France, Germany, the Low Countries and America – and as inner, mental withdrawal. In the process, a strikingly wide variety of contemporary sources comes under scrutiny, including letters, diaries, plays, treatises, translations and poetry. The extent to which the richness and disparateness of these modes of writing militates against or constructs a recognizable 'rhetoric' of exile is one of the book's overriding themes. Also under consideration is the degree to which exilic writing in this period is intended for public consumption, a product of private reflection, or characterized by a coalescence of the two. Importantly, this volume extends the chronological range of the English Revolution beyond 1660 by demonstrating that exile during the Restoration formed a meaningful continuum with displacement during the civil wars of the mid-century. This in-depth and overdue study of prominent and hitherto obscure exiles, conspicuously diverse in political and religious allegiance yet inextricably bound by the shared experience of displacement, will be of interest to scholars in a range of disciplines.

Philip Major teaches English at Birkbeck College, University of London. He has published widely on seventeenth-century literature and is currently writing a monograph on the works of Thomas, 3rd Lord Fairfax.

Literatures of Exile
in the English Revolution
and its Aftermath, 1640–1690

Edited by

PHILIP MAJOR
Birkbeck College, University of London, UK

Routledge
Taylor & Francis Group

LONDON AND NEW YORK

First published 2010 by Ashgate Publishing

2 Park Square, Milton Park, Abingdon, Oxfordshire OX14 4RN
711 Third Avenue, New York, NY 10017

Routledge is an imprint of the Taylor & Francis Group, an informa business

First issued in paperback 2018

British Library Cataloguing in Publication Data
Literatures of exile in the English Revolution and its aftermath, 1640–1690. – (Transculturalisms, 1400–1700)
    1. Exiles' writings, English – History and criticism. 2. Exile (Punishment) in literature – History – 17th century. 3. Great Britain – History – Commonwealth and Protectorate, 1649–1660 – Historiography. 4. Great Britain – History – Charles II, 1660–1685 – Historiography.
    I. Series II. Major, Philip.
    820.9'3552'09032–dc22

Library of Congress Cataloging-in-Publication Data
Major, Philip.
  Literatures of exile in the English Revolution and its aftermath, 1640–1690 / by Philip Major with a foreword by Lisa Jardine.
    p. cm. – (Transculturalisms, 1400–1700)
  Includes bibliographical references and index.
    1. Great Britain—History—Civil War, 1642–1649—Literature and the revolution. 2. Great Britain—History—Puritan Revolution, 1642–1660—Literature and the revolution. 3. English literature—Early modern, 1500–1700—History and criticism. 4. Exile (Punishment) in literature. 5. Exiles' writings, English—History and criticism. 6. Exiles in literature. 7. Revolutionary literature, English—History and criticism. 8. Royalists in literature. 9. Literature and history—Great Britain—History—17th century. I. Title.
  PR435.M28 2010
  820.9'358—dc22

                  2010005635

ISBN 978-1-4094-0006-6 (hbk)
ISBN 978-1-138-37958-9 (pbk)

Contents

List of Figures

List of Contributors

Christopher D'Addario is Assistant Professor of English at Towson University, where he teaches early modern English literature. In addition to other essays, he is the author of *Exile and Journey in Seventeenth-Century Literature* (Cambridge, 2007). He is currently working on a study of the aesthetics of everyday life in seventeenth-century London.

Katrien Daemen-de Gelder is a postdoctoral researcher at Ghent University. Her primary areas of interest include sixteenth- and seventeenth-century Scottish and English literature, particularly Anglo- and Scoto-Dutch relations during the reign of James VI and I (1566–1625). She is currently conducting research with Jean-Pierre Vander Motten into the literary and intellectual impact of the English exiles in the Spanish Netherlands between 1603 and 1688.

Ann Hughes is Professor of Early Modern History at the University of Keele, and has published widely on the religion, politics and print culture of mid-seventeenth-century England. Her latest book is *Gangraena and the Struggle for the English Revolution* (Oxford, 2004).

Marika Keblusek is Professor of Book History at the University of Amsterdam and lecturer in art history at Leiden University. She recently co-curated the exhibition 'Royalist Refugees: William and Margaret Cavendish at the Rubenshuis, 1648–1660' at the Rubenshuis Museum, Antwerp. She is working on several book projects, including *'Minds of Winter': Literary Life and Book Culture of Royalists in Exile in the Netherlands, 1642–1660*, and *Double Agents: Cultural and Political Brokerage in Early Modern Europe*. In 2006 *Your Humble Servant: Agents in Early Modern Europe* (ed. and introduction) was published.

James Loxley is Senior Lecturer in English Literature at the University of Edinburgh. He is the author of *Royalism and Poetry in the English Civil Wars: The Drawn Sword* (Macmillan, 1997), *The Complete Critical Guide to Ben Jonson* (Routledge, 2002) and *Performativity* (Routledge, 2006). Published articles include: 'On Exegetical Duty: Historical Pragmatics and the Grammar of the Libel', *Huntington Library Quarterly*, 69 (2006); 'Cavalier Poetry', in David Scott Kastan, ed., *The Oxford Encyclopaedia of British Literature* (New York: Oxford University Press, 2006); and 'Performatives and Performativity: Ben Jonson Makes His Excuses', *Renaissance Drama*, 33 (2004).

Philip Major teaches English at Birkbeck, University of London. He has published widely on seventeenth-century literature and is currently writing a monograph on the works of Thomas, 3rd Lord Fairfax, and editing a volume of essays on the life and works of Thomas Killigrew.

Sarah Mortimer is Student and Tutor at Christ Church, Oxford. She is the author of *Reason and Religion in the English Revolution: The Challenge of Socinianism* (Cambridge, 2010), based on her doctoral work, and is co-editing a volume of essays on *The Intellectual Consequences of Religious Heterodoxy 1650–1750* for Brill.

Jason Peacey is Lecturer in History at University College London. In addition to writing a number of articles on the politics and political culture of civil war Britain, he has published *Politicians and Pamphleteers: Propaganda During the English Civil Wars and Interregnum* (Ashgate, 2004), edited *The Regicides and the Execution of Charles I* (Palgrave, 2001), and co-edited (with Chris R. Kyle) *Parliament at Work* (Boydell, 2002). He is currently preparing a monograph on print culture and political participation in seventeenth-century Britain.

Timothy Raylor is Professor of English at Carleton College, Minnesota. His publications include *The Essex House Masque of 1621: Viscount Doncaster and the Jacobean Masque* (2000), *Cavaliers, Clubs, and Literary Culture: Sir John Mennes, James Smith and the Order of the Fancy* (1994), and the edited collection *The Cavendish Circle* (a special issue of *The Seventeenth Century*, 1994), and articles on various aspects of the literary and intellectual history of seventeenth-century England in *English Manuscript Studies, English Literary Renaissance, Historical Journal, Huntington Library Quarterly, Renaissance Quarterly*, and *Renaissance Studies, Review of English Studies*, and *The Seventeenth Century*. He is currently working, with Stephen Clucas, on an edition of *De corpore*, for the Clarendon Hobbes.

Julie Sanders is Professor of English Literature and Drama at the University of Nottingham. She has published widely on seventeenth-century literature. She recently published an edition of James Shirley's *The Bird in a Cage* as part of the Revels edition of *Three Seventeenth-Century Plays on Women and Performance* (MUP, 2006), which she co-edited with Hero Chalmers and Sophie Tomlinson.

Nigel Smith is Professor of English at Princeton University. He has published widely on early modern literature, especially the seventeenth century. His major works are the Longman Annotated English Poets edition of Andrew Marvell's *Poems*, a *TLS* 'Book of the Year' for 2003; *Literature and Revolution in England, 1640–1660* (Yale UP, 1994); and *Perfection Proclaimed: Language and Literature in English Radical Religion 1640–1660* (Oxford UP, 1989). He has also edited the *Journal* of George Fox (1998), and the Ranter pamphlets (1983). He has co-edited (with Nicholas McDowell) *The Oxford Handbook of Milton* (Oxford, 2009), and a biography of Marvell is forthcoming.

J.P. Vander Motten is Professor of English Literature at Ghent University. He has published widely on various aspects of seventeenth-century English literature, especially Restoration drama. He is currently editing (with Olivia Smith) a collection of essays on the northern and southern Netherlands as a literary and cultural 'entrepôt' for seventeenth-century British letters, to be published in a special issue of *English Studies*.

Acknowledgements

Much of the initial stimulus for this book derived from doctoral work undertaken on exile during and after the English Revolution. A debt of gratitude is therefore owed to the stimulating research environment of Birkbeck, University of London, and, more particularly, to my supervisor, Thomas Healy. Tom, it was, who first suggested to me the idea of a conference on the subject of seventeenth-century exile. I am glad he did so, since many of the essays presented here derive from the subsequent international symposium held in London in the summer of 2006. I wish to thank the Institute of English Studies, Michael Baron, my co-organizer Laura Jacobs, and all participants, for making that event such a convivial and intellectually fruitful one.

Along the way, I have had the substantial benefit of discussing exile with a number of distinguished scholars, including Nigel Smith, Paul Davies, Jonathan Scott, Paul Seaward, Susan Wiseman, Geoffrey Smith, Jason McElligott and Colin Brooks. My thanks go to all of them for helping, in one way or another, to shape this book, and my sincere apologies to anyone in this regard whom I have omitted. Finally, I would like to thank Erika Gaffney, Whitney Feininger and Kathy Bond Borie at Ashgate for steering this project through to publication with a happy blend of expertise and good humour.

Abbreviations

Add. MS	Additional Manuscript
BL	British Library
CClSP	*Calendar of the Clarendon State Papers*, ed. O. Ogle et al., 5 vols (Oxford: Clarendon Press, 1869–1970)
CSPC	*Calendar of State Papers Colonial, America and West Indies*
CSPD	*Calendar of State Papers Domestic*
JHC	*Journals of the House of Commons*
JHL	*Journals of the House of Lords*
ODNB	*Oxford Dictionary of National Biography*
TSP	*A Collection of the State Papers of John Thurloe, Esq.*, ed. Thomas Birch, 7 vols (London, 1742)

Foreword

Lisa Jardine

Those of us who studied seventeenth-century Britain at the end of the twentieth century were taught that the 'English Revolution' – as we were encouraged to call the period 1642–1660 – was a seamless period of intellectual growth, inventiveness and creativity, interrupted temporarily by Charles II's return to the throne, then reinvigorated with the arrival of the joint constitutional monarchs William III and Mary Stuart, in 1688. The great Marxist historian Christopher Hill showed us that English literature and political understanding were fostered by the Cromwellian Republic; the brilliant historian of science Charles Webster explained how Francis Bacon's 'Great Instauration' was converted from Royalist romance to achieved reality in the energetic, forward-looking environment of Republican Britain.

In those days, we paid scant attention to those who preferred to refer to the period as the 'Interregnum' – an unfortunate interruption to deep-rooted indigenous literary and artistic traditions. For them the continuity of culture had been interrupted by the English Civil Wars. They treated the period as a deep and damaging fissure across British history, implying that all that was intellectually great and productive fled to the continent (as we called mainland Europe), returning to active life only once republican rule was finally over. Cut off from their homeland, the royalists suffered emotional distress, dislocation and penury. Those they met and mingled with were merely a distraction until they were able to return to the newly restored Stuart kingdom, at which time they reconnected with the agendas and tradition from which they had so long been cut off.

The reality was, of course, far more complex, and there has long been a need for corrective scholarly work, a period of reassessment, regardless of which 'camp' one had previously belonged to. The present book is part of a grand and widespread current rehabilitation of the cultural and intellectual life of Britain in the period 1640–1690 which has been taking place in recent years. Its most important revisionist feature, I believe, is the fact that it engages with its 'exiles' in a Europe without national boundaries to literary and cultural creativity. It does not allow its attention to rest – or be arrested – at national boundaries, but instead extends its historical attention so as to include the experience of Britons during the period 1640–1690 in the mainland European countries where first the so-called royalists and then (after 1660) ardent republicans sought refuge.

There was, Philip Major argues in his 'Introduction', a particular quality of attention which those who continued their intellectual and literary lives as exiles displayed. 'Exile' is a condition which places a special kind of strain on every aspect of a person's life. Nevertheless, what these exiles learned from those they sometimes reluctantly engaged with contributed in important ways to their ways of thinking and writing once they returned. There were, too, continuous currents of intellectual exchange between those in exile and those who remained behind. Only if we recognize this and take account of it can the intellectual and cultural history of the British Isles in the second half of the seventeenth century be fully understood.

The essays in *Literatures of Exile* are eloquent testimony to the increased depth and richness to be discovered, if we scrutinize the surviving literary materials from this tumultuous political period inclusively – from both inside and outside Britain. I add one further example here, which I came across in my own research into the early Royal Society in London (which received its first Royal Charter in 1662), which came entirely as a surprise to me, and which has permanently altered my view of the distinguished individual it concerns. It will serve, I hope, additionally to underline the importance of examining English-language literary works from this period in a broad European context, in order properly to understand them.

An early biographer of Robert Boyle (1627–1691), seventh son of the Earl of Cork, and prominent member of the Royal Society in London, records that 'in February 1647–8, [he] made a voyage to Holland, partly to visit the country, and partly to accompany his brother Francis in conducting his wife from The Hague. But he did not stay long there, for on the 15th of April, 1648, he was at London'.[1]

Robert Boyle's personal fortunes were closely tied to those of his brother Francis, five years older, with whom he had spent four years being educated at Eton. In 1638, when Francis was 15 and Robert going on 10, an advantageous marriage was arranged for the older boy, somewhat precipitately (at the behest of the king), to one of Queen Henrietta Maria's ladies-in-waiting, Elizabeth Killigrew – sister to Thomas Killigrew, the Restoration playwright and theatre manager. Since I am going on to talk about Elizabeth's adventures in Holland, we might note that Thomas Killigrew's life was also permanently altered by his only recently uncovered period of exile there, during the Commonwealth years.[2]

Robert and Francis went together to the court at Whitehall, to pay court to the bride, and were fêted and flattered there, ahead of the main Boyle family party. The extravagant wedding ceremony took place at the palace shortly afterwards, in the presence of the king and queen. Francis's father would have preferred a betrothal, considering his son too young for marriage. Four days later, to the young bridegroom's disappointment, the Earl of Cork prudently arranged for his two sons to leave for France, on a Grand Tour from which they did not return until 1642. Francis's new wife remained at court with Queen Henrietta Maria. On his

---

[1]   *The Life of the Honourable Robert Boyle by Thomas Birch, M.A. and F.R.S.*, (London: A Millar, 1744; reprinted in vol. I of *Works of the Honourable Robert Boyle*, ed. Thomas Birch, 6 vols [London, 1772]). Birch gives his source in a footnote: 'Mr. Boyle's letter to Mr. Marcombes, dated from London, Febr. 22, 1647–8, in which he mentions his intentions of setting out for Holland the next day'.

[2]   See J.P. Vander Motten, 'Thomas Killigrew's "Lost Years", 1655–1660', *Neophilologus*, 82 (1998), 311–34.

return from his Tour, he enlisted to fight for the king as captain of one of the foot companies in Ireland.[3]

In August 1646, when, after the fall of Oxford, the situation for royalists had worsened dramatically, Francis and Elizabeth Boyle were granted a passport to leave England for The Hague with their entire household, to join the court of Mary Stuart, Princess of Orange (Charles I and Henrietta Maria's eldest daughter).[4] Like many others they were presumably expecting to stay there until the outcome of the civil war was decided. However, a year and a half later, in late February 1648, Robert Boyle went to The Hague, hurriedly and at short notice, 'to accompany his brother Francis in conducting his wife from The Hague'.[5] In spite of the urgency, Robert – the inveterate intellectual tourist – took a detour in order to visit a number of places of scientific interest, including the famous anatomy school at Leiden, on which he reported back to the avid information-gatherer Samuel Hartlib. The brothers arrived at The Hague around 24 February.[6]

The real reason Robert Boyle made the trip to Holland in 1648 was to come to the aid of his brother Francis, and to hush up, as far as possible, a major Boyle family scandal. Francis Boyle's wife, Elizabeth Killigrew, was pregnant by the exiled Prince Charles, the future King Charles II. Her daughter, Charlotte Jemima Henrietta Fitzcharles (whom Charles acknowledged as his), was brought up as a Boyle. We may imagine that the 25-year-old Francis Boyle, who had been married, in the presence of royalty, at such an impressionably young age, with such high expectations, was both shocked and shamed. He was, however, as was customary, well taken care of in recompense for his agreement to turn a blind eye to the whole affair, come the Restoration.

Samuel Pepys, who was very close to the negotiations just prior to Charles II's return to England in 1660, records in his diary for 20 March that he provided 'Mr. Boyle' with 'an order for a ship to transport him to Flushing', evidently to meet the king: 'This evening came Mr Boyle on board, for whom I writ an order for a ship to transport him to Flushing. He supped with my Lord [Edward Montagu],

---

[3] *JHC*, 14 October 1642, ii, p. 809.

[4] *JHL*: 'Boyle et al – pass to go to Holland, 22. Car. 1 viii 468 a. "Ordered, That Mr. Boyle and his Wife shall have a pass to go in to Holland; carrying with them Servants, and such Necessaries as are fit for his Journey."' This was exactly the moment when Charles II left Jersey to join his mother at the French Court.

[5] 'In February 1647–8, [he] made a voyage to Holland, partly to visit the country, and partly to accompany his brother Francis in conducting his wife from the Hague. But he did not stay long there, for on the 15th of April, 1648, he was at London; and on the 13th of May at Stalbridge, whence he wrote to his sister Ranelagh, giving her an account, that he should possibly soon send her his thoughts upon the subject of Toleration, in an essay of his, intitled, *Of Divinity*' (Birch, *Life of Boyle*). Birch adds the footnote: 'Mr. Boyle's letter to Mr. Marcombes, dated from London, Febr. 22, 1647–8, in which he mentions his intentions of setting out for Holland the next day.'

[6] Letter from Boyle to Marcombes, 22 February 1647/8, saying that he is leaving for Holland the next day.

my Lord using him as a person of honour.' Shortly afterwards, Charles II elevated Francis Boyle to the Irish title of First Viscount of Shannon, and Francis and his family took up permanent residence in Ireland.

Back at Stalbridge House, which Robert Boyle had made his home in England, in summer 1648, Francis's younger brother sat down to write *Seraphic Love* – a work referred to in the literature as marking a 'deep spiritual crisis at age 21'. In this semi-fictional series of letters to a close cousin and personal friend, who has been heartlessly let down by the woman he passionately loves, Boyle meditates on female wiles, and contrasts the woes of earthly love of woman to the sublimity of angelic love of God. An inveterate, youthful reader of romances, he has learned at first hand that erotic love can lead to heartbreak and disaster. He had watched as the promise of his brother's Whitehall wedding disintegrated into sordid scandal. His observation of his older brother's pain and humiliation is, I suggest, plainly there in the text:

> For the Repulses, the Regrets, the Jealousies, the Fears, the Absences, the Despairs, and the rest of the afflicting Disquiets of Lovers; though in well-writ Romances they are soon read over by the diverted Peruser; yet they are not so soon Weather'd out, nor so easily Supported by the disconsolate Lover, whose infelicities, though they may be perhaps so handsomely deplored, as to Delight the Reader; yet trust me, Lindamor [the name Boyle gives his supposedly fictional addressee], 'tis a much happier condition to be Free from misfortunes, than to be able to Complain eloquently of them.

> And as I have with delight beheld a Storm excellently drawn by some rare Artists Pensil; but when I was this Spring tost by the rude winds, that blew me out of Holland, I found a real Storm a very troublesome and uneasie thing. So the condition of a Lover, though drawn by a smooth Pen, it is wont strangely to affect and please us; yet when men are really engaged in it, they find it full of hardships and disquiet.

> 'Tis a much better condition to be Look'd on, than Embrac'd; and Experience gives men of it much (sadder and) more unwelcome notions than Description did. Nor phancy, Lindamor, that the Troublesomness of your sufferings in Love proceeded but from their not being Acceptable to her for whom you endur'd them; for, had your Mistresse crown'd them with Myrtle, & prov'd as kind to you as Hymen could have made her, yet, I fear, she could have Recompenc'd you but by Disabusing you, and could not have freed you from the Need of happinesse, but onely from a Mistake concerning it.[7]

Ten years later, when he eventually published *Seraphic Love*, Robert Boyle was still adamant, in response to the uxorious John Evelyn's extolling of the bliss of matrimony and the advantages of the company of an educated woman, that celibacy was the only way to avoid pain and disappointment at the hands of the opposite sex. The veiled allusion to the disturbing 'storms' of love – so unlike the

---

[7]   *Seraphic Love* (London, 1660 [second edition]), pp. 45–6.

passions read about in contemporary romances – that he had encountered in The Hague, pointedly 'places' Boyle's preference for devoted love of God over that of any woman.[8] *Seraphic Love* is no abstract, theoretical treatise, in other words, but a young man's visceral response to vicarious erotic pain and disappointment.

Robert Boyle has traditionally been treated as an almost insularly British figure, who in adult life never left the British Isles. His most recent biographer, Michael Hunter, fails to mention the Dutch episode I have just recounted at all.[9] Yet *Seraphic Love* is increasingly acknowledged to be a work which captures essential features of Boyle's complicated intellectual personality, as practising scientist and devout Christian. Meanwhile, the complex formation of that personality, and the progress and development of seventeenth-century science, have increasingly come to be seen as importantly interrelated.[10] Ought we not therefore to notice that a moment of high emotional drama, in exile, formed the basis for Boyle's first articulation of his personal attitude towards both?

Neither Robert Boyle nor any other mid-seventeenth-century intellectual left their lives of the mind behind in the Thames Estuary as they set sail for mainland Europe. Nor did they cease to engage with the intellectual lives of those around them, as they circulated as exiles in communities in France and the Netherlands (in both of which countries significant groups of ex-patriot men and women congregated), and beyond Europe, in the newly formed communities of the New World. Once we recognize this, we retrieve an intricate, continuous web of influence stretching backwards and forwards across the English Channel, the Narrow Sea and the Atlantic Ocean, which both complicates and clarifies developments in art and literature in Britain in the second half of the century.

---

[8] Strictly speaking, the reference to the rescue trip to The Hague is added in 1659 when Boyle published the expanded printed version of *Seraphic Love*, and in its reworked form added some more direct 'clues' to the original occasion, including the reference to the sudden storm at sea and its fearful consequences during the crossing to The Hague, and the age at which he had first encountered disappointment with women. See Lawrence M. Principe, 'Style and Thought of the Early Boyle: Discovery of the 1648 Manuscript of *Seraphic Love*', *Isis*, 85 (1994), 247–60 (pp. 255–6).

[9] Michael Hunter, *Boyle: Between God and Science* (London: Yale University Press, 2009). At pp. 68–9 he asks the question, what decided Boyle to devote himself to a 'Love causing in him a noble heat without the trouble of desire', and never to marry, but he still overlooks the Dutch episode.

[10] See, for example, Steven Shapin, 'Personal Development and Intellectual Biography: The Case of Robert Boyle', *British Journal for the History of Science*, 26 (1993), 335–45; Lawrence M. Principe, 'Virtuous Romance and Romantic Virtuoso: The Shaping of Robert Boyle's Literary Style', *Journal of the History of Ideas*, 56 (1995), 377–97; Michael Hunter, 'Robert Boyle (1627–91), A Suitable Case for Treatment?', *British Journal for the History of Science*, 32 (1999), 261–75.

Introduction

Philip Major

I

Exile, and exilic literature, has long and powerfully imposed itself upon our imagination. Ever since individuals and peoples first sought refuge in foreign climes from political, religious or racial persecution, the written word has attempted to inscribe the myriad psychological, social and cultural experiences of the displaced on readers' hearts and minds. Such writing, it should be conceded, has not always evoked the complexities of exile; one well-placed commentator has observed that 'literature tends to show the romantic side of exile. In reality, people live in exile submerged in trauma'.[1] There is little question, however, that the resurgence of exilic writing precipitated by the seismic geopolitical upheavals and forced migrations of the last century has genuinely extended our knowledge and deepened our understanding of exile. Consequently, there is rich potential for marshalling this modern sensibility to the momentous deracination of earlier centuries. In this respect, the mid-to-late seventeenth century is an abundantly fertile area of enquiry. There are many different ways of looking at the English Revolution and its aftermath, and exile provides a fruitful new lens through which to view this pivotal period in the history of England and the British Isles.

Yet, while exile remains a conspicuous feature on seventeenth-century England's political and literary landscape, surprisingly little of its territory has been mapped. As Christopher D'Addario has observed:

> we have yet to apply this increased knowledge of and sensitivity to the ruptures of exile to the early modern period, where, particularly in seventeenth-century England, an unprecedented number of men and women were forced to flee England or to remain in "internal exile", unreconciled to the ruling authority.[2]

From one angle, the apparent marginalization of exile in the historiography of the English Revolution can be linked to a broader issue – the disproportionately modest levels of modern scholarship devoted towards numerically the most

---

[1] Dubravka Ugrešić, *Nobody's Home*, trans. by Ellen Elias-Bursać (London, San Francisco and Beirut: Telegram, 2007), p. 16. For an influential amplification of this view, see Ian Buruma, 'The Romance of Exile', *The New Republic* (February 12, 2001), 33–8. I am grateful to the publisher's anonymous reader for the helpful comments provided on an earlier version of this Introduction.

[2] Christopher D'Addario, *Exile and Journey in Seventeenth-Century Literature* (Cambridge: Cambridge University Press, 2007), p. 3.

prominent body of mid-seventeenth-century English exiles: royalists. It is difficult to dispute that scholars of the English Civil Wars, from Victorian titans such as S.R. Gardiner onward, have focused predominantly on parliamentarians, with supporters of the monarchy treated essentially as counterfoils rather than as figures of intrinsic importance.[3] Given the range of valuable studies which this focus has yielded, and given the uniqueness of the English republican epoch, it has in many ways been both a productive and an understandable imbalance of attention. Unquestionably, the contours of our understanding of the mid-seventeenth-century have been dramatically reshaped by the plethora of monographs and articles on its panoply of radicals, republicans and revolutionaries. It has been well written, nevertheless, that 'a full understanding of a revolutionary era demands a study of the conservatives as well as the revolutionaries'.[4] The experiences of royalists are inherently important, but they are also, and perhaps more significantly, essential to a wider comprehension of the period as a whole.

The gap is narrowing. Far more critical attention has been trained on royalists over the last two decades, and as a result they no longer seem such a strangely unknowable presence orbiting the edges of the mid-century. We now have an array of studies identifying and exploring constitutional, social and literary aspects of royalism and, relatedly, key features of the royalism/Church of England dyad.[5] One of the aims of this interdisciplinary collection of essays is to augment this growing volume of work illuminating the lives of Stuart supporters. Superficially, at least, it achieves this through its subject matter: seven of the ten essays assembled here mainly concern themselves with royalists. At a deeper thematic level, it engages with important ongoing scholarly discussions about precisely what royalism was. The most fundamental of these centres on royalism's perceived one-dimensionality.

---

[3]   As Jason McElligott has succinctly asserted, 'Royalism has never been particularly fashionable among historians of the English Civil Wars.' *Royalism, Print and Censorship in Revolutionary England* (Woodbridge: Boydell, 2007), p. 2.

[4]   David Underdown, *Royalist Conspiracy in England* (New Haven: Yale University Press, 1960), p. viii.

[5]   See, for example, David L. Smith, *Constitutional Royalism and the Search for Settlement* (Cambridge: Cambridge University Press, 1994); Jerome De Groot, *Royalist Identities* (Basingstoke: Palgrave, 2004); *Royalists and Royalism during the English Civil Wars*, ed. Jason McElligott and David L. Smith (Cambridge: Cambridge University Press, 2007); *Royalists and Royalism during the Interregnum*, ed. Jason McElligott and David L. Smith (Manchester: Manchester University Press, 2010); McElligott, *Royalism, Print and Censorship*; Robert Wilcher, *The Writing of Royalism, 1628–1660* (Cambridge: Cambridge University Press, 2001); James Loxley, *Royalism and Poetry in the English Civil Wars: The Drawn Sword* (Basingstoke: Palgrave, 1997); Lois Potter, *Secret Rites and Secret Writing: Royalist Literature 1641–1660* (Cambridge: Cambridge University Press, 1987); Andrew Lacey, *The Cult of King Charles the Martyr* (Woodbridge: Boydell, 2003); Anthony Milton, *Laudian and Royalist Polemic in Seventeenth-Century England* (Manchester: Manchester University Press, 2007); Hero Chalmers, *Royalist Women Writers 1650–1689* (Oxford: Clarendon Press, 2004).

Until recent years, most of those accounts which were indifferent or faintly hostile to the royalist side, and a good few of those that were sympathetic, tended to paint an unsatisfactorily spare, monochrome picture of royalism, an image only reinforced by the multileveled sectarianism and colourful eclecticism of its parliamentarian counterpart. In this settled view, allegiance to the king was pre-determined, rigid, and uniformly elitist, the notion of women royalists of any moment at best inchoate. If they were distinguishable at all, royalists were constrained within the reductive taxonomy of 'constitutionalists' or 'absolutists'.[6]

Today, the picture is more crowded, more vivid. The conviction grows that royalists are an appreciably more heterogeneous, fluid and, by extension, interesting, topic; their loyalty more individuated, their literature more variegated. The striking pageant of royalists and royalist writing presented in this volume argues for a creed that resists distillation, and reinforces our understanding of 'the diverse opinions and varying degrees of commitment that lay under the broad umbrella of royalist allegiance'.[7] It is the disjunctions as well as the continuities between chapters which contribute to these effects, which ultimately force us to think in terms of 'royalisms' rather than 'royalism'. For modern scholars, if not always for the exiles themselves, displacement generates a paradoxically enabling marginal status: exile is a singularly extreme environment in which people behave in fresh and informative ways; its scrutiny can therefore be used as a tool to prise open traditional assumptions. Filtered through the prism of exile, royalist allegiance to the monarch, for example, can take on the qualities of both imperturbability and perishability: the loyalism of the Duke of Buckingham's co-procurators, Endymion Porter and William Aylesbury, the focus of Katrien Daemen-de Gelder's and Jean-Pierre Vander Motten's chapter, can seem radically different in kind from that of Thomas Hobbes, the cynosure of James Loxley's.

As with royalism generally, though by no means to the same extent, there has been more sustained analysis of the royalist exile in recent years, evidenced in the emergence of penetrating new studies, most notably by Geoffrey Smith and, with a more literary focus, Anna Battigelli and Christopher D'Addario, as well as in the staging of several germane international conferences.[8] This volume positions itself within the wider purview of both Smith and D'Addario, though the respective

---

[6]   For a lucid amplification of which, see David Scott, 'Rethinking Royalist Politics: Faction and Ideology 1642–49', in *The English Civil War: Conflict and Contexts, 1640–49*, ed. John Adamson (Basingstoke: Palgrave Macmillan, 2009), pp. 36–60 (pp. 37–44).

[7]   *Royalists and Royalism during the English Civil Wars*, ed. McElligott and Smith, p. 4.

[8]   *The Cavaliers in Exile* (Basingstoke and New York: Palgrave, 2003); *Margaret Cavendish and the Exiles of the Mind* (Lexington: University of Kentucky Press, 1998); *Exile and Journey*. Reflecting the historiographical bias already alluded to, Smith's was the first comprehensive study of the royalist exile for half a century; that is, since Paul Hardacre's 'The Royalists in Exile During the Puritan Revolution', *Huntington Library Quarterly*, XVI (1953), 353–70. Relevant conferences include 'Royalists and Royalism', University of Cambridge, 23–5 July 2004; 'Englishmen Adrift', Ghent University, 27–9 April 2006; 'Exile in the English Revolution and its Aftermath', University of London,

nodal points vary. Smith's emphasis is on the multiplicity of royalist experiences in exile, and, as I have indicated, both individually and collectively, implicitly and openly, most chapters dovetail neatly with his accent on the royalist 'crowd of fugitives', and 'the diversity of behaviour they exhibited in response to the unfamiliar and difficult situations with which they were confronted'.[9] D'Adddario's starting point, which finds echoes in the literary preoccupations of this book, is the meaning with which exilic writing is invested, the 'centrality of language to the perception of displacement by the exile'.[10] More significantly, for D'Addario the instability of language which he identifies in royalist literature, as the exilic text moves across linguistic, geographic and ideological boundaries, complicates the inflexibly partisan frames of reference with which the writings of this period have often been associated.[11] To a greater or lesser extent these essays pick up on and extend this idea of literary and semantic fragility and oscillation, of displacement as a destabilizing, entropic force. Exile shapes an instability that leaves words unmoored from their former meaning and application, and makes them occupy, like the exiles themselves, a space of tantalizing liminality. This has significant repercussions for the exiles under discussion here; to use Hobbes as an example once more, it can inform a concomitantly wavering political identity.

As this book also illustrates, however, exile in these years was by no means the sole preserve of royalists. It also impacted, at the Restoration, on republican sympathizers. These included two of Cromwell's Major-Generals, the regicides William Goffe and John Dixwell, the focus of the book's two concluding chapters. Here, the relative sparseness of scholarship clearly cannot be explained by a parliamentarian-dominated historiography; yet on the evidence of both essays, there is little doubt that detailed study of the exilic experiences of such men throws new light on the political dynamics and socio-cultural cadences of the period. It is the juxtaposition of figures of diverse political and religious allegiances, royalist and non-royalist, Anglican and puritan alike, yet bound, inextricably, by the experience of exile, through which the originality of this book is most clearly conveyed. This inclusive approach illustrates significant and sometimes surprising contrasts and comparisons between political and religious adversaries. At the same time, the highly individual nature of exile is recognized. In this way, the book offers up new ways of understanding important historical and social issues about mid-seventeenth-century English society, particularly English exile communities, under pressure. These centre on royalist and republican, Church of England and puritan attitudes, self-imagery and propaganda as they relate to notions of victory and defeat, power and impotence, inclusion and exclusion, and the many additional consequences that exile had for family relations.

29–30 July 2006, where most of the studies in this book were first aired; and 'Exile in Early Modern Europe', University of York, 21–2 September 2006.

[9]   *The Cavaliers in Exile*, p. 208.
[10]   *Exile and Journey*, p. 4.
[11]   *Ibid.*, p. 16.

It fails to dim the new light shone on royalism and republicanism in this book that this approach simultaneously helps to demonstrate a blurring, as much as a reinforcement, of long-established factional divides. In some respects it thereby continues the recent movement away from a dominant scholarly paradigm which has tended to polarize seventeenth-century literature into 'royalist' and 'parliamentarian', strictly oppositional, categories. Such binaries have begun to be challenged by analyses which still recognize the politicized inflections of these writings but also, and increasingly, discern their contingency and ambiguity, the traits they share as well as those which distinguish them. Correspondingly, on the resurgent subject of readership, such studies emphasize the overlapping constituencies to which these texts appealed.[12]

II

Until recent years, 1660 was held by the majority of historians and literary scholars to provide an appropriate cut-off point for studies of the English Revolution. However, by extending the chronological range beyond this date to examine the exilic experiences of parliamentarians after the Restoration, this volume shows that, born, as it is, of the same original conflict, exile during the Restoration is irrevocably tied to the displacement of the English Revolution. Indeed, the overlaps and intersections highlighted by a focus on exile contribute meaningfully towards the continuing debate over just when – and where – the English Revolution actually ended.

In this way, the collection aligns itself with two ongoing and interlinked historiographical arguments positing a wider conspectus on and remapped vision of seventeenth-century English history. The case for each has been lucidly made by Jonathan Scott.[13] Put simply, Scott called for the seventeenth century to be seen as a unity, and for England to be seen as European. Of the two, it would be fair to say that the former perspective has been taken up more readily and widely.[14] Pointing to a revisionist-induced dearth in modern explanatory accounts of the century as a whole, Scott persuasively claimed that accounts of the crises of 1618–48, 1678–83 and 1688–89 too often reflect 'the fragmentation of seventeenth-century

---

[12]   For example, by D'Addario, *Exile and Journey*, and Steven Zwicker, *Lines of Authority: Politics and English Literary Culture 1649–1689* (Ithaca and London: Cornell University Press, 1993); Edward Holberton, *Poetry and the Cromwellian Protectorate: Culture, Politics, and Institutions* (Oxford: Oxford University Press, 2008).

[13]   *England's Troubles: Seventeenth-Century English Political Instability in a European Context* (Cambridge: Cambridge University Press, 2000). The central arguments in this work built on those in two earlier studies by Scott: *Algernon Sidney and the English Republic, 1623–1677* (Cambridge: Cambridge University Press, 1988), and *Algernon Sidney and the Restoration Crisis, 1677–1683* (Cambridge: Cambridge University Press, 1991).

[14]   Most recently, D'Addario, for instance, has emphasized the interconnectedness of the exilic writing produced across the century by, among others, puritan exiles in the New World, Hobbes, Milton and Dryden. *Exile and Journey*, passim.

historiography, rather than the continuity of seventeenth-century history'. In this formulation, 1660 is an arbitrary, artificial landmark created in part by a modern fixation on revolution: 'The modern (post-Marxist) assumption both of mid-century revolution, and of revolution implying discontinuity, has reinforced this division of the century into two halves'. Whereas, Scott asserted, the Restoration period has been presented as 'artificially wedded to its future, and severed from its past', in reality it is, on the contrary, 'uniquely under the shadow of its past'.[15] Coalescing as it does around the idea of a continuum of exile and exilic writing running through the English Revolution and the Restoration, this book provides supporting evidence for this position; it thus orientates itself among those studies hoping to reframe critical understandings of the 'long' seventeenth century.

As I have indicated, if the methodology of going beyond traditional seventeenth-century dividing lines, at least in a chronological sense, is now more firmly established, Scott's call for the Europeanization of seventeenth-century English history has so far received a more cautious reception. It is not difficult to ascertain why the depth of research on mid-century exile remains incommensurate with its historical and literary importance: almost by definition the topic demands that we widen our horizons from the traditionally Anglocentric, if more recently increasingly British-oriented, scholarship which has characterized studies of this period. The reward for this wider focus, as amply evidenced by the essays that follow, is twofold: first, discovery of the ways in which exiles adapt to, or isolate themselves from, their new environment, a process which in turn reveals imperatives of assimilation, integration, acculturation and separation; and second, insight into the multifarious ways in which governments and individuals of the host communities to which they flee respond on a political, religious and – as witnessed in Nigel Smith's chapter – cultural level to their new guests.

In this volume the shift in focus is on two fronts: the New World as well as the European mainland. The direction of travel westwards taken in the final two chapters, on the regicide exiles, is again coordinate with D'Addario, who in his study of New England settlers casts further light on the profoundly transatlantic nature of émigré textual production and readership, building on recent scholarship which has established the considerable extent of political, social and cultural cross-fertilization between Old and New England.[16] If we believe that the forces that shaped and constituted the English Revolution only ramified outwards centrifugally, untouched by centripetal European influences, then we must at least recognize that these ramifications did not stop at Dover or at Plymouth, any more

---

[15]   *England's Troubles*, pp. 25–6.

[16]   *Exile and Journey*, pp. 22–56. Another important recent study emphasizing England's enduring Atlantic connections is *Shaping the Stuart World 1603–1714: The Atlantic Connection*, ed. Allan I. Macinnes and Arthur H. Williamson (Leiden, Boston: Brill, 2006). For a recent qualification of this transatlantic approach, particularly as it relates to the literature of New England, see John Kerrigan, *Archipelagic English: Literature, History, and Politics 1603–1707* (Oxford: Oxford University Press, 2008), esp. pp. 57–9.

than they ceased at 1660. In more ways than one, then, this volume is Janus-faced: looking back from the perspective of the later seventeenth century to the English Revolution (and earlier), and telescoping forward from the opposite position; surveying continental Europe, but also, and to equal effect, gazing west across the Atlantic to the shores of New England.

Scott's appeal for a European outlook followed on from his criticism of the New British History, a methodology which, as defined by an early exponent, Glen Burgess, seeks to 'escape a British history written purely and simply in terms of the inexorable growth of English dominance', and which 'for that reason [...] must recognise the existence of separate English, Scottish, Irish and Welsh histories'.[17] For Scott, the New British History represents merely a recrudescence, or at best enhancement, of narrow national foci which have continued to dominate studies of the period and obscure the wider picture. Though now more British than English in scope, it is hard to disagree that the mainstream historiography of the seventeenth century remains almost entirely national. Beyond studies of foreign policy there has been a clutch of accounts operating in and advocating a European framework,[18] but it is revealing that one of the most enthusiastic of these predates *England's Troubles*.[19] Even where otherwise excellent modern studies take a seventeenth-century-wide approach to the English Revolution, engagement with Europe can remain markedly minimal.[20]

This collection neither embraces nor ignores the New British History. Its radar is turned, rather, towards the breaking down, or at least the traversing, of continental boundaries, its methodological model Scott's Anglo-European, and the more recent transatlantic, scholarly paradigm. If it does not go as far as Scott in denationalizing English or British history, in restoring its pre-modernity, it nevertheless breathes new life into the idea that Europe (and the New World) played a more central role in the English Revolution and its aftermath than has previously been acknowledged. In this it is assisted by its wide geographic arc, encompassing Ireland, Spain, France, the Dutch Republic, the Spanish Netherlands, Italy and

---

[17] *The New British History: Founding a Modern State 1603–1715*, ed. Glenn Burgess (London and New York: I.B. Tauris, 1999), p. 8.

[18] *The Anglo-Dutch Moment: Essays on the Glorious Revolution and its World Impact*, ed Jonathan Israel (Cambridge: Cambridge University Press, 1991); *Roger Morrice and Britain in the late 1680s*, ed. Jason McElligott (Aldershot, Burlington: Ashgate, 2006); Lisa Jardine, *Going Dutch: How England Plundered Holland's Glory* (London: Harper, 2008). Moving beyond Europe, for a conceptually sophisticated and notably boundary-crossing study of a key aspect of English seventeenth-century history, see Alison Games, *The Web of Empire: English Cosmopolitans in an Age of Expansion, 1560–1660* (New York: Oxford University Press, 2008).

[19] *The Stuart Court and Europe: Essays in Politics and Political Culture*, ed. R. Malcolm Smuts (Cambridge: Cambridge University Press, 1996). I am grateful to Professor Scott for his reflections on the influence of his arguments.

[20] See, for example, *The English Revolution, c.1590–1720: Politics, Religion and Communities*, ed. Nicholas Tyacke (Manchester: Manchester University Press, 2007).

Germany, as well as New England. Indeed, with its attendant investigation into material exchanges, movements of peoples, and belief systems, it seems wholly apposite that this volume forms part of a series on the theme of *Transculturisms, 1400–1700*.

Of course, a genuinely transnational, integrated European approach to the English Revolution and its aftermath requires not simply greater acknowledgement of this European dimension, but also further and closer interrogation of continental sources, echoed in Jason McElligott's urgent plea for scholars to 'take notice of at least some of the vast array of relevant print and manuscript sources on the continent [...], to stop merely talking about the importance of Europe and to start showing its importance in practice'.[21] Though its Anglophone sources still predominate, this volume takes important steps forward in this regard, with Katrien Daemen-de Gelder's and Jean-Pierre Vander Motten's mining of the City Archives of Antwerp complementing Nigel Smith's work on Dutch, German and Italian literature. Nonetheless, it is difficult to draw precise conclusions from this small sample of material: it is both a sobering and exciting thought that the continental primary sources examined here represent but a tiny fraction of the available material, driven home by Nigel Smith's revelation that 669 literature concerned with the English Revolution were published between 1640 and 1669 in German alone. These and other such sources hold out the promise of richly informing our still incipient understanding of the complex inter-relations between English exiles and their hosts.

In its definition of exile the scope of this book is broad, without diluting the essential integrity of the exilic experience, or discounting the potential benefits of more restrictive designation. Its main focus is on physical displacement in countries outside of England, but it also accommodates the inner, mental withdrawal of royalists who chose to remain in England in the 1640s and 1650s, or who returned from overseas during that period, seeking a *modus vivendi* with various republican regimes. As with its treatment of revolutionaries as well as royalists, this holistic method allows for the complexity of the experiences and literary strategies of exile in these years to be more fully investigated. This leads to a wider, more nuanced comparison of responses to exile and defeat than would be possible if, say, consideration were given only to those who remained exiled abroad.

Yet, such an inclusive approach is not without its problems. In his essay, Timothy Raylor rightly draws attention to the dangers of spreading our notion of exiles of the mid-century too thinly: 'Exiles in England? Exiles in the mind? As we loosen the term, the subject begins to dissolve.'[22] Raylor's thesis, that we have underplayed the pre-war intellectual and cultural links between England and the continent, fits neatly with Scott's templates of Anglo-Europeanism and seventeenth-century continuity; however, it qualifies the notion that the royalist exile in and of itself was a significant catalyst for or conduit of European transculturalism. Pre-existing roots, Raylor argues, had already been established by Grand Tourists, ambassadors,

---

[21]   *Roger Morrice*, p. 9.
[22]   See below, p. 20.

travelling tutors (such as Hobbes and Marvell), and religious refugees. In this way, then, Raylor actually, and interestingly, questions one of the premises of the volume. Moreover, the caution we need to exercise in defining exile is further informed by the fact that even if we limit our ambit, as Geoffrey Smith does, to the 'Cavaliers', that is 'those active and committed adherents of Charles I or Charles II who, as a consequence of their beliefs and activities, went into exile in Europe between 1640 and 1660', very few of them were formally banished: 'their lives would not have been in danger if they had remained in England'.[23] These are valid and vexed questions of definition and categorization, though it might be added with some assuredness that they are not – and are not held to be – germane to the regicide exiles; their exiles were also technically voluntary, but the danger to their lives, both in New England and upon any possible return home, was all too apparent.

Whether written by exiles or 'exiles', however, it strikes me that there remains a tangible and ubiquitous sense of rupture, loss, and marginalization, of real or 'imagined alterity',[24] about the majority of the texts scrutinized here, informed by the – for all the writers knew – permanent and irreversible reality of displacement, around which the volume as a whole profitably coheres. To some degree, that is, most of the case studies presented in these essays experience 'an immediate loss of an entire world that they had known'[25] which finds vivid literary expression in recognizably exilic writings. The extent to which the book's coherence extends to the identification of a broadly systematized rhetoric of exile – beyond already familiar factional and solipsistic topoi – is more questionable, not least because exilic modes of thought, argument and expression vary considerably: the disruptions of exile allow for illuminating self-reflexivity as well as considered literary strategy. Nevertheless, the literary focus of these chapters suggests the palpable sense of unity to be derived from an overarching and increasingly productive theoretical perspective. This sees the written text, across multiple idioms, as both social determinant and material object, as 'a social and cultural phenomenon embedded in the circumstances of its production and consumption, and relatedly as an object that can provide us with a particular knowledge of these circumstances'.[26]

III

A good deal more research remains to be undertaken on exile in the English Revolution and its aftermath. We still know relatively little, for example, about the decorum maintained and exhibited by the Stuart court-in-exile, about the full extent of the public and private nature of exilic correspondence, and about

---

[23]   Smith, *The Cavaliers in Exile*, p. 5.

[24]   Nico Israel, *Outlandish: Writing Between Exile and Diaspora* (Stanford: Stanford University Press, 2000), p. 11.

[25]   D'Addario, *Exile and Journey*, p. 19.

[26]   *Ibid.*, p. 4.

the role of externals, such as religious ceremonies, in exilic survival strategies of the period.[27] Nevertheless, fresh ground has been charted here, in a book which actively participates in contemporary scholarly discussions and sets new methodological and theoretical parameters for the challenges that lie ahead. These essays contribute significantly, in the first instance, to emergent and divergent notions of royalism and royalist literature. In doing so, they do not shy away from the problems of – and rewards for – accessing and interpreting the relevant continental primary sources; nor do they disregard the difficulty of defining with any precision the cultural and intellectual impact on royalist exiles of living on the European mainland. And yet, in providing a substantial re-examination of figures like the Cavendishes, the Carys, Aylesbury and Hobbes, they help to re-vivify exilic experiences of the mid-century, affording new insights into the pressures that bore down on – and opportunities that presented themselves to – supporters of the Stuart monarchy and adherents to the Church of England, when displacement and dispossession followed swiftly upon political and military defeat.

It follows, then, that these studies argue, by turns implicitly and forthrightly, for a less Anglo-centric and more European approach towards the English Revolution and its aftermath. But it is worth reiterating that the exilic lives and writings captured here are not solely those of royalists. In exploring the post-1660 experiences of Goffe and Dixwell, the book also opens up new, equally important vistas of enquiry into onetime parliamentarians who sought refuge across the Atlantic, and, in the process, calls for a perspective of seventeenth-century continuity. This newly exposed North American dimension to exile (rather than simply migration) in this period is of intrinsic value, and, catalyzing a residual Good Old Cause mindset in New England which continued to influence Anglo-American relations long after the regicide exiles were dead and buried, it also had far-reaching political and ideological implications.

Another common thread running through the book is the friction generated by the potent dislocations and ruptures of exile, demonstrating how these stressors frequently cause people to think and act revealingly. Perhaps the most interesting dialectic contributing to this tension is between fluidity and stability. As we will witness, the sense of flux engendered by dislocation, which encompassed exposure to new cultures and creeds, and which also betrayed, for the exile, the linguistic instability of the English language itself, influenced the philosophical, literary and theological choices of exiles. On the other hand, the exigencies of displacement could cause exiles to turn in on themselves, to attempt to retain, through the familiarity of their books and the company they kept, the patterns of life they had previously known. Edges are regularly blurred: several of the subjects under

---

[27] For a germane recent account of Church of England ceremonies in the royalist exile, see Philip Major, 'Funerary Rites in the Royalist Exile: George Morley's Ministry in Antwerp, 1650–1653', *Renaissance and Reformation/Renaissance et Réforme*, 31.3 (2009), 35–50.

investigation undergo an extraordinarily wide spectrum of experiences that defies easy patterning. In this way the book attempts to convey something of the caboodle of often competing imperatives and priorities – familial, survivalist, cultural, ideological – in which the seventeenth-century exile swims. One corollary of this is that the often life-changing experience of exile, and the mixed reactions and wide-ranging literary genres it elicits, help to illustrate once more the error of making cosy, simplistic divisions between traditional factions of the mid-century. While reactions and attitudes to exile and defeat reinforce notions of political, religious and cultural bifurcation, they can also create unlikely bedfellows, and, conversely, betray the hybridity of notionally homogeneous groups.

A further feature of this study is the compromise it negotiates between a narrow and wide focus: quotidian exilic episodes both inform and vie with macrocosmic social and literary trends. For example, the strains placed by exile on familial ties inform the tensions played out within specific family units, such as the Carys, but also help construct a wider narrative of the changing domestic and cultural role of women, and dynamics of authority and hierarchy, in the 1640s and 1650s; preferment afforded to individual royalist exiles, and the travails of individual divines, provide a clearer picture of the culture of the Restoration court and Church respectively. Well-known, in some cases canonical, texts are blended with newly ventilated writings to inform this analysis. Moreover, the range of works under scrutiny is instructively wide – poems, plays, histories, philosophical and theological treatises jostle for attention with journals, diaries, correspondence and legal documents.

Above all, this book is concerned with self-identity. When to military and political defeat, catastrophic in themselves, is added the psychological and physical thunderbolt of displacement and dispossession, what coping mechanisms – if, indeed, they need them – do exiles in this period employ to adapt and reconcile themselves to their new circumstances, and how effective are they? For some, the wretchedness of their lot wore a grim aspect; the mental and material wounds inflicted by separation from family and native country, compounded by severe material deprivation, were too deep to heal. At another extreme, exile could be a stimulating cultural and intellectual experience; or, on a spiritual level, a liberating means toward finding a New Jerusalem, exemplified in the New England experiences of the regicides. The majority of exiles, it seems, navigated a no less interestingly contoured *via media* between the two. These chapters, then, speak to each other in relaying hopeful as well as harmful facets of exile. That accepted, if there is one theme that hovers most spectrally over the book it is the relentless poverty from which few exiles, at one point or another, were immune. It is this poverty, trammelling the lives of exiles of all social, political and religious persuasions, to which we should remain alive when engaging with this topic. The fact that in an early modern age when success betokened divine sanction, and defeat godly disfavour, poverty could be transformed into a consolatory mindset of persecution, often shading over into a paradoxical patriotism, or, in the case of Hobbes, inform a controversial political philosophy, does little to diminish its pathos. On the evidence of this study, at least, for all the arrestingly diverse means by which it is resisted, embraced, denied and articulated in this period, it is exile's irreducible poignancy that still leaves, as it should, the deepest impression.

IV

This volume features contributions from a number of prominent as well as emerging academics, and will be of interest, I hope, to many students and scholars in the fields of both history and literary criticism. It commences with a discussion by Timothy Raylor of the methodological and evidential problems involved in defining exile and, relatedly, in viewing the royalist exile as a 'watershed' intellectual and cultural phenomenon. Though from a viewpoint – ironically – that subverts the book's stance on the importance of exile, Raylor nevertheless makes a persuasive case for one of its central arguments: a European rather than an English approach.

The collection then furnishes a brace of three pertinent case studies emphasizing, *inter alia*, the multiple individual experiences of royalist exiles and their families. The chapter by Ann Hughes and Julie Sanders brings a feminist perspective to the question of the family by considering the exile of Charles I's relatives and the literary families, the Cavendishes and the Carys. The authors call attention to a number of important exilic ramifications for elite families: disrupted power structures and hierarchies, divergent literary representations, and expedient political accommodations. The essay by Katrien Daemen-de Gelder and Jean-Pierre Vander Motten draws on archival sources pertaining to the Spanish Netherlands, a significant refuge for English royalist exiles. In this chapter, the patron-client relationship between the second Duke of Buckingham and William Aylesbury provokes consideration of the grinding material poverty and debt which could afflict royalist exiles, and shows how even close relations with affluent royalist networks might fail to mitigate its effects.

The next chapter, by Marika Keblusek, elucidates the scholarly communities forged by royalist and Anglican exiles on the continent, particularly in terms of their book culture. It opens a window onto the key role of reading and writing as an exilic survival strategy, as both a unifying intellectual force and emotional lifeline. The impact of displacement on Anglicans and Anglicanism is a theme developed further by Sarah Mortimer. Her chapter argues the case for understanding in a European context the debate between Anglican episcopacy on the one hand, and Catholicism, parliamentarian Presbyterianism, and Erastianism on the other, among exiled royalists and those who remained in England.

The following three essays focus with greater intensity on literary production in the royalist exile, including drama, poetry and philosophy, and its continental influences and reception. Nigel Smith reverses the usual direction of discussing exiles in relation to the England they left behind to examine, rather, their impact on Europe, particularly European literature. Special attention is paid to the influence of the English Revolution on Dutch, German and Italian literary culture. Smith sets himself in dialogue with other contributors by making a strong case for civil war and Commonwealth literature being seen as in part belonging to the history of European letters and its politics, part of the interrelated histories of emergent vernacular literatures and nation states. In his study, Christopher D'Addario analyzes the 'poetics of exile' of Abraham Cowley from a European standpoint, following recent scholarship in placing him in relation to royalist exiles in France as well as French intellectuals such as Gassendi. His evocation of the 'the pervasive polyvalence of language itself' is followed by an important consequent argument concerning the political meanings of form. James Loxley's chapter considers the significance of the concept of exile in Hobbes political philosophy, drawing on theorists such as Arendt, Agamben and Schmitt. The author argues that exile was associated with the state of being conquered but also with the state of nature, so that exiles escaped subjection under law to enjoy natural liberty.

The final two essays introduce a transatlantic dimension by exploring the experiences of regicides who fled to New England after the Restoration. My chapter appraises the significance of William Goffe's exile in Hadley, Massachusetts, observing, in the process, the curious blend of millenarianism and mundanity which suffuses his correspondence. I also consider Goffe's survival strategy of immersing himself in the local community, and the ambivalence he exhibits towards his adopted land. Jason Peacey gives an account of John Dixwell's reclusive life in New Haven, Connecticut, lived under an assumed name. His essay examines the powerful influence over the mind of an exile that the mother country could still exert. In bringing the story to the next generation by discussing Dixwell's correspondence with his niece, and his son who returns to England to lay claim for his patrimony, it provides a fitting conclusion to a volume in which the theme of continuity bulks large.

Chapter 1

Exiles, Expatriates and Travellers: Towards a Cultural and Intellectual History of the English Abroad, 1640–1660

Timothy Raylor

I

Half a century has passed since Paul Hardacre offered the first full-length survey of the fate of the royalists during the puritan revolution.[1] Hardacre's monograph cannot claim to have inaugurated the modern professional study of royalism – that honour must go to Sir Charles Firth, who discussed it in a paper published posthumously in 1937.[2] Hardacre's book can nevertheless claim to have offered the first thorough mapping of the territory. But it did not provide a complete map. Hardacre excluded from it two significant areas: the royalist exile, and the royalist contribution to intellectual history. The exile had already formed the subject of an earlier article, which had also presented a preliminary sketch of the exiles' contribution to intellectual history, asserting their importance in bringing England into contact with European life and culture, and suggesting several areas for further investigation – Anglican clerics and Grand Tourists; the fields of literature, philosophy, and science.[3]

Some of the areas pointed out by Hardacre have proven fruitful for subsequent research. We have, for instance, excellent work on the Grand Tour by John Stoye, Edward Chaney, and Michael Brennan;[4] and on the Anglican clergy by

[1]   P.H. Hardacre, *The Royalists During the Puritan Revolution* (The Hague: Nijhoff, 1956). I am grateful to the Dean and President of Carleton College and my colleagues in the Department of English for their support of my work. This material is based upon work supported by the National Science Foundation under Grant No. 0526068.

[2]   C.H. Firth, 'The Royalists under the Protectorate', *English Historical Review*, 52 (1937), 634–48.

[3]   'The Royalists in Exile During the Puritan Revolution, 1642–1660', *Huntington Library Quarterly*, 16 (1952–1953), 353–70.

[4]   John Stoye, *English Travellers Abroad 1604–1667*, rev. edn (New Haven and London: Yale University Press, 1989); Edward Chaney, *The Grand Tour and the Great Rebellion: Richard Lassels and 'The Voyage of Italy' in the Seventeenth Century*, Biblioteca del Viaggio in Italia, Testi, xix (Geneva: Slatkine, 1985); Michael G. Brennan, *English Civil War Travellers and the Origins of the Western European Grand Tour* (London: Hakluyt Society, 2002); Brennan (ed.), *The Origins of the Grand Tour: The Travels of Robert Montagu, Lord*

John Spurr.[5] But no clear consensus about the cultural significance of the royalist exile has yet emerged. In the field of literary study there have been attempts to identify a distinctive and coherent character in the poetry and literary theory of the exiles, usually by reference to literary or philosophical developments in France; the revival of Epicurean atomism and ethics by Gassendi and others has provided a particularly attractive explanatory framework.[6] In the history of science and philosophy, however, the argument that contact with the atomism of Gassendi effected any fundamental shift in the scientific investigations of the exiles has been strongly contested.[7] Historians of science have undertaken important primary research among the English who were abroad at this time – though without a strong sense that it can usefully be framed by the notion of a royalist exile.[8] One area about which Hardacre did not comment has attracted more attention than any of those on which he did: the experience of women in exile. Recent study of the royalist exile has in large part been driven by the surge of scholarly interest in Margaret Cavendish.[9] The exile of Cavendish and her husband formed the basis

---

Mandeville (1649–1654), William Hammond (1655–1658), Banaster Maynard (1660–1663) (London: Hakluyt Society, 2004); see also John Marciari, *Grand Tour Diaries and other travel manuscripts in the James Marshall and Marie-Louise Osborn Collection*, Yale University Library Gazette, Occasional Supplement, ii (New Haven: Yale University Press, 1999); Isaac Basire, *Travels through France and Italy (1647–1649)*, ed. Luigi Monga and R. Chris Hassel, Biblioteca del Viaggio in Italia, Testi, xxv (Geneva: Slatkine, 1987). For the attribution to Basire, see Edward Chaney, *The Evolution of the Grand Tour* (London and Portland: Frank Cass, 2000), p. 87 n. 2; John Lough, *France Observed in the Seventeenth Century by British Travellers* (Stocksfield: Oriel Press, 1985).

[5]   John Spurr, *The Restoration Church of England, 1646–1689* (New Haven and London: Yale University Press, 1991); among important earlier work in this area is Robert S. Bosher, *The Making of the Restoration Settlement: The Influence of the Laudians, 1649–1662* (London: Dacre Press, 1951), esp. pp. 49–87, 284–94.

[6]   See, most notably, Charles K. Smith, 'French philosophy and English politics in interregnum poetry', in *The Stuart Court and Europe: Essays in Politics and Political Culture*, ed. R. Malcolm Smuts (Cambridge: Cambridge University Press, 1996), pp. 177–209.

[7]   Stephen Clucas, 'The Atomism of the Cavendish Circle: A Reappraisal', *Seventeenth Century*, 9 (1994), 247–73.

[8]   See, for instance, Jean Jacquot, 'Sir Charles Cavendish and his Learned Friends', *Annals of Science*, 3 (1952), 13–27, 175–91; Noel Malcolm, *Aspects of Hobbes* (Oxford: Oxford University Press, 2002), Chapters 6, 7, and 9; Noel Malcolm and Jacqueline Stedall, *John Pell (1611–1685) and His Correspondence with Sir Charles Cavendish: The Mental World of an Early Modern Mathematician* (Oxford: Oxford University Press, 2005).

[9]   For work in this vein, see, *inter alia*, Anna Battigelli, *Margaret Cavendish and the Exiles of the Mind* (Lexington: University of Kentucky Press, 1998), and Emma Rees, *Margaret Cavendish: Gender, Genre, Exile* (Manchester: Manchester University Press, 2003). Also valuable and pertinent is Katie Whitaker's biography of Cavendish, *Mad Madge: The Extraordinary Life of Margaret Cavendish, Duchess of Newcastle, the First Woman to Live by Her Pen* (New York: Basic Books, 2002).

of a lavish recent exhibition in Antwerp.[10] We now also finally have, 50 years after Hardacre, a book-length survey of the royalist exile, in Geoffrey Smith's *The Cavaliers in Exile*.[11] Smith's is a generous, discriminating and appealing social history of the exile; but one in which the possibility that it might have involved an intellectual or cultural dimension scarcely surfaces.

At first blush this seems a little odd. On the face of it, the study of the intellectual and cultural activities of the exiled royalists seems a rich and attractive topic. At Paris in the later 1640s, for instance, many leading English philosophers, poets and patrons were gathered. Edmund Waller famously remarked to John Aubrey 'that (William) the Lord marquisse of Newcastle was a great patron to Dr. Gassendi, and M. Des Cartes, as well as Mr. Hobbes, and that he hath dined with them all three at the marquiss's table at Paris'.[12] The most perfunctory tally of philosophical and literary works written or published by the English at Paris during the 1640s yields impressive results: Hobbes's *De cive*, *Leviathan* and about half of his *De corpore*; his Answer to Davenant's Preface to *Gondibert* (1650) and Davenant's Preface (1650) and the first half of *Gondibert* itself (1651); Cowley's *The Mistress* (1647); Sir Kenelm Digby's *Two Treatises* (1644). A wider lens would include the first version of Clarendon's great *History*, drafted on Jersey in the middle to late years of the decade. A slower shutter would register the numerous poetic and philosophical works of Margaret Cavendish, written in Antwerp and published at London, and her husband's influential manual on the managing of horses, not to mention his unpublished manual on fencing and his letter of advice to Charles II.[13] Attention to ephemera and polemic would include numerous works of Anglican apologetic and controversy – Bramhall against Hobbes and de la Milletière, for instance.[14] Taking a still longer view, we might include works written in the immediate or longer-term aftermath of the exile: the translations of Richard Fanshawe, John Evelyn, or Walter Charleton; the travel memoirs of Evelyn, Raymond, and others.

---

[10] *Royalist Refugees: William and Margaret Cavendish in the Rubens House 1648–1660*, ed Ben van Beneden and Nora de Poorter (Antwerp: BAI, Rubenianum, 2006).

[11] *The Cavaliers in Exile, 1640–1660* (Basingstoke and New York: Palgrave, 2003).

[12] J. Aubrey, *Brief Lives*, ed. Andrew Clark, 2 vols (Oxford: Clarendon Press, 1898), i, 366. William Petty, dedicating a work to Newcastle in 1674, reminded the then duke of the way in which, some 30 years earlier at Paris, Mersenne, Gassendi, Hobbes, Descartes, Roberval, Mydorge 'and other famous men', 'all frequenting, and caressed by, your Grace and your memorable Brother, Sir *Charles Cavendish*, did countenance and influence my Studies as well by their Conversation as their Publick Lectures and Writings'; *The Discourse Made before the Royal Society the 26. of November 1674. Concerning the Use of Duplicate Proportion* (London, 1674), sigs. A9r–v; qtd in Emil Strauss, *Sir William Petty: Portrait of a Genius* (Glencoe, IL: Free Press, 1954), p. 28 (corrected).

[13] See above, n. 10.

[14] On which, see Bosher, *Making of the Restoration Settlement*, pp. 63–6; Nicholas D. Jackson, *Hobbes, Bramhall and the Politics of Liberty and Necessity: A Quarrel of the Civil Wars and Interregnum* (Cambridge: Cambridge University Press, 2007).

If we expand our focus to consider, more broadly, intellectual activity, we can look at evidence of book collecting.[15] Among those collections susceptible to examination are the purchases, both English and continental, of Christopher, Lord Hatton; those of Sir Richard Browne, who passed his taste for fine bindings, along with many of his books, to his son-in-law, John Evelyn; and those of Sir Kenelm Digby. All three assembled major collections in Paris during the years of exile.[16] We might examine the evidence left by readers, attending to the commonplace books of Hyde on Jersey, which record his reading of Tacitus, Livy, and Cicero, Bacon and Grotius, Machiavelli and Hobbes.[17] We could examine the commonplace book prepared by Evelyn's cousin, the erstwhile army officer, Sir Samuel Tuke, during the later 1650s.[18] Tuke's commonplace book lets us glimpse a more serious and contemplative side to a figure we might have been forgiven for dismissing as something of a lightweight. He read widely in ancient and modern history, *belles lettres*, and moral and political philosophy: Caesar and Strada, Donne and Voiture, Bacon, Montaigne, and Senault. Tuke was surprisingly keen on modern philosophy, taking a critical interest in the mechanistic systems of Descartes, Gassendi and Hobbes.[19] To write a history of all this seems worth attempting. Why has it not been done?

The difficulty becomes clear once we start to try to define more precisely the scope of the subject. Yes, there was clearly much activity among the English abroad, but can it be comprehended by the notion of a royalist exile, or distinguished from the more general history of the period? What, in fact, do we mean by an exile, or by a royalist?

---

[15]   Marika Keblusek has forthcoming a study of the purchases of the exiled cleric, Michael Honywood; she is also working on a broader study of English exiles and book collecting: see her 'The Exile Experience: Royalist and Anglican Book Culture in the Low Countries, 1640–60', in Lotte Hellinga et al. (eds), *The Bookshop of the World: The Role of the Low Countries in the Book-Trade 1473–1941* (Houten: HES & De Graaf, 2001), pp. 151–8.

[16]   Stoye, *English Travellers Abroad*, pp. 316–18. For more on Evelyn, see Mirjam Foot, 'John Evelyn's Bookbindings', in *John Evelyn and his Milieu*, ed. Francis Harris and Michael Hunter (London: British Library, 2003), pp. 61–70; on Digby, see Robert T. Petersson, *Sir Kenelm Digby: The Ornament of England 1603–1665* (London: Jonathan Cape, 1956), pp. 241–5; Davida Rubin, *Sir Kenelm Digby F.R.S 1603–1665: A bibliography based on the collection of K. Garth Huston, Sr., M.D.* (San Francisco: Jeremy Norman & Co., 1991), pp. 75–94.

[17]   Bodleian Library, Oxford, MSS Clarendon 126–7.

[18]   BL, Add. MS 78423; a subsequent volume (Add. MS 78424) dates from the early 1660s. On Tuke, see C.H. Firth, 'Tuke, Sir Samuel', rev. A.J. Hopper, *ODNB*.

[19]   On Tuke's admiration for Hobbes, see Gillian Darley, *John Evelyn: Living for Ingenuity* (New Haven and London: Yale University Press, 2006), p. 105.

II

Taken in the strictest sense, exile implies banishment from one's homeland; but a little loosening allows the notion of voluntary expatriation.[20] Such loosening is necessary, because very few of those who went abroad were, like Edmund Waller, formally banished (and Waller, though banished, was not really a royalist).[21] But the introduction of voluntariness immediately opens the door to a whole range of figures who might more aptly be thought of as émigrés, or expatriates, or even as cultural tourists than as royalist exiles. The three writers featured in Michael Brennan's valuable collection of travel accounts from the period were embedded in family alliances and social networks which defy simplistic classification as either 'parliamentarian' or 'royalist'.[22] With pragmatism and self-discipline, Geoffrey Smith restricts the scope of his study to the cavaliers: the soldiers and statesmen who had fought and lost the war and who (along with their families and households) remained abroad for significant periods. Smith's tight focus on the Jermyns and the Wilmots explains why intellectual history is almost entirely absent from his book: it excludes most of those on whom such a history would have to be based – the dispossessed Anglican clergy; the long-term expatriates; young gentlemen on the Grand Tour. Defined thus narrowly, the intellectual history of the royalist exile would be little more than a biography of Clarendon.

We clearly need a looser focus, but deciding where and how to draw the line between the history of the royalist exile and the general history of the period is not easy.[23] Does exile, for example, entail travel abroad? It rather depends on where one feels at home. Ann, Lady Fanshawe and her family were driven from home by the parliamentary army, fleeing penniless to royalist Oxford, where they eked out a miserable existence, eating one dish a day, and sleeping in a 'very bad bed' in a baker's garret.[24] While Lady Ann seems to have felt that she was exiled *to* Oxford, many of the 575 scholars who were turned out of the university may reasonably have felt banished *from* it.[25] So, probably, did many of the 1850 other scholars and clergy from around the country who were extruded from their livings after the fall of the monarchy. Although Robert Herrick may have felt a frisson at returning from his Devonshire living to London, reversing what he regarded sourly as a 'banishment' to 'the dull confines of the drooping West', his fellow West-country

---

[20]   *OED*, 1, 1b.

[21]   Of the 225 'long-term exiles' who form the core of Smith's study, only 60–70 had no alternative but to leave the country; *Cavaliers in Exile*, p. 58.

[22]   *Origins*, ed. Brennan, pp. 1–2.

[23]   Smith, *Cavaliers in Exile*, p. 35; Stoye, *English Travellers Abroad*, pp. 282, 292.

[24]   *The Memoirs of Anne, Lady Halkett and Ann, Lady Fanshawe*, ed. John Loftis (Oxford: Clarendon Press, 1979), p. 111.

[25]   *Walker Revised: Being a Revision of John Walker's Suffering of the Clergy during the Great Rebellion, 1642–60*, ed. Arnold G. Matthews (Oxford: Clarendon Press, 1948), pp. xiii–xiv.

clergymen, Thomas Flavell and John Smith, who were reduced to hiding among the rocks, cannot have been so sanguine.[26] The various Commonwealth and Protectoral acts for banishing delinquents from London created exiles from the capital – a subject whose literary repercussions have been sensitively explored by Philip Major.[27] What about the notion of 'inner exile'? It depends again on whether it involves a retreat one might not otherwise have chosen from a place one might have considered to be home. For this reason 'exile' seems to me not quite the right term for the situation of Margaret Cavendish in respect of her being 'a woman trying to write in a hostile culture'.[28] Exiles in England? Exiles of the mind? As we loosen the term, the subject begins to dissolve.[29]

Problems of definition are not the only ones that should give us pause when we consider the intellectual and cultural history of the royalist exile. There is also the problem of evidence. We currently lack a documentary base with enough breadth and depth to allow many confident generalizations. The exiles brought little home with them; anyone who has ever moved house will understand why. Rich deposits like the Evelyn archive at the British Library or the Cavendish papers at Nottingham and Welbeck are rare. Continental archives undoubtedly contain more information than we have yet uncovered. Recent research on English exiles in the Low Countries has been especially illuminating, shedding valuable light on figures like Thomas Killigrew, Samuel Tuke, and Thomas Ross, and on the court of Princess Mary.[30] But it would be unwise to expect to uncover many large caches

---

[26] *The Poetical Works of Robert Herrick*, ed. L.C. Martin (Oxford: Clarendon Press, 1956), p. 242 ('His returne to London') (see also, 'To Dean–bourn', p. 29; 'To his Houshold gods', p. 111); *Walker Revised*, ed. Matthews, pp. 96, 100.

[27] Philip Major, '"Twixt Hope and Fear": John Berkenhead, Henry Lawes, and Banishment from London during the English Revolution', *Review of English Studies*, n.s. 59 (2008), 270–80.

[28] Rees, *Margaret Cavendish*, p. 5.

[29] For some suggestive reflections on such methodological problems, see Christopher D'Addario, *Exile and Journey in Seventeenth-Century Literature* (Cambridge: Cambridge University Press, 2007), pp. 18–21.

[30] See, on Killigrew, J.P. Vander Motten, '"The Saucy Zeal of Layman": The Religious Views of Thomas Killigrew (1612–1683)', *Lias*, 20 (2002), 81–110; Vander Motten, 'Thomas Killigrew's "Lost Years", 1655–1660', *Neophilologus*, 82 (1998), 311–34; on Tuke, J.P. Vander Motten and Katrien Daemen-de Gelder, 'Sir Samuel Tuke (c. 1615–1674) at the "Little Court" of Mary Stuart (1631–1660)', *Notes and Queries*, 251 (2006), 168–70; on Ross, Katrien Daemen-de Gelder and J.P. Vander Motten, 'Thomas Ross's *Second Punick War* (1661 and 1672): Royalist Panegyric and Artistic Collaboration in the Southern Netherlands', *Quaerendo*, 38 (2008), 32–48; J.P. Vander Motten and Katrien Daemen-de Gelder, 'A "Copy as Immortal, as its Original": Thomas Ross' *Second Punick War* (London, 1661 and 1672)', in *Living in Posterity: Essays in Honour of Bart Westerweel*, ed. Jan Frans van Dijkhuizen et al. (Hilversum: Uitgeverij Verloren, 2004), pp. 185–90; on Princess Mary, see Nadine N.W. Akkerman and Paul R. Sellin, 'A Stuart Masque in Holland: *Ballet de La Carmesse de La Haye* (1655)', *Ben Jonson Journal*, 11 (2004), 207–58, 12 (2005), 141–64.

of material in continental holdings. Nor should we underestimate the obstacles to finding those documents which remain unnoticed. Continental archives are not, in my experience, calendared in a way that easily allows the wide trawls historians of Britain are used to carrying out through the volumes issued by the Historical Manuscripts Commission or the Calendars of State Papers. Finally, the major documentary accounts of the exile experience on which we are obliged to build are frequently of questionable value as primary evidence for the period of the exile itself. These were written with a complex set of motives, often many years after the experiences they described. It is well known that John Evelyn's account of his travels of the 1640s was written up in the 1670s, partly from notes taken at the time, but partly also from guidebooks, some of which were not published until long after his tour.[31] Michael Brennan has recently shown that the travel diary of Robert Montagu, Lord Mandeville, was carefully overseen and in part written by his travelling tutor, a Mr Hainhofer, to demonstrate the value of his pedagogy.[32] The memoirs of Ann, Lady Fanshawe – on which I drew above to illustrate her experience in the mid-1640s – were in fact written in 1676.[33] In preparing retrospective accounts of their itineraries travellers were prone to favourable framing: in 1654 John Milton insisted that he had rushed home from his tour in order to help fight for liberty in England – despite the fact that the civil war would not break out for several years after his return, in 1639;[34] after 1660, Robert, Lord Mandeville and Sir John Reresby would present their peregrinations as driven by loyalty to the royal cause.[35] It would, in sum, be hazardous to rely too heavily on anyone's post-Restoration reconstruction of their actions or motives during the 1640s and 1650s. In too many cases, however, that is all we have to go on.

III

I want to move now from these preliminary ruminations on the historiography of the exile to the heart of my chapter: a consideration of the cultural and intellectual implications of the phenomenon we think of as the royalist exile. The main drift of Hardacre's preliminary survey was that the royalist exile introduced the English, for the first time to any significant degree, to continental forms and practices; that this encounter had a dramatic impact on the exiles; and that they, on their return, changed profoundly the intellectual and cultural life of their country.

---

[31]   *The Diary of John Evelyn*, ed. E.S. de Beer, 6 vols (Oxford: Clarendon Press, 1955), i, 69–114; *Origins*, ed. Brennan, pp. 33–4.

[32]   *Origins*, ed. Brennan, pp. 61–5, 69, 77.

[33]   *Memoirs*, p. 101; Loftis comments on their genre and restricted value as historical evidence: *Memoirs*, pp. xiv–xv.

[34]   Chaney, *Grand Tour*, p. 249.

[35]   *Origins*, ed. Brennan, pp. 2, 36; compare with Reresby, *Memoirs and Travels of Sir John Reresby*, ed. Albert Ivatt (London: Kegan Paul, 1904), p. 1. For more examples, see Chaney, *Grand Tour*, pp. 352–5.

This thesis – we might call it a 'watershed' thesis – has been echoed, with varying degrees of refinement, in much subsequent scholarship. Christopher D'Addario, for example, characterizes the experience of a figure like Hobbes in Paris as one of linguistic and cultural alienation, confusion, and loss; while Michael Brennan claims that, for such figures, 'there was now a necessity to refine their own concepts of Englishness; and for that matter, the position of a previously insular England within a broader continental context'.[36]

Watershed moments and ruptures have a dangerous attraction; it is always tempting to find them (particularly in places where no one else has). Having done so, it is tempting to overestimate their significance. In what follows I want to urge a case for caution, arguing against the tendency to filter all English experience on the continent during the revolutionary period through the lens of a royalist exile, and against the view that this experience represented a significant rupture with the recent past. I shall, on both these points, be making a case for continuity, arguing that continental travel had already become a well-established convention for young men of means, and suggesting that many so-called exiles might rather be thought of as educational tourists. And I shall suggest that the cultural impact of the English experience in Europe only looks like a significant rupture if we underestimate the extent and the profundity of pre-war contacts. What I have to say will echo the judgement of John Stoye, in his classic *English Travellers Abroad*. In writing that book, Stoye had been drawn to explore the possibility that the royalist exile both involved and occasioned a major shift in English life; he even expanded the chronological span of his study in order to address the issue. Having done so, he concluded, 'the truth is not so spectacular':

> During the reigns of James I and Charles I foreign travel had evidently become an important and conventional element in the upbringing, sometimes in the adult life, of many Englishmen. If an important minority chose temporary exile after the Parliamentary victory, it was by no means electing to go into the wilderness. They went partly because western Europe was familiar ground; only the circumstances, particularly the poverty, of this second residence abroad, were strange to some of them. In most cases they returned long before 1660, and they were in any case always outnumbered by ordinary travellers. For this reason, that special quality of life often associated with the Restoration [...] does not owe too much to the new court and the returned cavaliers; it owes even more to the steady stream of travellers over sixty years.[37]

Now Stoye has been criticized for pushing the formalization of the Grand Tour too early and for arguing too strongly for the persistence and importance of 'ordinary travellers' during the period: travellers who, in his view, outnumbered the genuine 'exiles'.[38] It seems to me that these are mainly objections about terminology.

---

36 D'Addario, *Exile and Journey*, pp. 57–86; Brennan, *English Civil War Travellers*, p. 16.
37 *English Travellers Abroad* (1952), p. 458.
38 Chaney, *Grand Tour*, pp. 63–5.

We may question at what point the term 'Grand Tour' came into use, but the available evidence shows that educational travel on the continent following a fairly well-established itinerary had become a convention of upper-class English life by the end of the 1630s.[39] Certainly, Stoye's distinction between 'exiles' and 'ordinary travellers' is too rigid – though the alternative of presenting all who went abroad as, in some sense, exiles seems hardly preferable;[40] but Stoye's essential point is not that these 'ordinary travellers' were oblivious to the war: it is that they were, in travelling, continuing an established tradition.

The 1630s witnessed what Chaney himself has described as a 'travel boom' – a boom, in particular, in educational and cultural tourism.[41] The preconditions for it were Charles I's peace treaties with France and Spain in 1630, which reopened to English travellers territories that had previously been closed or dangerous; it was encouraged by the cosmopolitan tastes of this most sophisticated of courts.[42] During the 1630s, the vogue for educational travel spread well beyond the upper echelons of the aristocracy. James Howell's *Instructions for Travell* (1642) speaks to this vogue, addressing not only noblemen and their tutors but also private gentlemen of smaller means to sketch out a tour of France, Spain, Italy and the Low Countries as an educational experience suitable for a young man between leaving university and attending the Inns of Court.[43] The tour of France, Italy, and Switzerland undertaken in 1638–39 by John Milton, the son of a London scrivener, is a telling instance of such broadening.[44] The publication, in the early 1640s, of guidebooks like Howell's, and grammars and phrasebooks, furnish evidence that the convention was already established; they appeared too early to be responses to the phenomenon of royalist exile. Giovanni Torriano's *Italian Tutor* was published

---

[39]   Against Stoye's thesis, Chaney ranges a statement in Clarendon's late dialogue 'Concerning Education': 'We can all remember when very few Men travelled beyond the Seas, except it was to be a Soldier' (*Grand Tour*, p. 65). But Chaney elides Clarendon a little too easily with the character of the Old Lawyer who makes this remark, and ignores the same character's insistence in the preceding dialogue, 'Of the Want of Respect due to Age', that 'our Fathers travelled, and sent their Sons abroad, who returned richly improved by their Observation and Experience'; Edward Hyde, Earl of Clarendon, *Two Dialogues: 'Of the Want of Respect due to Age' and 'Concerning Education'*, ed. Martine W. Brownley, Augustan Reprint Society, 227–8 (University of California, Los Angeles: Clark Memorial Library, 1984), p. 293.

[40]   Chaney's chapter heading is '"Doom'd to Wander": the Royalist Exile, 1640–1660', *Grand Tour*, p. 49. The value of Chaney's assembly of evidence for the contemporary view of travel during this period as a form of royalist exile is undermined by his admission that it includes material from after 1660, or is fictitious, and by his acknowledgement that not all who left were royalists; *Grand Tour*, pp. 352–5.

[41]   Chaney, *Evolution*, p. 86.

[42]   Stoye, *English Travellers Abroad*, p. 117; Chaney, *Grand Tour*, p. 11.

[43]   James Howell, *Instructions for Forreine Travell*, ed. Edward Arber (London, 1869), pp. 18, 26–7, 16, 75–6.

[44]   *Origins*, ed. Brennan, pp. 30–32; Stoye, *English Travellers Abroad*, p. 11.

in 1640; James Wadsworth's *European Mercury*, published in 1641, received its imprimatur on 23 March 1639[/40].[45] Howell's book was entered in the Stationers' Register on 28 September 1641.[46] By this point, only a small number of 'court papists' and army plotters had fled abroad;[47] the exodus to come could hardly have been predicted even by the most enterprising of stationers.

If the outbreak of hostilities in the summer of 1642 did not create the market for such books, it certainly expanded it. When men like John Evelyn, Roger Pratt, or Robert, Lord Montagu went abroad in the 1640s, when men like Sir John Reresby and Francis Mortoft travelled in the 1650s, they were not going into exile. They were, to varying degrees, strategically absenting themselves from troubles at home.[48] But they were engaging in a well-established educational convention, and they took with them works like Howell's.[49] The itineraries they followed differed little in their essential goals (primarily, cultural education) or in their broad outlines (France, Italy, Switzerland; occasionally Spain) from those undertaken by Englishmen during the 1630s. I believe that this point holds good. When he published a revised edition of his book in 1989, Stoye saw no reason to alter a word of his earlier judgement.[50]

I shall base my argument for continuity on a consideration of two areas: philosophy and poetry. That argument will be divided into two parts: I shall look first at the assumption that England was, prior to the exile, intellectually isolated from Europe; I shall then try to assess just how much of a turning point, in respect to my chosen topics, the period of the exile really was.

IV

The belief that pre-war England was in some significant way isolated from continental intellectual and cultural life is founded, it seems to me, upon a grave underestimation of the nature and extent of pre-war contacts between England and the continent. Let me try to sketch briefly the main means of contact, before trying to assess their significance.

Contacts between England and Europe were established primarily through travel. This took several forms, the most conspicuous of which was ambassadorial. The great embassies plied between the capitals of Europe, carrying diplomats, agents and their entourages, taking Englishmen abroad, and bringing foreigners

---

[45]   Chaney, *Grand Tour*, p. 299.

[46]   *A Transcript of the Registers of the Worshipful Company of Stationers from 1640–1708 A.D.*, ed. George E.B. Eyre and Charles R. Rivington, 3 vols (London, 1913–14), i, 34.

[47]   Smith, *Cavaliers in Exile*, pp. 8–13.

[48]   Chaney himself reads Evelyn's travels in this way. *Grand Tour*, pp. 354–5; Brennan aptly characterizes the Tour undertaken by Robert, Lord Montagu, during the 1640s as 'tactically astute'. *Origins*, p. 32.

[49]   Chaney, *Grand Tour*, pp. 395–6.

[50]   *English Travellers Abroad* (1989), p. 328; compare with *ibid.*, p. 282.

to England: Wotton to Venice; Herbert and Doncaster to Paris; Gondomar and Bassompierre to London. Ambassadors themselves often forged significant links between England and Europe. But those established by the more junior figures in their entourages could be more lasting. The long-standing links between Constantijn Huygens and England, for instance, date from his presence in an ambassadorial entourage to London.[51] Georg Rudolf Weckherlin, who slipped into English government service during the 1620s, working in various official and semi-official capacities as Secretary for Foreign Tongues, and, for a time, licenser for news, settled in London after serving in embassies from Württemberg.[52]

Less visible than the embassies, but often providing greater continuity, were the diplomatic links established by the official, or semi-official, Residents: Sir William Boswell at The Hague from 1632 until his death in 1650;[53] Balthasar Gerbier at Brussels between 1631 and 1641.[54] Boswell, a great collector of manuscripts and an energetic correspondent, was a vital link between intellectuals in England and the Low Countries.

Of great importance for the intellectual development of the English nobility and gentry were the travelling tutors who, from the early part of the century, traversed France, Switzerland, and Italy with their charges, as war and opportunity allowed.[55] Travelling tutorships allowed young men of sound education but small means to gain international experience, add social and cultural polish, and thereby expand their horizons. Several figures who later achieved distinction in public, clerical, or university life, served apprenticeships as travelling tutors.[56] The most famous of these was Thomas Hobbes, who took two generations of Cavendishes on tours of France and Italy in 1614–15 and 1634–36, in addition to making a tour to France and Switzerland with Gervase Clifton in 1629–30.[57] Another was Andrew Marvell, who travelled in France, Italy and Spain as tutor to some (as yet unidentified) noblemen in the mid-1640s, and again in France with Cromwell's

---

[51] On Huygens see Rosalie L. Colie, *'Some Thankfulnesse to Constantine': A Study of the English Influence upon the Early Works of Constantijn Huygens* (The Hague: Nijhoff, 1956). Huygens also figures prominently in Lisa Jardine, *Going Dutch: How England Plundered Holland's Glory* (London: Harper, 2008).

[52] S.A. Baron, 'Weckerlin, Georg Rudolph', *ODNB*.

[53] Boswell had earlier served in the Parisian embassies of Doncaster and Herbert. A. Stewart, 'Boswell, Sir William', *ODNB*.

[54] Born in the Netherlands, Gerbier had come to London as part of a 1616 embassy of the States General, attached himself to Buckingham and settled there. J. Wood, 'Gerbier, Sir Balthazar', *ODNB*; Chaney, *Evolution*, pp. 215–25.

[55] Stoye, *English Travellers Abroad*, pp. 17–46 (tutors), pp. 63, 281 (war).

[56] For some examples, see Timothy Raylor, 'Milton, Hartlib, and the Education of the Aristocracy', in *The Oxford Handbook of Milton*, ed. Nicholas McDowell and Nigel Smith (Oxford: Oxford University Press, 2009), pp. 382–406 (p. 390, n. 32).

[57] On these journeys, see Malcolm, *Aspects*, pp. 6, 11–12, 9.

nephew, William Dutton, in 1656.[58] Another was Isaac Marcombes, who travelled in France, Switzerland and Italy with Robert Boyle (and his brothers) in the late 1630s and early 1640s.[59] During the 1640s and 1650s several dispossessed clergymen travelled as tutors: in the later 1640s, for example, Isaac Basire, Archdeacon of Northumberland, escorted John Andrews, William Ashburnham and Thomas Lambton through France and Italy.[60]

Educational tourism was largely a one-way street, but the movement of religious refugees flowed in both directions. Foreign Protestants came to England – like the Huguenot medical professor Theodore Turquet de Mayerne, who became a prominent court physician,[61] or the Dalmatian cleric Marc Antonio De Dominis, sometime Archbishop of Spalato, who converted and served, for a few years, as Dean of Windsor, before recanting and returning to Rome for trial and, as it turned out, death in prison.[62] English Catholics went abroad, among them the priest, Thomas White, who was a student and then professor at Douai.[63] Travelling abroad also were freelance intellectuals, like the Aberdonian William Davisson, who emigrated for financial reasons and became Professor of Chemistry and royal physician at Paris; and merchants, like Robert Bargrave.[64] And then there was Sir Kenelm Digby, that unclassifiable gadfly, who spent time at the courts of Paris, Madrid, London and Rome, converted from Roman Catholicism to Anglicanism and back again, engaged in piracy in the Mediterranean, and chemical experiments at both Gresham College and the Collège de Boncourt.[65]

---

[58]   Nicholas von Maltzahn, *An Andrew Marvell Chronology* (Basingstoke and New York: Palgrave, 2005), pp. 30–31, 43–4; Chaney, *Grand Tour*, pp. 347–50. An unnoticed reference to Dutton's being at Saumur with his tutor (Marvell) appears in a letter of James Scudamore to Sir Richard Browne of 30 June 1656, in which he notes the presence there of 'yong Mr Dutton with an English Tutour & Gouerno^r'; Misc. English, Pierpont Morgan Library, New York. This precedes by some six weeks Scudamore's well-known chararcterization of Marvell as 'a notable English Italo-Machavillian'; von Maltzahn, *Chronology*, p. 44.

[59]   R.E.W. Maddison, *The Life of the Honourable Robert Boyle, F.R.S.* (London: Taylor & Francis, 1969), pp. 21, 26–53.

[60]   Chaney, *Grand Tour*, pp. 58, 331–2; [Basire], *Travels*.

[61]   Hugh Trevor-Roper, *Europe's Physician: The Various Life of Sir Theodore de Mayerne* (New Haven and London: Yale University Press, 2006).

[62]   Noel Malcolm, *De Dominis (1560–1624): Venetian, Anglican, Ecumenist and Relapsed Heretic* (London: Strickland & Scott, 1984).

[63]   Beverley Southgate, *'Covetous of Truth': The Life and Work of Thomas White, 1593–1676* (Dordrecht, Boston, and London: Kluwer Academic Publications, 1993), pp. 21–33.

[64]   L. Principe, 'Davisson, William', *ODNB*; Robert Bargrave, *The Travel Diary of Robert Bargrave, Levant Merchant 1647–1656*, ed. Michael G. Brennan (London: Hakluyt Society, 1999), Ser. III, vol. 3.

[65]   Stoye, *English Travellers Abroad*, pp. 315–16; M. Foster, 'Digby, Sir Kenelm', *ODNB*; Petersson, *Ornament of England*.

Contacts established through travel could be and were maintained by means of correspondence, as in the case of the regular newsletters sent by the Venetian friar Fulgenzio Micanzio to the Devonshire Cavendishes after the tour of 1615. (Micanzio's letters were translated by Hobbes for domestic circulation.)[66] By means of correspondence, even those who had never been abroad could be, and perhaps more widely than we have hitherto realized, were, connected to a continent-wide web of intellectual exchange. Such contacts were facilitated by the intelligencers: those crucial hubs in the republic of letters, who took it upon themselves to act as clearing houses for the exchange of information. These included Marin Mersenne in Paris, with contacts in France, Italy and the Low Countries; and Samuel Hartlib in London, with contacts in the Imperial territories, Bermuda and New England. Through Hartlib, a provincial gentleman like Sir Justinian Isham in Northamptonshire could find out about the latest theories of the Moravian educational philosopher, Jan Amos Comenius.[67]

While the main traffic of travellers, expatriates and émigrés was undoubtedly from England to the continent, we should not underestimate the impact of continental travellers and emigrants to England, of whom Hartlib, of course, was one. Nor should we downplay foreign interest in England. Descartes was planning a visit to England, perhaps with a view to settling here, in 1630; a decade or so later the possibility of a formal invitation was discussed in the Mersenne circle; it probably came from Sir Kenelm Digby.[68] Comenius did of course visit England, under the sponsorship of Hartlib and his supporters, in 1642: not, as it turned out, the most propitious moment for the realization of the pansophic dream. Even intellectuals who presumably had not the slightest intention of visiting England nonetheless took an interest in it that may surprise us. Stefano Villani has recently shown that Giovanni Francesco Loredano, of the Venetian Academy of the Incogniti, took English lessons from Sir Aston Cokayne, while that Derbyshire gentleman was on his tour of Italy in the 1630s.[69]

All this is a brief and inadequate sketch of some very broad territory. There are more points of contact than I have indicated, and many of those I have touched upon await full exploration. But I hope I have provided sufficient evidence to suggest the truth of Stoye's claim that, when they went abroad, many – like

---

[66]   Fulgenzio Micanzio, *Lettere a William Cavendish (1615–1628)*, trans. by Thomas Hobbes, Scrinium Historicale, XV (Rome: Istuto storico O.S.M., 1987).

[67]   George H. Turnbull, *Hartlib, Dury and Comenius: Gleanings from Hartlib's Papers* (London and Liverpool: Hodder & Stroughton, 1948), pp. 347, 361, 362.

[68]   Stephen Gaukroger, *Descartes: An Intellectual Biography* (Oxford: Clarendon Press, 1995), pp. 361, 463, n. 27.

[69]   Stefano Villani, 'The English Civil Wars and the Interregnum in Italian Historiography in the 17th century', in *Cromohs Virtual Seminars. Recent historiographical trends of the British Studies (17th–18th Centuries)*, ed. M. Caricchio and G. Tarantino (2006–07), pp. 1–4; http://www.cromohs.unifi.it/seminari/villani_ecv.html.

Hobbes to France, Fanshawe to Spain, or Arundel to Italy – were returning to familiar territory.

V

I have tried to show that strong contacts between England and the continent existed before the war; but this does not of course prove that anything significant for the study of intellectual or cultural history was communicated through them. Those familiar with the work of the intelligencers Hartlib in London or Mersenne in Paris will need little persuasion of the validity of such a claim. For those who are not, let me try to illustrate a little more particularly the richness of some of these connections. I shall offer two examples of English visitors to France: one an ambassador, the other a travelling tutor.

Our ambassador is Edward, Lord Herbert of Cherbury, who composed the bulk of *De veritate*, his treatise on epistemology and metaphysics, while resident at Paris in the early 1620s. On its completion, he sent drafts to two local readers for comment. Such readers may have been local, but they formed an international audience. One was Hugo Grotius, then also serving as a diplomat in Paris; the other, the Silesian cleric Daniel Tilenus, Professor of Theology at Sedan. Pressed by both Grotius and Tilenus to publish the book he did so – though not before praying for and receiving a sign of divine encouragement, in the form of 'a Loud though yet Gentle noise' from the heavens.[70] The book was published at Paris, but the Parisian link does not end there. In 1639 Mersenne distributed copies of a French translation to Descartes and others for comment. Campanella, Peiresc, and Gassendi all offered criticism; some circulated it still wider: from Gassendi, for instance, it passed to Elia Diodati.[71] Through Hartlib, the book was distributed in the German-speaking world; a letter about it from Hartlib's young associate, Joachim Hubner, survives among the Herbert papers.[72] Such comments and criticisms furnished the basis for future recensions of and additions to the work.

Our travelling tutor is Hobbes. Reconstructing Hobbes's intellectual development prior to the 1640s is a hazardous enterprise: the records are fragmentary, the corpus unclear, the datings in dispute. Nonetheless, I think we can safely endorse the claim that the 1630s were crucial years, and that the contacts he made as a travelling tutor were key in effecting his shift from humanist scholar to natural philosopher. It was in a private library in Geneva in 1630 that he allegedly experienced his 'Euclidean eureka' – that moment when he caught sight of an open copy of Euclid in a gentleman's library and grasped, for the first time, the

---

[70]   Edward Herbert, *The Life of Edward, Lord Herbert of Cherbury*, ed. James M. Shuttleworth (Oxford: Oxford University Press, 1976), pp. 120–21.

[71]   Mario M. Rossi, *La Vita, Le Opere, I Tempi di Edoardo Herbert di Chirbury*, 3 vols (Florence, 1947), ii, 496, 518–39; iii, 435–7.

[72]   Rossi, *La Vita*, iii, 437–42.

broad philosophical implications of the geometric method of deduction.[73] And it was during his extended stay in Paris in 1634–36 that he first entered Mersenne's circle and began, as he later tells us, to be counted a philosopher. It was here that he started to 'investigate the principles of natural science', and to do so, moreover, in terms of the nature and varieties of motion.[74] In Paris, he was in daily contact with Mersenne, and he met or befriended other French intellectuals in Mersenne's orbit: Gassendi, Mydorge, and Roberval. Also involved in this same community were expatriated British intellectuals like Kenelm Digby, with whom he discussed philosophy, and William Davisson, whose chemical experiments he observed. On his return to England Hobbes kept up a correspondence with both Mersenne and Digby. Digby, for instance, sent him a copy of Descartes's *Discourse of Method*, soon after its appearance.[75] It was on his return that Hobbes seems to have set about expounding a system of philosophy based upon the ideas he had begun to develop in Paris. In a letter of 1637, Digby enquires about the progress of Hobbes's 'Logic', by which he seems to refer to an early version of what became the opening part of *De corpore*.[76] Although Hobbes's ideas would undergo expansion, refinement and, in certain areas, significant change over the next two decades, the fundamental principle of his philosophy – that all phenomena are the product of motion – appears to have been set in place during his stay in Paris in the late 1630s.

There is almost certainly nothing in the preceding sketches to surprise a historian of science or philosophy. In such disciplines (which, unlike the study of literature, are not organized by national or linguistic categories), the richness of pre-war intellectual links between London and the continent is taken for granted. And this, I think, is why historians working in such fields have largely ignored the suggestion that the royalist exile was a discrete phenomenon, or a special case, involving a sudden and dramatic end to England's isolation.

Let us turn now from philosophy to examine the case of poetry, retaining our focus on France. The Frenchification of English culture is popularly thought of as a Restoration phenomenon. Recent scholarship, however, has been assiduous in detecting French influences on English literature at a much earlier date. The main focus of such work has, naturally, been the court of Henrietta Maria. Scholarship by John Peacock, Erica Veevers, and more recently Melinda Gough and Karin Britland has shown how Davenant and Jones employed French attitudes and themes, French topics and devices in their composition of masques for the queen.[77] The influence of the Parisian salons and the précieux literary culture

[73]   Malcolm, *Aspects*, p. 9.

[74]   Hobbes, *Thomas Hobbes malmesburiensis opera philosophica quae latine scripsit omnia*, ed. William Molesworth, 5 vols (London: Bohn, 1839–45), i, p. xiv; Malcolm, *Aspects*, p. 12.

[75]   Hobbes, *Correspondence*, ed. Noel Malcolm, 2 vols (Oxford, 1994), i, 51.

[76]   *Ibid.*, i, 42–3; Malcolm, *Aspects*, p. 12.

[77]   John Peacock, 'The French Element in Inigo Jones's masque designs', in *The Court Masque*, ed. David Lindley (Manchester: Manchester University Press, 1984), pp. 149–68;

which flourished in them has been examined by Julie Sanders and others.[78] A strong argument for this kind of influence is Thomas Kaminski's reading of the Caroline lyrics of Edmund Waller as instances of what he calls 'English préciosité'.[79] What Kaminski demonstrates is the way in which Waller translates the distinctive tone and the idiom of Parisian salon poetry – above all, that of Voiture – into a Francophile but decidedly English setting.

Such scholarship speaks for itself; I shall simply make two additional points about French influence on English literature in the early seventeenth century. One is that it predates the French marriage. This is becoming increasingly clear through the work of scholars like Marie-Claude Canova-Green, Barbara Ravelhofer, and James Knowles.[80] One of the key figures here was the Francophile courtier, James Hay, Viscount Doncaster, and later Earl of Carlisle. Doncaster's Paris embassy of 1616 elicited a complimentary ode from the court poet Marc de Mailliet. In the following winter, and presumably through Doncaster's offices, de Mailliet visited London and wrote a ballet, which was performed before Queen Anne by a group of French musicians. Knowles plausibly suggests that it was to this ballet that Jonson replied three days later in the Doncaster-sponsored *Lovers Made Men*.[81] This masque, like others sponsored by Doncaster, reveals a sophisticated understanding of the principles of the French *ballets de cour*, which were loose and linear in structure, featuring a series of entries, allowing courtiers to make multiple appearances.

Peacock, *The Stage Designs of Inigo Jones: The European Context* (Cambridge: Cambridge University Press, 1995); Erica Veevers, *Images of Love and Religion: Queen Henrietta Maria and Court Entertainments* (Cambridge: Cambridge University Press, 1989); Melinda Gough, 'A Newly Discovered Performance by Henrietta Maria', *Huntington Library Quarterly*, 65 (2002), 435–47; Gough, '"Not as Myself": The Queen's Voice in *Tempe Restored*', *Modern Philology*, 101 (2003), 48–67; Karen Britland, '"All emulation cease, and jars": Political Possibilities in *Chloridia*, Queen Henrietta Maria's Masque of 1631', *Ben Jonson Journal*, 9 (2002), 87–108; Britland, *Drama at the Courts of Queen Henrietta Maria* (Cambridge: Cambridge University Press, 2006). See also Barbara Ravelhofer, *The Early Stuart Masque: Dance, Costume, and Music* (Oxford: Oxford University Press, 2006).

[78] Julie Sanders, 'Caroline Salon Culture and Female Agency: The Countess of Carlisle, Henrietta Maria, and Public Theatre', *Theatre Journal*, 52 (2000), 449–64; see also Raymond Anselment, 'The Countess of Carlisle and Caroline Praise: Convention and Reality', *Studies in Philology*, 82 (1985), 212–33; and the seminal article on the subject: J.B. Fletcher, 'Précieuses at the Court of Charles I', *Journal of Comparative Literature*, 1 (1903), 120–53.

[79] Thomas Kaminski, 'Edmund Waller: English Precieux', *Philological Quarterly*, 79 (2000), 19–43.

[80] Marie-Claude Canova-Green, *La Politique-spectacle au grand siècle: les rapports franco-anglais* (Paris, Seattle and Tübingen: Biblio 17, 1993); Barbara Ravelhofer, 'Burlesque Ballet, a Ballad, and a Banquet in Ben Jonson's The Gypsies Metamorphos'd (1621)', *Dance Research*, 25 (2007), 144–55; James R. Knowles, 'The "Running Masque" Recovered: A Masque for the Marquess of Buckingham (c. 1619–20)', *English Manuscript Studies 1100–1700*, 8 (2000), 79–135.

[81] Knowles, 'The "Running Masque"', 102.

Doncaster's masques responded by incorporating multiple appearances, but without abandoning the Jonsonian antithesis between masque and antimasque. This was achieved by means of the structural device of metamorphosis, lovers made men. Or, as in the masque he offered to the visiting ambassador extraordinary, marèchal de Cadenet, in January 1621: giants made stones made lovers.[82]

The second claim I want to make about the French impact on pre-war English literature is that we need to investigate not merely French influences on English writing, but the presence in England of French poets.[83] Among de Cadenet's entourage in the embassy of 1621 was Theophile de Viau, who presented an ode to Buckingham.[84] In 1631 Saint-Amant visited London and wrote a long manuscript ode to the king and queen. In the dedicatory epistle to it he grumbled about the large number of rotten French rhymers ('miserable rimailleurs') then hanging around the English court.[85] Who were they? We do not know, but Voiture visited England in 1633, and Tristan l'Hermite in the following year, later composing a *roman à clef* on the basis of his experiences (*Le Page disgracié*).[86] The possible payoffs for investigating this territory are suggested by Karen Britland's attribution of *Floriméne*, the queen's pastoral of 1635, to the poet and academician, Boisrobert.[87]

It seems, in sum, that neither the strong claim that intellectual or literary contacts between England and the continent began with the exile, nor the more measured one that the exile precipitated the redefinition of 'a previously insular England within a broader continental context', can be regarded as proven. The case I have been trying to urge is that we have underestimated – and quite seriously underestimated – the nature and extent of contacts between England and the continent prior to the civil war. I do not regard myself as having proven this case; but I hope I have at least been able to raise the possibility that it is just, and that more research on such contacts would be profitable.

VI

I turn now to the second part of my argument, in which I attempt to assess the impact of the exile for intellectual and cultural history, focusing still on France,

---

[82] Timothy Raylor, *The Essex House Masque of 1621: Viscount Doncaster and the Jacobean Masque* (Pittsburgh: Duquesne University Press, 2000).

[83] For a general overview, see Canova-Green, *La Politique-spectacle*, pp. 183–218.

[84] Theophile de Viau, *Oeuvres poétiques*, ed. Guido Saba (Paris: Classiques Garnier, 1990), pp. 41–4.

[85] Margaret Pickel, *Charles I as Patron of Poetry and Drama* (London: Frederick Muller, 1936), p. 167.

[86] Canova-Green, *La Politique-spectacle*, pp. 270, 201; Britland, *Drama at the Courts*, pp. 133–4.

[87] Karen Britland, '*Florimène*: The Author and Occasion', *Review of English Studies*, n.s. 53 (2002), 475–83; Britland, *Drama at the Courts*, pp. 156–63.

and remaining on the ground of philosophy and of poetry. Was it, as Hardacre and others would have it, a turning point? I noted earlier the dangerous attractiveness of watersheds: our desire to discover them; our tendency to exaggerate their significance. The case at hand seems particularly liable to this kind of exaggeration because, if I am right about our failure to take the measure of England's contacts with Europe before the war, then we lack an accurate yardstick by which to assess the distinctiveness of travel during and after it.

Doubtless for many of those who went abroad the experience was transformational. But I am not sure that such changes led to repercussions sufficiently broad or fundamental to be thought of as a cultural watershed. Nor should we be too quick to attribute changes directly to the impact of continental culture. In addition to sparking fresh interests and changes of direction in some, the experience of exile or emigration gave many of those who went abroad the time and the freedom to pursue established interests. This was perhaps particularly true of the older generation. The Marquess of Newcastle, for instance, was developing his new method of horsemanship by the mid-1630s; not until his retreat at Antwerp in the 1650s did he find the time to write up an account of it. His long letter of political advice, presented to Charles II at the end of the 1650s, differs, as Conal Condren has shown us, in its scope and its level of detail from that he delivered to him in the 1630s, but not in its fundamental perspective.[88] For poetry and for philosophy, the exile involved significant repercussions, but in neither case are these necessarily quite the ones envisaged by Hardacre. Starting again with philosophy, let us look once more at Hobbes.

I have already made the claim that the foundations of Hobbes's philosophical system were laid in Paris in the 1630s. His decade in Paris saw changes of mind on local issues – the vacuum, for instance, the existence of which he first denied and then accepted – and responses to new works and new points of view. There was a massive expansion of his system. But there was not, I think, any fundamental change in direction from the analysis by motion he had first postulated in the middle 1630s. The main impact of his Paris period seems to have been that it allowed him the time and the freedom to develop his philosophy – time to work out its various component parts and to determine the logical relations between them; and freedom to write most of it up. Anticipating an international rather than a narrowly English readership, he did so in Latin. We can illustrate this by contrasting Hobbes's philosophical output in the four years following his return from Paris in the autumn of 1636 with his output in the four years following his return to Paris at the end of 1640.

The difficulty of finding the time and the freedom to study is a running theme in Hobbes's correspondence. A letter from Digby of January 1637 illustrates both the fact and, inadvertently, the causes of this concern. In his letter, Digby writes

---

[88]   Conal Condren, 'Casuistry to Newcastle: *The Prince* in the World of the Book', in *Political Discourse in Early Modern Britain*, ed. Nicholas Phillipson and Quentin Skinner (Cambridge: Cambridge University Press, 1993), pp. 164–86.

'I am exceeding glad to heare you haue so perfect freedome both of minde and time to study; and do expect proportionable effects of them'. Digby then goes on to ask a question about Hobbes's position on logic, to request copies of anything he has recently written, and to thank him for managing his packets of mail. He also encloses, for Hobbes to read, a copy of a paper he had recently written on the devils of Loudun.[89] Hobbes's concern about lack of freedom to work comes through especially strongly in the letters he wrote to Newcastle in the summer and autumn of 1636.[90] From these it appears that Hobbes was entertaining the possibility of a move to Welbeck, in order to focus on his studies. He did not go; but after his return Hobbes became heavily involved in serving the Welbeck Cavendishes in their wide-ranging intellectual interests. During this period he wrote nothing entirely independently of the Cavendish family. The only original work he certainly produced at this time was *The Elements of Law*, an economical vernacular exposition of the rudiments of his system, followed by a more particular and detailed statement of its implications for civil philosophy. This he wrote at Newcastle's request and presented to him. The picture changes somewhat if we include the digest of Aristotle's *Rhetoric* he was involved in preparing in the course of his work as tutor to young William Cavendish of the Devonshire branch.[91] It changes still further if we include also the so-called 'Short Tract on First Principles', a brief work of disputed authorship.[92] But even if we include these works, the picture does not change radically. Hobbes was writing with at least one eye on the Cavendish family.

Hobbes's first four years in Paris were, by contrast, and in large part thanks to Mersenne, perhaps the most stimulating and probably the most productive of his life. Soon after his arrival, around December 1640, he responded, at Mersenne's request, to Descartes' *Meditations*, penning a series of objections which were soon published and which opened up an acrimonious dispute between the two men over questions of priority and indebtedness. At around the same time – and again with an eye on Mersenne – he brought to completion at least part of a substantial Latin treatise, the surviving portion of which concerns optics and is conceived, in large part, as a critique of Descartes's *Dioptrique*.[93] He also composed and had printed in a limited edition the third section of his tripartite *Elements of Philosophy*,

---

[89]   Hobbes, *Correspondence*, i, 42, 43–5.

[90]   *Ibid.*, i, 32, 37.

[91]   On which, see Malcolm, *Aspects*, p. 9.

[92]   On the authorship dispute, see Malcolm, *Aspects*, pp. 80–145; Timothy Raylor, 'Hobbes, Payne, and A Short Tract on First Principles', *Historical Journal*, 44 (2001), 29–58; Karl Schuhmann, 'Le *Short Tract*: première oeuvre philosophique de Hobbes', *Hobbes Studies*, 8 (1995), 3–96.

[93]   For this dating, see Timothy Raylor, 'The Date and Script of Hobbes's Latin Optical Manuscript', *English Manuscript Studies, 1100–1700*, 12 (2005), 201–9; Noel Malcolm, 'Hobbes, The Latin Optical Manuscript, and the Parisian Scribe', *English Manuscript Studies, 1100–1700*, 12 (2005), 210–32.

De cive (1642). While this drew on work he had undertaken in the later 1630s – much of it recasts material from *The Elements of Law* – this was material which had not, as far as we know, been disposed in such a manner or formally written out in Latin until then. Almost immediately after completing *De cive* he must have launched into his extended response to the *De mundo* of Thomas White, which appeared in the same year. White was, as we have already seen, an English Catholic priest and philosopher; his *De mundo* was an attempt to negotiate a rapprochement between the new physics and mechanics of Galileo, and the Aristotelian physics and metaphysics of the Schools. Hobbes's critique of it was almost certainly undertaken at the suggestion of Mersenne. The result, which survives in a manuscript in the Bibliothèque nationale, is a massive series of animadversions on White's book, covering around 450 folio sheets. It seems to have been written in a torrent, with White serving as the occasion for the ad hoc unpacking of Hobbes's own views on philosophy, physics and metaphysics.[94] These ideas appear to have been in a state of flux, with sheets, chapters and clusters of chapters undergoing revision and replacement as the scribal fair copy, eventually presented to Mersenne, was prepared.[95]

Much of the material in Hobbes's lengthy manuscript, now generally known as the *Anti-White*, covered ground designated for discussion in the first part of *The Elements of Philosophy*, *De corpore*. Indeed, he appears to have begun work on *De corpore* at about the same time as he was writing against White. A perplexing manuscript fragment, probably dating from the same period and now in the National Library of Wales, contains material which later surfaces in the early chapters of the printed text of *De corpore*.[96] In the case of Hobbes (and also, to a lesser extent, of Digby), the early years of exile look less like a watershed than a dam-burst. It is not hard to see why: exile gave Hobbes an unprecedented degree of liberty from the obligations of patronage – obligations that had played, and would once again play – a significant part in his life.

To clinch this point, and to emphasize once again the way in which the intellectual history of the period is in some ways at odds with the history of the royalists in exile, let us look briefly at what happened to Hobbes's progress in the years immediately following the royalist defeat at Marston Moor. The collapse of the king's northern forces at Marston Moor brought a wave of cavaliers to the continent[97]; among them were two of Hobbes's strongest well-wishers and patrons, William, Marquess of Newcastle and his scholarly brother, Sir Charles. The arrival of his patrons at Paris in 1645 sucked Hobbes into their orbit, bringing him additional support, companionship and stimulation, but also time-consuming

---

[94]   Malcolm, *Aspects*, p. 17.

[95]   The best extant account of the manuscript is Thomas Hobbes, *Critique du 'De mundo' de Thomas White*, ed. Jean Jacquot and Harold W. Jones (Paris: Librarie philosophique J. Vrin, 1973), pp. 89–96.

[96]   National Library of Wales, MS 5297. On the dating, see Malcolm, *Aspects*, pp. 13, 18.

[97]   Chaney, *Grand Tour*, pp. 54–5.

obligations. Following the arrival at Paris of the Cavendish brothers in the spring of 1645, Hobbes's activities and output undergo a visible shift. In the summer Newcastle obliged him to take part with Bishop Bramhall in a staged debate on the question of free will. This may not in itself have been too onerous, but it required a written position paper. And when this found its way into print a decade later it set off another long and diverting quarrel. By the end of the same year he had written, at Newcastle's urging, a substantial treatise on optics – in English, so that the Marquess could read it. More informally, he assisted the Cavendish brothers with a range of enquiries – offering his assessments of Descartes and Rheita, reviewing mathematical theorems, and assisting Sir Charles with his geometrical investigations.[98] It was probably around this time that he composed, again for Newcastle, the essay on the relative strength of two swords that the Marquess subsequently marked up for incorporation into his own treatise on fencing.[99] In the spring of 1646 he managed to see through the press the second edition of *De cive*, but it is hard to imagine that progress on *De corpore* was unaffected by the responsibilities of clientage. By the summer of 1646, Hobbes was planning a rural retreat, to the estate of a friend in Languedoc, where he might be able to get some work done. As Sir Charles put it in a letter of July 1646: 'M^r: Hobbes is goeing out of towne to a more retired place for his sudies [*sic*] so that you must not nowe direct your letters to him but to Monsr: de Bose'.[100] At this very moment, however, Prince Charles appeared at Paris, and Hobbes was invited to serve him as mathematics tutor.[101] Not only did this put paid to his planned retreat, it also took him away, for long periods, from Paris and Mersenne: took him, moreover, to what one imagines must have been the rather uncongenial hothouse of the court of Henrietta Maria at Saint Germain-en-Laye. On one occasion, in November 1646, Hobbes visited Paris briefly, but did not even have time to see Mersenne. Sir Charles was unconcerned about the impact of Hobbes's teaching on his research, assuring Pell in October 1646 that 'I beleeue he hath spare time enough besides to goe on with his philosophie'; but as modern academics can imagine only too well, such a view was overly optimistic.[102] We should not exaggerate the uncongeniality or the impact of Hobbes's teaching post; he evidently found some stimulating company among the courtiers at S. Germain: a fascinating letter from Adrian May, for example, picks up on a discussion of perception the two men had held while walking in the garden at S. Germain.[103] Nor can Hobbes's failure to make progress

---

[98] Malcolm, *Aspects*, p. 18.

[99] BL, Harleian MS 5219: see Timothy Raylor, 'Thomas Hobbes and "The Mathematical Demonstration of the Sword"', *Seventeenth Century*, 15 (2000), 175–98.

[100] Malcolm and Stedall, *John Pell*, p. 487.

[101] While it would seem reasonable to imagine that Newcastle had some hand in securing this appointment, he seems to have had nothing to do with it: compare with Malcolm, *Aspects*, p. 18; Malcolm and Stedall, *John Pell*, p. 495.

[102] Hobbes, *Correspondence*, i, 147; Malcolm and Stedall, *John Pell*, p. 490.

[103] Hobbes, *Correspondence*, i, 148–50.

be blamed entirely upon his teaching responsibilities: in 1647 he fell seriously ill. But not until after the departure from Paris in the summer of 1648 of both the prince and the Cavendish brothers do we once again hear that Hobbes has resumed work on *De corpore*. He appears to have worked on it for most of that year, quietly setting it aside in the autumn of 1649 to write *Leviathan*.[104]

Hobbes's French sojourn does not, in sum, fit neatly within the paradigm of a royalist exile as involving either intense intellectual dislocation or a profound cultural turning point. Yes, Hobbes invariably presents his flight to Paris as an escape from danger – and it was clearly a kind of self-exile; but he also presents it as a return: to a beloved city, to old friends, to an intellectual community. He wrote in his verse autobiography of returning to his 'beloved Paris' ('dilectam ... Lutetiam').[105] Writing from Paris to Viscount Scudamore in April 1641, he remarked that 'Here I liue contentedly wth my old frend Monsr du Bosc'.[106] In both verse and prose autobiographies, Hobbes celebrates the period as one in which he engaged in philosophical study with Gassendi and Mersenne, lauding the latter as 'the axis' around which turned all the planets in the intellectual cosmos.[107] Until the fortunes of war brought Welbeck and St. James's to Paris, he appears to have thrived as a member of the Parisian intelligentsia, just as he had done on his visit there in the 1630s. During this period, he looks more like an émigré than an exile; and neither at the time nor in his late autobiographies does Hobbes himself present his Paris period as an exile.[108] Not until the death of Mersenne and the departure of Gassendi in the autumn of 1648 robbed him of his closest intellectual companions did Hobbes seem to give serious thought to the possibility

---

[104] *Ibid.*, i, 177 (in which he notes that obligations of clientage continue to retard his progress); Malcolm, *Aspects*, p. 19.

[105] Hobbes, *Opera philosophica*, i, xc; cp. pp. xv, xxix–xxxii.

[106] Hobbes, *Correspondence*, i, 115.

[107] *Opera philosophica*, i, pp. xv, xci–xcii; there are readily accessible translations in Thomas Hobbes, *The Elements of Law Natural and Politic*, ed. J.C.A. Gaskin (Oxford and New York: Oxford University Press, 1994), pp. 247, 258–9. This is very much the burden also of the Aubrey-Blackburne biography of Hobbes; *Opera philosophica*, i, pp. xxix–xxxvii.

[108] As D'Addario notes, the anonymous English translation of Hobbes's Latin verse autobiography deploys the term to characterize Hobbes's position after his rejection by the court of Charles II in the wake of *Leviathan*: '[I] stood amazed, like a poor Exile'; *Exile and Journey*, p. 78; but this denotes banishment from the royal court rather than country; and in the Latin original Hobbes uses the more precise term 'proscripto': an outlaw or proscribed person, which aptly characterizes Hobbes's new situation as *persona non grata* at court; Hobbes, *Opera philosophica*, i, p. xciii. For Hobbes's understanding of exile as legal banishment, see *The Elements of Law*, XXI.14; *Leviathan* (London, 1651), p. 165. In a careful analysis of the text of Hobbes's verse *Vita*, John K. Hale notes that it is the return to London, rather than the sojourn in Paris, that Hobbes presents as an exile: 'Thomas Hobbes' Poem of Exile: 'The Verse *Vita* and Ovid's *Tristria* 4.10', *Scholia: Natal Studies in Classical Antiquity*, 17 (2008), 92–105 (pp. 100–103).

of returning to England.[109] In sum, rather than leading to alienation and isolation, Hobbes's flight to Paris brought him to the centre of the European republic of letters and precipitated a period of intense productivity. But it did not mark a major turning point in his intellectual development.

VII

In turning from philosophy to poetry, we are confronted with Hardacre's claim that 'The banishment of the literary leaders of the day had pronounced repercussions'.[110] Among these leaders he identifies Denham, Davenant, Cowley and Waller. 'In their travels' he writes, 'such men came into contact with Continental tendencies which they transplanted to England after their return'.[111] Unfortunately, Hardacre's prime example of such influences is Sir John Mennes, whom Hardacre supposes, on the basis of the publication of some of his verses in collections of the mid-1650s, to have picked up what he calls 'the French art of burlesque' in exile. The problem with this claim is that these verses were not new. Mennes and his associates had been writing and circulating them since the mid-1630s – even, it appears, before the French master of burlesque, Paul Scarron, had adopted the mode. Mennes did pen at least one poem during his exile – a light-hearted account of a drunken court entertainment at Cologne – but it differs in no significant ways from his pre-war productions.[112]

Hardacre's second example of pronounced repercussions is the fashion for writing critical prefaces to poems and plays – a claim which suggests a lack of familiarity with Spenser or Jonson. If we look closely at Davenant's Preface to *Gondibert* we see that its main continental sources are of no recent vintage: Tasso's *Discorsi*, which had appeared in the previous century, and Jean Chapelain's prefatory 'Lettre ou Discours' to Marino's *L'Adone*, which first appeared in 1623.[113] Nor do such sources provide its foundations, which are, as Dowlin showed long ago, classical (the Horatian-Aristotelian tradition) and English (that tradition as interpreted by Sidney and Jonson).[114] To the extent that both the poem and the Preface are inflected with a new approach, this derives less from the field of literary criticism than from the introduction to that field of the psychology and

---

[109] Malcolm, *Aspects*, pp. 119–20; Hobbes, *Correspondence*, i, p. 179; compare with *ibid.*, 170 (May 1648), in which he expresses anxiety at the prospect – raised by his patron – of a return to England.

[110] 'Royalists in Exile', 362.

[111] *Ibid.*, 363.

[112] Timothy Raylor, *Cavaliers, Clubs, and Literary Culture: Sir John Mennes, James Smith, and the Order of the Fancy* (Newark: University of Delaware Press, 1994), pp. 196–7.

[113] Cornell M. Dowlin, *Sir William Davenant's 'Gondibert', its Preface, and Hobbes's Answer: A Study in English Neo-Classicism* (Philadelphia: Pennsylvania University Press, 1934), pp. 21–44.

[114] Dowlin, *Sir William Davenant's 'Gondibert'*, pp. 45–72.

political theory of Hobbes.[115] Such innovations are clearly the product of exile: Davenant encountered Hobbes at the Louvre and S. Germain during his tutorship of the prince. But they are the product of conversations among the émigrés rather than of continental influence.

We have already insisted upon French influence on English court poets before the war – especially on those who were, like Davenant and Waller, associated with the queen's court. What do we find once they go into exile? We are struck first by how little most of them seem to have written, next by how lacking in ambition or significance those works generally are, and finally by how many of these writers seem to have wrestled with anxieties about the value and purpose of poetry. The exception, of course, is Davenant, with his grandiose plans for a new kind of poem, and his insistence that such a poem would be a necessary arm of government. But even Davenant would be driven to despair, penning a lachrymose postscript from his prison in Cowes Castle, where he anticipated a sentence of death, and renounced further work on the poem.[116]

Waller and Denham afford rather different pictures. Waller, I have recently argued, explicitly abjured poetry after the recall of parliament, trying to re-launch himself as a political orator, an English Cicero.[117] During the same period, Denham by contrast tried, in *Coopers Hill,* to use poetry to resolve the constitutional crisis. After the royalist defeat the king himself, in the summer of 1647, urged him to abandon poetry as an occupation unsuited for one who wished to be 'thought fit for more serious Employments'.[118] Denham later claimed that he had followed the king's advice – though years later, at the Louvre, Charles II would present him with 'arguments to divert and put off the evil hours of our banishment'.[119] When we look at the poetic corpuses of Waller and Denham from this period, we notice how small, in all senses of the term, they are. It is, in this respect, telling that both men seem to have contributed to the collaborative debunking of *Gondibert,* in which they punctured the laureate's high hopes for his new romance-epic, and

---

[115] See Cowley's and Waller's commendatory poems on *Gondibert* (Davenant, *Gondibert,* pp. 269–71); Cowley's ode 'To Mr. Hobs' (*Poems,* pp. 188–92); and, for a general overview, Richard Hillyer, *Hobbes and his Poetic Contemporaries: Cultural Transmission in Early Modern England* (Basingstoke and New York: Palgrave, 2007). See also, for detailed discussion of Hobbes's impact on Davenant, James R. Jacob and Timothy Raylor, 'Opera and Obedience: Thomas Hobbes and *A Proposition for Advancement of Moralitie* by Sir William Davenant', *Seventeenth Century,* 6 (1991), 205–50.

[116] *Sir William Davenant's 'Gondibert',* ed. David F. Gladish (Oxford: Clarendon Press, 1971), pp. 250, 252; Mary Edmond, *Rare Sir William Davenant* (Manchester: Manchester University Press, 1987), pp. 116–18; Arthur Nethercot, *Sir William D'Avenant: Poet Laureate and Playwright-Manager* (Chicago: University of Chicago Press, 1938), pp. 267–9.

[117] Timothy Raylor, 'The Early Poetic Career of Edmund Waller', *Huntington Library Quarterly,* 69 (2006), 239–65 (pp. 262–5).

[118] *The Poetical Works of Sir John Denham,* ed. Theodore H. Banks, 2nd edn (Hamden: Archon Books, 1969), p. 59.

[119] *Ibid.,* p. 60.

his large ambitions for poetry.[120] Although he would take up (or return to) his ambitious translation of *The Aeneid* after returning to England, Denham's surviving output from the period of his exile consists of a few pieces of bantering comic doggerel, the general character of which may be inferred from the title of a single poem: 'To Sir John Mennis Being Invited from Calice to Bologne to eat a pig'.[121]

Waller's output is smaller, but more interesting. To the best of our knowledge it consists of four minor complimentary poems for friends and associates, along with whatever hand he may have had in the anti-*Gondibert* verses. (One of the four poems is, in fact, a poem in commendation of *Gondibert*.) Two poems written on his visit to Padua in 1646 appear to mark the resumption of his poetic persona. One of these, on the graduation from the medical school there of his countryman, George Rogers, was probably the first poem he wrote, or at least presented, after his poetic retirement; it is interesting for its oblique meditation on the value of poetry in a time of civil war.

> Verses to Dr. George Rogers
> On his taking the degree of Doctor of Physic at Padua, in the year 1646
>> When as of old the earth's bold children strove,
>> With hills on hills, to scale the throne of Jove,
>> Pallas and Mars stood by their sovereign's side,
>> And their bright arms in his defence employ'd;
>> While the wise Phoebus, Hermes, and the rest,
>> Who joy in peace, and love the Muses best,
>> Descending from their so distempered seat,
>> Our groves and meadows chose for their retreat.
>> There first Apollo tried the various use
>> Of herbs, and learned the virtues of their juice,   10
>> And framed that art, to which who can pretend
>> A juster title than our noble friend?
>> Whom the like tempest drives from his abode,

---

[120] The verses are reprinted by Gladish in *Sir William*, pp. 272–86. For discussion, see Nethercot, *D'Avenant*, pp. 273–7; Edmond, *Davenant*, pp. 109–10; Raylor, *Cavaliers, Clubs*, pp. 198–9.

[121] Denham, *Poetical Works*, p. 100. On Denham's Virgil and the difficulties of dating, see Jerome de Groot, 'John Denham and Lucy Hutchinson's Commonplace Book', *Studies in English Literature*, 48 (2008), 147–63; Brendan O. Hehir, *Harmony from Discords: A Life of Sir John Denham* (Berkeley and Los Angeles: University of California Press, 1968), pp. 11–13, 101–8. The slimness of their surviving corpuses from the period may in part be the result of depredation – a continual hazard for historians of the exile. Several poems from this period remained uncollected during their authors' lives and only subsequently came to light – two poems from Waller's visit to Padua, for example, surfaced relatively recently: a poem on George Rogers (discussed below), which was first included in Waller's corpus in Thorn Drury's edition of 1893, and a poem on the physician Vesling, first noticed by E.S. de Beer in 'An Uncollected Poem by Waller', *Review of English Studies*, 8 (1922), 203–5. Denham inscribed his anti-*Gondibert* verses, including some not printed in the 1653 edition, into an exemplar of his 1668 *Poems and Translations*; Denham, *Poetical Works*, pp. 311–25.

And like employment entertains abroad.
This crowns him here, and in the bays so earned,
His country's honour is no less concerned,
Since it appears not all the English rave,
To ruin bent; some study how to save;
And as Hippocrates did once extend
His sacred art, whole cities to amend;   20
So we, great friend suppose that thy great skill,
Thy gentle mind, and fair example, will,
At thy return, reclaim our frantic isle,
Their spirits calm, and peace again shall smile.[122]

The poem is an ephemeral production, designed for donation to a particular recipient on a particular occasion; but it has ambitions, as a good occasional poem should, to acknowledge the larger implications of the moment: ambitions which here involve reflection on the problem of the war, and on one's duties and obligations to one's country. (In light of the tendency to regard Waller as a royalist turncoat, it is worth pointing out how clearly he conceives of this as duty to country [ll. 16, 23], rather than to king or parliament.) It is an elegant apologia for Rogers: let no one criticize him for fleeing abroad at the start of the war (Rogers had taken his BM from Oxford in December 1642 and headed straight off to Padua);[123] by taking up medicine instead of arms he will, on returning home, provide the example and the skills with which to heal his country.

And yet we cannot help noticing how much more the poem suggests than it actually says. Hovering behind the discussion of medicine, lurking in the conventional but hardly necessary presentation of university study as a pastoral retreat, is an argument about poetry, and an apologia for the poet himself. Elsewhere in Waller's work Phoebus is invariably a figure for the poet (as in his famous 'Fable of Phoebus and Daphne applied'); why else, if not to establish this association, does he here invoke 'the rest,/Who … love the Muses best' (ll. 5–6)? But for all that Waller obviously wishes to associate his own poetry with Rogers's medicine he is, in the end, unable to do so – unable at least to make the connection explicit. The closure of the parallel may be permitted by the choice of 'spirits', as opposed to 'bodies', in the final line (poets, too, calm spirits) – but the reader has to work at it. Even the resolution of the poem's main argument seems to betray doubts about its strength. There is a typically Wallerian sleight of hand in the way the final clause does not, as at first it seems to, either depend upon the verbs of which Rogers is the agent ('reclaim', 'calm'), or follow necessarily from them. It tries but does not quite manage to articulate the claim that Rogers's medicine – and, by implication, Waller's poetry – will restore peace to England.

Cowley's case is different again. His collection of love lyrics, *The Mistress*, was published in London in 1647. Its considerable bulk and recent claims for its

---

[122] Waller, *The Poems of Edmund Waller*, ed. G. Thorn Drury, 2 vols (London, 1901), ii, 5.

[123] N. Moore, 'Rogers, George', rev. M. Bevan, *ODNB*.

innovativeness require some comment. I am not persuaded by the oft-repeated view that the collection represents a lyric watershed; this is supported by no contemporary evidence of reception and rests wholly on Cowley's own playful claim therein to be 'Love's Columbus'.[124] Charles Kay Smith's attempt to promote its novelty on the grounds of French *libertin* and Epicurean thought seems to me to blur together several rather different discourses.[125] The *libertins* were not necessarily Epicureans. And though Cowley occasionally poses as the Epicure of popular imagination – 'No *bound* nor *rule* my pleasures shall endure,/In Love there's none too much an *Epicure*' – it is a mistake to equate such playful posturing with the serious philosophical researches of a Gassendi.[126] Even the collection's bulk may be deceptive. Thomas Corns points to the way in which *The Mistress* 'assiduously rehearses the values and enthusiasms of the Caroline court';[127] but this might in part be because many of the poems in it are, as the Delaware edition suggests, of Caroline vintage.[128] Cowley did, of course, engage in some significant poetic experimentation and innovation; but he did so later, on Jersey, and following an encounter with Pindar, rather than in an immediate response to his French contemporaries. Even he would come publicly to abjure poetry, along with the royal cause, after the failure of Penruddock's rising in 1655; the despondent Preface to his *Works* of 1656 announces his intent: 'to make my self absolutely dead in a Poetical capacity, my resolution at present, is never to exercise any more that faculty'.[129]

The most remarkable immediate effect of the civil war exile on the leading English poets who went abroad appears, therefore, to have been varying degrees of pessimism about the value of poetry, or, at best, vacillation between optimism and despair. There is less evidence here of a watershed than of a drought. And to the extent that a degree of excitement infected the poets, it seems to have been inspired not by French neoclassicism, but by the philosophical ideas of their countryman, Hobbes.

On their return to England things changed. As the poets made their several accommodations with the Protectorate, most would again recur to the composition of poetry with serious ambitions: Waller in his *Panegyrick* on Cromwell; Denham in his revision and expansion of *Coopers Hill* and his *Aeneid* translation. Davenant would find an even more ambitious project than *Gondibert*

---

[124]   A. Cowley, *The Collected Works of Abraham Cowley*, ed. Thomas O. Calhoun et al., 6 vols (Newark, London, and Toronto: University of Delaware Press, 1989), ii.1, p. 62 (the phrase comes from the poem 'The Prophet').

[125]   Smith, 'French philosophy and interregnum poetry', pp. 197–8.

[126]   Cowley, *Collected Works*, ii.1, p. 77.

[127]   Thomas N. Corns, *Uncloistered Virtue: English Political Literature, 1640–1660* (Oxford: Oxford University Press, 1992), p. 251.

[128]   Cowley, *Collected Works*, ii.1, pp. 223–5.

[129]   Abraham Cowley, *Poems*, ed. Alfred R. Waller (Cambridge: Cambridge University Press, 1905), p. 6 (see also pp. 6–8); for discussion, see Corns, *Uncloistered Virtue*, pp. 255–9.

for pressing poetry into the service of government, through the multimedia art of opera.[130] But even this project, which seems at first so promising for the watershed argument, does not, in the end, constitute a complete rupture with the past. No doubt its immediate inspiration was Mazarin's introduction of Italian opera to Paris during the period of Davenant's residence there.[131] But the idea has a longer pedigree, traceable to March 1639, when Davenant secured a patent to build a large 'Theatre or Playhouse' behind the Three Kings in Fleet Street, 'wherein', for a paying audience, 'Plays, musical Entertainments, Scenes or other like Presentments, may be presented'.[132] This is clearly an attempt to establish something like the 'operas' Davenant would later stage at Rutland House.[133] Nor was this proposal a home-grown affair; it was probably inspired by the recent commercial success of the public opera houses of Venice, no less than three of which had opened in the three years prior to 1639.[134] Davenant's theatrical proposal suggests, once again, the existence of strong, pre-war contacts between England and the continent.

VIII

To the extent that it might be narrowly focused on royalist exiles, the intellectual and cultural history of the English presence on the continent during the period 1640–60 is a less promising subject than it might at first appear. Widened to include all those who, for whatever reason, travelled abroad during the years of trouble at home – the émigrés, expatriates and travellers – a richer field emerges. Thus understood, the cultural and intellectual importance of the civil war lies less in its creation of a discrete community of royalist exiles than in its stimulation of what was already a significant fashion among the English aristocracy and gentry for educational tourism on the continent. Once we follow Brennan (and ultimately

---

[130] Jacob and Raylor, 'Opera and Obedience'.

[131] Neal Zaslaw, 'The First Opera in Paris: A Study in the Politics of Art', in *Jean-Baptiste Lully and the Music of the French Baroque: Essays in Honor of James R. Anthony*, ed. John H. Heyer et al. (Cambridge: Cambridge University Press, 1989), pp. 7–23.

[132] *The Jacobean and Caroline Stage*, ed. Gerald E. Bentley, 7 vols (Oxford: Clarendon Press, 1941–68), vi, 304–9 (305); Edmond, *Davenant*, p. 75; also L.B. Campbell, *Scenes and Machines on the English Stage During the Renaissance: A Classical Revival* (Cambridge: Cambridge University Press, 1923), p. 210.

[133] Citing lack of commercial viability, Bentley doubts that the two schemes can be identified; but he recognizes a close relationship between them: *Jacobean and Caroline Stage*, vi, 306; compare with Glynne Wickham, *Early English Stages, 1300–1600*, 5 vols (London and New York: Routledge & Kegan Paul, 1972), ii.2, p. 205. The evidence cited in the following note suggests that Davenant had reason for imagining that his scheme might be profitable.

[134] Per Bjurström, *Giacomo Torelli and Baroque Stage Design*, Acta Universitatis Upsaliensis. Figura. n.s. ii (Stockholm: Nationalmuseum, 1972), pp. 34–7.

Stoye) in defining our topic as 'English Civil War Travellers' rather than 'royalist exiles' we no longer have a self-contained story, beginning in 1640 and ending in 1660, with the Restoration as its epilogue; rather, we are faced with the prospect of writing a single chapter in a longer and wider history of travelling and – still more broadly – of cultural contact between England and Europe. Such a history would require a more sustained attention to contacts between the British Isles and the continent in the earlier seventeenth century than we have yet mustered, and would demand an approach that is European rather than English in scope.[135]

---

[135] For important recent examples of this approach, see Jardine, *Going Dutch*; J.P. Vander Motten and Katrien Daemen-de Gelder, '"*Les Plus Rudes Chocs de la Fortune*"; Willem Frederik, Stadholder of Friesland (1613–64), Thomas Killigrew (1612–83), and Patronage in Exile', *Anglia*, 127 (2009), 65–90.

Chapter 2
Disruptions and Evocations of Family Amongst Royalist Exiles

Ann Hughes and Julie Sanders

I

On 20 May 1656 Charles Cheyne wrote from Chelsea to his brother-in-law Charles Cavendish, Viscount Mansfield, at Welbeck, to report the birth and baptism of his first child, a daughter: 'its weakness made us give itt presently a sprinkling of Christianity under much confusion'. Indeed, the haste with which a distinctly unPuritan baptism with ample godparents had been arranged meant that the occasion had fallen foul of Cromwellian legislation on Sabbath observation:

> My Lord of Bullingbrooke was pleased though not here at first upon request to come & stand for my Lord of Newcastle such was my Deare Lady's desire & his kindnesse, but some unchristian Justice, it being Sunday made him pay 10s for breaking the sabbath & then gave him then a license to doe itt. Such use we make of the laws of God and man.[1]

This chapter discusses the impact of defeat, separation and exile on family ties amongst English royalists in the 1640s and 1650s, exploring how relationships were experienced and imagined, disrupted and renegotiated.[2] We will consider how exile complicated hierarchical relations amongst the royal family itself, and posed dilemmas for many of its followers.

Our main focus is on two literary families, the Cavendishes and the Carys. The affection of Cheyne's wife, Lady Jane Cavendish, for her absent, exiled father, William, Earl or Marquis of Newcastle (the ambiguities of title reflect greater irritations of political defeat) was revealed through her desire for his symbolic presence at her daughter's baptism, a key familial event. The pleasures of family

[1]   Department of Manuscripts and Special Collections, University of Nottingham: Portland MS, PW 1/84. The Earl of Bolingbroke was married to Frances Cavendish, sister of Jane Cheyne. This episode is also discussed in Linda Levy Peck, *Consuming Splendor: Society and Culture in Seventeenth Century England* (Cambridge: Cambridge University Press, 2005), p. 289.

[2]   The research for this chapter was made possible by a British Academy small grant for work on 'Women and Royalist Exile in the Low Countries'. It was originally presented at the conference, 'Exile in the English Revolution and its Aftermath, 1640–1685', University of London, 29–30 June 2006, and we thank those present for their comments.

life, and attachment to household and place, are major themes in the poems and drama of Jane and her younger sister Elizabeth, wife of the Earl of Bridgewater, that circulated in manuscript, and featured also in the better known printed works of her step-mother Margaret Lucas/Cavendish, Duchess of Newcastle, two-years' Jane's junior.

In this chapter we will juxtapose these literary and visual constructions with analyses of the various survival stratagems used by the Cavendishes, at home and in exile. The Cavendish example shows how compromise and resistance, complementary rather than sharply contracting stances, intensified tensions within family structures that would have been complex in any circumstances. The second case study, of the Carys, involves siblings calling on family connections as cultural or rhetorical resources, ways of appealing for help despite profound religious and political disagreements with potential patrons such as Edward Hyde.

II

With Charles II a 'stateless king in exile', a peripatetic (until 1656) and often penniless monarch, accustomed hierarchies within the royal family itself were often shaken.[3] Charles, the nominal head, was dependent on his mother in Paris, and on his sister Mary and his doubly exiled aunt Elizabeth of Bohemia in The Hague for money, patronage and diplomatic support in ways that would have been unthinkable for an established monarch. Exile, indeed, was represented in drama associated with Henrietta-Maria as disempowering and emasculating.[4] The formalities due to Charles II as the titular head of the family were usually observed. Thus Charles confirmed his father's appointment of Jehan van der Kerckhove, Lord of Heenvliet, as Superintendent of his sister's household in January 1651, and Elizabeth of Bohemia obtained his consent for a projected marriage for her daughter Sophia in October 1654.[5] But Charles 'found it challenging to impose his own authority upon members of the royal family'.[6] Charles and his advisers worried about Mary's independence and were perennially anxious about the influence over her of Heenvliet and his English wife, Lady Katherine Stanhope, Mary's old governess: 'the great Governors here in the Princess Royal's family and business are the Lady Stanhope and her Husband; and the great men with them

---

[3] Hero Chalmers, *Royalist Women Writers 1650–1689* (Oxford: Clarendon Press, 2004), p. 104.

[4] Karen Britland, *Drama at the Courts of Queen Henrietta Maria* (Cambridge: Cambridge University Press, 2006), pp. 202–5.

[5] *CClSP*, ii, 449; *Diary and Correspondence of John Evelyn*, ed. William Bray (London: Routledge, n.d.), p. 832, Elizabeth of Bohemia to Edward Nicholas, 2 and 19 October 1654.

[6] Nicole Greenspan, 'Public Scandal, Political Controversy, and Familial Conflict in the Stuart Courts in Exile: The Struggle to Convert the Duke of Gloucester in 1654', *Albion*, 35 (3) (Autumn 2003), 398–427 (p. 402).

are Lord Percy and Dan[iel] O'Neile', wrote Secretary of State Edward Nicholas disapprovingly to Lord Hatton in November 1650. Following the death of her husband, William of Orange, in November 1650, Mary engaged in a bitter dispute with her mother-in-law Amalia von Solms over her jointure and the guardianship of her baby son. Charles and his advisers repeatedly urged compromise as such conflicts hampered help for the royalist cause, but met with little success.[7]

Mary frequently resented her brother's interference, as when she objected to criticism about her close relationship with Lord Jermyn's son: 'To justifi any of my actions to you in this occasion were, I think, to do as much wrong to both my brothers as my own innocency'.[8] Royal family dramas could not be purely private affairs but inevitably had political and religious implications. The most serious concerned the struggles over the religious allegiance of Prince Henry, Duke of York. Released from captivity in England, Henry made his way in April 1653 to his mother's court in Paris after a brief spell in The Hague. According to Nicholas, the Princess Royal feared this was 'an artifice of some papists powerful with the Queen'.[9] Henrietta Maria's attempts to convert Henry were supported by her Catholic advisors, as well as her sister-in-law, Anne of Austria, the Dowager Queen of France. They argued that Henry should obey his mother rather than his brother, while from The Hague, Protestant royalists waited anxiously. Elizabeth of Bohemia observed/reflected, 'I believe my deare Nephue has a good resolution, but there is no trusting to one of his age. I confess I did not think the Queene would have proceeded thus', while Princess Mary's Chamberlain, Sir Alexander Hume, wrote to Nicholas, 'I am heartely glade to heare of the sweete castle of Gloucesters constancy [...] I assure you the Princesse Royall is much troubled for what hath been don.'[10] Hume's confidence was justified and Henry, still a Protestant, joined his brother in Germany. The English republican press reported these developments as a foul design by Henrietta Maria and the Jesuits to undermine English religion, and royalists responded, with some misgivings (because it entailed public criticism of Henrietta Maria), by publishing in 1655 *An Exact Narrative of the Attempts Made upon the Duke of Gloucester*, stressing Henry's constancy and Charles's opposition to his mother.[11]

The female-headed households of Henrietta Maria, Elizabeth of Bohemia and Mary Stuart, Princess of Orange, disrupted Stuart power structures, while their patronage had complex effects on other royalist families. Hatton commented to

---

[7]   See, for example, *The Nicholas Papers: Correspondence of Sir Edward Nicholas, Secretary of State*, ed. G.F. Warner, 4 vols (London: Camden Society, 1886–1920), i, 219–20 (February 1651); *CClSP*, ii, 119, 137, 156, 169 (February 1652–January 1653), 355 (May 1654); Jonathan I. Israel, *The Dutch Republic* (Oxford: Oxford University Press, 1998 paperback), pp. 729–32. Mary frequently resisted dispensing patronage as her brother wished: *CClSP*, ii, 197, 218, 256–7 (April and September 1653).

[8]   *TSP*, i, 664, 2 February [1655?].

[9]   *Nicholas Papers*, ii, 7 (1653–1655).

[10]   *Diary and Correspondence of John Evelyn*, p. 833; *Nicholas Papers*, ii, 137.

[11]   Greenspan, 'Public Scandal', offers a full account of these conflicts.

Nicholas in September 1654 'it is exceeding plesing to heare that brave Princess takes into her thoughts those that have served her father and brother with such signall fidelity'. He was discussing her favours to Hyde's family and Nicholas's son. Inevitably, however, positions for sisters and daughters were more easily available within these courts, so that female royalists sometimes had greater security than their fathers or husbands.[12] Lady Hyde and her children had a house provided free in Breda, while her daughter Anne joined Mary Stuart's household in September 1654.[13] Lady Hyde's sister Barbara Aylesbury had also been in Mary's service and, as Nicholas reported to Hyde in May 1652:

> Our sister Bab (who in earnest is very much in the Princess Royals esteem and confidence) hath lately upon occasion said so much good of you to the Princess Royal as hath not only satisfied her Highness concerning some malicious expression that the Lady Cornwallis made to the Princess of you (whereof you may not take notice) but as hath made her Highness deliver that she had a very gracious opinion and esteem of Sir Ed.[ward] Hyde.[14]

We risk overemphasizing the vulnerability and dependency of royalist women in exile since some, through service in the courts of Elizabeth or Mary, had stability their husbands and fathers lacked, and intimate connections that could benefit other members of their family. Anne Hyde wrote to her father in October 1654 that she regretted leaving her mother alone in Breda when she entered Mary's service, but she seems to have relished court life, and the favour of Mary and Elizabeth. Anne was 'verie fitt' for Mary's service, wrote Elizabeth to Nicholas, and 'a great favourit of mine'. In a later letter she found 'my favourit growen everie way to her advantage'.[15] Nicholas's own daughter, Susan, was also close to Elizabeth. Her letters to her father, like those of Anne Hyde to hers, insist on dutiful obedience, while revealing a privileged access to news and an independent responsibility for the family's financial transactions. Susan Lane arranged and repaid loans from merchants in Rotterdam and Dort, and had a freedom to travel to England which was impossible for the high-profile male politicians in her family. In January 1658 it was Susan who transmitted to her father the dramatic news that Princess Louise, Elizabeth's daughter, had absconded: 'the Queene is god be praysed resonable well in health but this unfortunat bisnes I feare will doe her much hurt. Her Matie comanded me to remember her kindly to you. wee heare yet nothing where Princes Leweis is'.[16]

---

[12] *Nicholas Papers*, ii, 89; see also Ann Hughes and Julie Sanders, 'The Hague Courts of Elizabeth of Bohemia and Mary Stuart: Theatrical and Ceremonial Cultures', *Early Modern Literary Studies*, Special Issue 15 (August 2007), 3.1–23.

[13] *CClSP*, ii, 275, 298.

[14] *Ibid.*, ii, pp. 139, 149; *Nicholas Papers*, i, 299. Barbara Aylesbury died in September 1652: *ibid.*, p. 308.

[15] *CClSP*, ii, 402; *Diary and Correspondence of John Evelyn*, pp. 829–30, 833.

[16] *Diary and Correspondence of John Evelyn*, p. 828; The National Archives, SP 77/32 f. 8, 11, 15, 286 (1658–9).

III

The Earl of Newcastle's daughters did not share their father's exile, yet Jane Cavendish (who married Charles Cheyne in 1654) was clearly devoted to her father and to her broader family and its estates. The poem written by Jane and her sister Elizabeth, later Countess of Bridgwater, when their father was away at the war, is often quoted:

> My Lord it is your absence makes each see
> For want of you, what I'm reduc'd to be […]
> So what becomes me better then
> But to be your Daughter in your Pen.
> If you're now pleas'd, I care not what
> Becomes of me, or what's my lot.[17]

Jane's own poems are suffused with a commitment to her 'great family', to ancestry, household and place broadly defined. A poem celebrating the arrival of a letter from her absent father – 'Thou happy Tuesday since that now I see/My fathers hand, that happy now I bee' – prompts an elaborate, idealized account of her father in all his relationships: as husband, father, master, commander and friend.

> Husband, your love unto your wife was such
> As she did thinke, she could not love too much
> For father, your children wishes every day
> That in their life, or death, they truly may
> Your kindness to diserve, and soe, thus wee,
> Our dayes will make, to onely study thee,
> Servants doe say their love to you makes feare
> And soe their service they doe hold most deare,
> For generally each one, may even, truely, say
> That souldiers soe serve you, not valews pay
> For friendship, all that knows you, will this own,
> That you for trueth of friend doth stand alone.[18]

---

[17]   Bodleian Library Rawl. Poet. 16, here quoted from Margaret J.M. Ezell, '"To be your daughter in your pen": The Social Function of Literature in the Writings of Lady Elizabeth Brackley and Lady Jane Cavendish', as reprinted in *Readings in Renaissance Women's Drama: Criticism, History, and Performance, 1594–1998*, ed. S.P. Cesarano and Marion Wynne-Davies (London and New York: Routledge, 1998), p. 255; for Jane and Charles Cheyne, who had served briefly in royal armies and spent the years 1643–50 abroad, see Peck, *Consuming Splendour*, pp. 283–306.

[18]   Jane Cavendish's verse here quoted from Yale University, Beinecke Library, Osborn MS b 233, p. 20. This is probably an earlier version than Bodleian Rawlinson, Poet 16. For recent discussions of Cavendish's work, see Alexandra G. Bennett, '"Now let my language speake": The Authorship, Rewriting, and Audience(s) of Jane Cavendish and Elizabeth Brackley', *Early Modern Literary Studies*, 11.2 (September, 2005), 3.1–13; *Early Modern Women's Manuscript Poetry*, ed. Jill S. Millman and Gillian Wright (Manchester: Manchester University Press, 2005), pp. 83–95.

Jane's verse praised her sisters, her 'sweete brothers' Charles and Henry, her grandparents, her aunts, and her recently dead mother:

> I had a mother which to speake was such
> That would you prayse, you could not praise too much
> For what of woeman, could bee perfect lov'd
> But shee was that, & the true stile of good
> Then in a word, she was the quincicence of best,
> And now sweete Saint, thy happy soules at rest[19]

One poem, 'The Corecter', was a humorous description of the family's chief household servants, while another, to her 'honorable Aunt Mary Countess of Shrewsbury', unashamedly celebrated their fortunate inheritance at a time when that good fortune was profoundly threatened by war and political defeat:

> And our Great familie may justly say
> Wee eate our bread the better every day
> For the bounty you did your brother give
> Thus will your greater gifts for ever live
> In your lov'd Nephews breasts.[20]

Jane Cavendish's surviving poetry pre-dates her father's second marriage, and no later poem about her young stepmother survives. That exiled stepmother's published works also presented constructions of family in prose, verse and visual image. The frontispiece in many copies of Margaret Cavendish's *Nature's Pictures* (1656) (see Fig. 2.1) portrayed Margaret and her husband presiding over a family group telling tales by the fire. As James Fitzmaurice has noted, this is the only frontispiece in any of her many books that Margaret Cavendish ever commented on, noting in verse:

> Those friends I did conceit
> Were gathered in a Company together
> All sitting by a Fire in cold weather,
> [...]
> My Lord and I, here in two Chairs are set,
> And all his Children, wives and husbands, met,
> To hear me tell them Tales, as I think fit,
> And hope they're full of Phancy, and of Wit,
> Ladies, I ask your pardons, mercies I,
> Since I talk all, and many Ladies, by.[21]

---

[19]   Osborn MS b 233, p. 31.

[20]   Osborn MS b 233, p. 33; see also a similar poem on Elizabeth Countess of Shrewsbury, p. 35. *Early Modern Women's Manuscript Poetry*, p. 92.

[21]   Margaret Cavendish, Countess of Newcastle, *Nature's Pictures Drawn by Fancies Pencil to the Life* (London, 1656), sig A2r, A3v. The poems are taken from the Huntington Library copy; they are missing from the British Library's copy [shelf mark G11599], from which the picture is taken.

Fig. 2.1   Margaret Cavendish, *Nature's Pictures* (1656). © British Library Board. All Rights Reserved. G. 1159.

Fitzmaurice suggests she may have been trying to 'mend fences' with her stepchildren and their spouses, with whom she had tense relationships, or, as Chalmers suggests, speaking for her exiled and politically marginalized husband, she was showing how a 'royalist family dispersed by the political realities of "the Time" are brought together in the text'. Fitzmaurice also points out that Cavendish added her own life at the end of the 1656 edition, in which her Lucas 'birth family' balances the Cavendish focus at the beginning. Significantly, both the frontispiece and the life are omitted from the 1671 edition when family issues were less pressing and negotiations of exile through paratexts no longer required.[22]

Where Jane Cavendish wrote of family members and servants recently dead or dispersed by war, Margaret's 'front matter' included stepdaughters and their spouses whom she had never or scarcely met portrayed together in a place they had never been. This was a trope of fantasizing the family unit that was repeated in Abraham van Diepenbeeck's engravings included in William Cavendish's great book on horsemanship, *Methode et invention nouvelle de dresser les chevaux*, published in Antwerp in 1658. The figure of 'Newcastle and his Family' after Diepenbeeck portrays the family together, including Margaret and William's daughters and their respective husbands sitting in the arches of the garden building at the Rubenshuis to watch William's sons execute complex equestrian manoeuvres. The daughters are seated according to the status of their husbands, so that Jane, although the eldest, is subordinated as the wife of a commoner to her sisters, who had married noblemen. The exaggerated equestrian endeavours add to the elements of fantasy and unreality that surround these family images, projected at great expense by the exiles.[23]

Jane and Margaret Cavendish construct rather different images of family, lineage and place in their cultural productions, yet both constructions are at odds with the more humdrum reality of exile and political marginalization. Newcastle was advised by the Duke of Buckingham in December 1650 to make his peace with the triumphant republican regime:

> the best Cowncell that I am able to give you, considering your owne condition, and the present state of our affayres, is to make your peace if it bee possible in England, for certaynly your Lordships suffering for the king has been great enough to excuse you, if you looke a little after your selfe now, when neither hee is able to assist you, nor you in a possibility of doing him service'.[24]

[22]   Chalmers, *Royalist Women Writers*, pp. 22, 131, and plate 133; James Fitzmaurice, 'Front Matter and the Physical Make-up of *Natures Pictures*', *Women's Writing*, 4:3 (1997), 353–6; Emma Rees, *Margaret Cavendish. Gender, Genre, Exile* (Manchester: Manchester University Press, 2003), pp. 26–33.

[23]   *Royalist Refugees: William and Margaret Cavendish in the Rubens House 1648–1660*, ed. Ben van Beneden and Nora de Poorter (Schoten: BAI, 2006), pp. 43–7; 220–23 (and Fig. 42); Peck, *Consuming Splendor*, p. 278.

[24]   B.L. Add. MS 70499, fol 317v, 5 December 1650.

Newcastle's two sons had accompanied him into exile in 1644, but returned to England in 1647. William and Margaret Cavendish persisted with their defiant exile, and perhaps had little alternative. Their defiance was made possible by the compromises and sacrifices of other members of the Cavendish family, notably William's younger brother Sir Charles, and his eldest daughter Jane. Jane's mother died in April 1643, and she and her younger sisters were virtual prisoners at Welbeck from its capture by the Earl of Manchester in August 1644; she took care to maintain good relationships with the parliamentarian commanders and did her best to preserve the family's treasures.[25] At the end of the war Jane negotiated with the parliamentarian authorities for the payment of the 'fifth' of the estate (the allowance granted to dependents) to herself and her siblings; this allowance was confirmed on her petition in April 1650 as the republican regime planned the sale of Newcastle's property. Sir Charles had first compounded for his estates in 1649, but returned (with Margaret) to England in November 1651 to resolve difficulties with his own property, and to save what could be saved of the Newcastle inheritance for his nephews and nieces. Over the next few months the main Cavendish properties, including Welbeck Abbey and Bolsover Castle, were brought back through trustees including Cavendish officials such as William Clayton and John Hutton, and prominent parliamentarian speculators such as John Rushworth and Edward Whalley.[26] This was clearly an agreed family strategy. Margaret Cavendish, in one of her many dedicatory epistles to her brother-in-law, wrote: 'your Bounty hath been the Distaffe, from whence Fate hath Spun the thread of this part of my Life'.[27] In the life of her husband she claimed that Sir Charles had to be persuaded to swallow his pride for the general good of the family. He

> was unwilling to receive his estate upon such conditions, and would rather have lost it, then compounded for it: but My Lord considering it was better to recover something, then lose all, intreated the Lord Chancellour, who was then in Antwerp, to perswade his brother to a composition, which his Lordship did very effectually.[28]

---

[25]   Katie Whitaker, *Mad Madge: Margaret Cavendish, Duchess of Newcastle, Royalist, Writer and Romantic* (London: Chatto and Windus, 2003), p. 86; Margaret Cavendish, *The Life of William Cavendish, Duke of Newcastle*, ed. C.H. Firth (London: Routledge, 1906), p. 116, n. Welbeck was briefly recaptured by the royalists in July 1645. Although Elizabeth Cavendish had been married at the age of 15 to John Egerton, Viscount Brackley before the civil war she did not live with her husband until the mid 1640s.

[26]   *Calendar of the Proceedings of the Committee for Compounding*, ed. Mary A. Green (London, 1889–92), pp 1732–7 (Jane Cavendish and Newcastle's estates), 2021–2 (Sir Charles); Whitaker, *Mad Madge*, pp. 131, 151–2. The Cromwellian official William Rushworth referred later to his help for Mansfield and Hutton: Portland MS, P1/E11/9/1/18.

[27]   Margaret Cavendish, Countess of Newcastle, *Poems and Fancies* (London, 1653), sig A2r–v. There was another epistle to Sir Charles in *The Worlds Olio* (London, 1655).

[28]   Cavendish, *Life of William Cavendish*, pp. 55–6.

IV

Like Margaret Cavendish, most scholars have seen the activities of royalist women (and younger brothers) as unproblematic, but we want to suggest that dilemmas of exile or return and accommodation produced real tensions amongst royalist families such as the Cavendishes. In the first place, in order to secure their positions in republican England, Newcastle's sons had to present themselves as their mother's, not their father's, children. Viscount Mansfield, Newcastle's eldest son, petitioned the parliamentary committee for the removal of obstructions in the sale of delinquents' estates as the son and heir of Elizabeth, late Countess of Newcastle, emphasizing that his father had only a life interest in her vast inheritance.[29] In 1653 the committee concluded that his actions in the civil war had been 'constrained' by his father and against his own will. On this account, in August 1641, Mansfield had been allowed by the House of Commons (of which he was an unlikely member):

> to goe into the Countrey & that thereupon he went to his father the Earle of Newcastle & continued with him for aboute two years during which tyme the said Earle was Engaged in the warr against the Parliament & that the said Lord Viscount Mansfeild was all that while under a Tutor, And that when his father tooke him with him he the said Viscount was of the age of 15 years & no more.

His mother (conveniently dead) had sought his return to the parliament:

> the said Lord Mansfeild & his Mother did aboute Aprill 1642 solicite the said Earle that the said Viscount might returne back to the Parliament which was denied & that he did endeavour by all means to procure his fathers leave, to travell beyond the seas which was also denied & that although he was constrained dureing the first two years of the warr, to waite sometimes on his father & when he rodd did weare a sword, yet he never acted any thing in the warr, by way of assistance or otherwise being weake of body & constitution, & that the earle gave express charge to the tutor & servants of the said Viscount and his Brother that if at any time there should happen any engagement with the Parliment forces that both the Viscount & his bro then with him should be carried away out of the danger which was accordingly done by those who had the care of them.

Although Mansfield had then gone abroad he was no more than seventeen years old, and in 1647 he had 'returned to London & hath stayed there And in the parliament quarters ever since'. The committee thus concluded, 'we are humbly of oppinion that the said Viscounts present with the said Earle in the Warrs, dureing the time aforesaid was not voluntary.'[30]

---

[29]   Portland MS, PW1/629, c. 1652, petition of Viscount Mansfield.

[30]   Portland MS, PW1/644, copy of the proceedings of the Committee for the removal of obstructions into the sale of delinquents' estates.

Thus Viscount Mansfield's sequestration was annulled, and he was free to reclaim Welbeck and to inherit his mother's vast estates, once his uncle had helped him buy out his father's life interest, Sir Charles acting so the lands 'may be setled in his name & Blood'.[31] When Mansfield and his brother Henry sold lands in Nottinghamshire to finance a marriage settlement for their sister Frances, in 1654, they had to indemnify the purchasers against any 'suit, trouble, eviccon molestacon, interrupcon, claime or demande' from their father. In the settlement itself Newcastle was firmly described under his pre-civil war title of Earl, 'formerly called by the name of the Marquesse of Newcastle', for parliament did not recognize the elevation to the title of Marquis granted by Charles I in 1643.[32]

While Newcastle's children used their inheritance from his first wife, his second, as we have already suggested, took the activities of his children in their father's interests entirely for granted. Newcastle's two sons were, she wrote in the *Life* of her husband, sent back to England in 1647 to make rich marriages, 'but they being arrived there, out of some reason best known to them, declared their unwillingness to marry as yet, continuing nevertheless in England, and living as well as they could'. The children 'did all what lay in their power to relieve my Lord their father', while hangings and pictures at Welbeck and Bolsover were saved 'by the care and industry of his eldest daughter'.[33] In her own autobiography, published in 1656, Margaret Cavendish made a virtue of their exile, bragging of their refusal to compromise and ridiculing those women who did petition for relief:

> indeed I did not stand as a begger at the Parliament doore, for I never was at the Parliament-House, nor stood I ever at the doore, as I do know, or can remember, I am sure, not as a Petitioner, neither did I haunt the Committees, for I never was at any, as a Petitioner, but once in my life […] the Customes of England being changed as well as the Laws, where Women become Pleaders, Atturneys Petitioners and the like, running about with their severall Causes, complaining of their severall grievances, exclaiming against their severall enemies, bragging of their severall favours they receive from the powerfull, thus Trafficking with idle words bring in false reports, and vain discourse; for the truth is, our Sex doth nothing but justle for the Preheminence of words, I mean not for speaking well, but speaking much, as they do for the Preheminence of place.

Although Margaret acknowledged that there were some 'Noble, Vertuous, Discreet and worthy Persons, whom necessity did inforce to submit', we might wonder what her stepdaughter Jane thought of this passage.[34]

---

[31] Portland MS Ne. D 455 (an extensive account of Sir Charles' recovery of the Cavendish estates; P1 E 1/1/1, 3, 4. Whitaker, *Mad Madge*, pp. 151–2.

[32] Portland MS, Ne D 1662; Ne D. 456.

[33] Cavendish, *Life of William Cavendish*, pp. 46, 69–70. Newcastle's sons had left England with him in 1644, returning in 1647.

[34] Margaret Cavendish, 'A True Relation of my Birth, Breeding and Life', from her *Natures Pictures* (1656), pp. 379–80 [also reprinted in Cavendish, *Life of William Cavendish*, pp. 155–78.]

Despite the literary and visual constructions of straightforward family harmony, other sources suggest that the Cavendish children were seeking rapprochement with the Cromwellian regime and running their own lives, independent of any paternal authority. Surviving letters between the Cavendish siblings and their spouses mention their father rarely and their stepmother never, while Margaret's writings always refer to them in formal terms, by title or as their father's sons or daughters. Although it is usually assumed she met the daughters for the first time on her visit to England in 1651–53, there is no evidence for any meeting in manuscript or printed material. Justified fears that the authorities were opening letters might account for some of this reticence, but the letter of Charles Cheyne quoted at the beginning included a reference to Newcastle.[35] Jane Cavendish and her brothers and sisters do express vividly their affection for each other and for their family estates, Jane insisting to her brother Charles in March 1656 on the superiority of Welbeck over London:

> as to Hid Parke, you judge very rightly of my Inclination, for I like much better the solitary walkes of Welbeck, then the crowd & dust of that Parke. I have not as yet been there, for which I am wondered at by those that affect such pleasures'.[36]

It may be significant that the few surviving letters between Newcastle and his children in the 1650s are to his younger son Henry. They concern the financial complications arising from the death of Charles, Viscount Mansfield in October 1659, and present the father as supplicant and dependent.[37]

However, the letters between Henry and his father-in-law, William Pierrepoint, are more affectionate (and in the 1650s of more advantage) than those from his own father. Pierrepoint's mother was a Talbot, and he was a prominent neighbour of the Cavendishes in Nottinghamshire, but he had been an active parliamentarian until 1648. He refused office under the Protectorate but remained a close personal associate of Oliver Cromwell and an effective informal operator within the regime.[38] Pierrepoint's letters are always endorsed 'To my Deer sonn the Lord Henry Cavendish', and, in between moving accounts of the deaths of his wife and a young son, he sent Henry minutely detailed instructions on how to ingratiate himself with the Protectorate:[39]

> I desire you when your owne and your wife's health will permit to goe see my Lord President Lawrence and to present your owne and my humble service

---

[35]   Whitaker, *Mad Madge*, pp. 139–40, for the assumptions of contact in 1651–52; William Pierrepoint did not write of public affairs to his son-in-law Henry Cavendish during the political crisis of May 1659 for fear of his letters being opened: NUL PW1/381.

[36]   Portland MS, PW1/86; see also Peck, *Consuming Splendor*, pp. 288–9.

[37]   Add. MS 70499, fols 351–6: see discussion below.

[38]   *ODNB* for Pierrepoint; Life of William for the help.

[39]   Portland MS, PW1/371–81, 377 (17 October 1657) is quoted.

to him and to let him know your wifes and your owne great sicknes hitherto
prevented you therein and to desire him to goe with you to my Lord Protector
and you then to let my Lord Protector know those causes which hindred you
from sooner waiting upon him.

Henry was to inform Cromwell of Pierrepoint's 'most great obligments to his
highnes and of my most devoted public service to him'. A fortnight later Pierrepoint
hoped his intervention with Lawrence and Oliver St John, the Lord Chief Justice,
had succeeded in freeing Henry from an expensive appointment as sheriff of
Derbyshire. The men had been 'satisfied in a good and true character of you. They
are not complementall but are very reall to their frends'.[40]

With Pierrepoint's encouragement, both Cavendish brothers as well as their
brother-in-law Bridgewater cultivated members of the Cromwellian regime.[41]
Mansfield was eager to do the parliamentary officer Colonel Saunders 'a
curtesye' in a matter of ecclesiastical patronage in April 1656, and later the same
month both brothers were in touch with Lord Lambert.[42] Mansfield avoided the
'decimation tax' imposed on ex-royalists in 1656 through the good offices of
the Major-General for the east midlands, Edward Whalley, with Henry's 'father
Pierrepoint' as intermediary. Henry wrote to his brother from his father-in-law's
house at Thoresby of meeting Whalley, who 'desired me to present his service
to you and to tell you he is sorry he could not wayte of you, but did intend it.
My father Pierrep[oint]t gave him many thankes for his kindness to you'.[43] The
very language of Cavendish's formal documents and business affairs expressed
compromise with the republic. In all estate settlements Newcastle, as we have
seen, was an Earl not a Marquis, while John Hutton, in a letter to Viscount
Mansfield, passed on 'certine newse upon the Exchange' about 'the pretended
King of Scots'.[44]

All this intensified the predictable hostility of adult stepchildren to their father's
young second wife. Compromise and accommodation with the parliamentarian
regimes may well have been a family strategy to avoid the full penalties of
Newcastle's royalism, but it inevitably shook his authority as a father. However,
exile and defeat in other contexts might intensify family ties, especially when the
bitterest protagonists were safely dead.

---

[40] PW1/378 (31 October 1657); about the same time Pierrepoint again urged Henry to
attend on the Protector and dine with him if possible: PW1/379, no date.

[41] Portland MS, PW1/120, 19 May 1655, Elizabeth to Charles Cavendish, Viscount
Mansfield: 'my Lords Busnis is now dune & he went to give the Protector thanks'.

[42] BL, Add. MS 70, 499 fols 333r, 335r, 337r.

[43] Add. MS 70499, fol. 341 (and see also fol. 339, where Mansfield was cleared from
'all sute or question of delinquency' by Whalley, the Protector and the Council).

[44] Add. MS 70499, fol. 345, June 1656.

V

In March 1650, Edward Hyde received a letter from 'Sister Clementia de Ste Maria Magdalena', otherwise Anne Cary, 'from the English Cloyster in Cambray': [45]

> My Lord,
> The great expressions you are pleased to make to all people of your affection to my Dead Brother & for his sake to us all & ye assurance you were pleased to give us of it, att yr beeing here hath given me the courage to presume upon yu, which if you bee not very favourable to mee, you must needes judge a great impudence, but yr Lordships undeserved favours to us & what I have heard of you, by all that have the honour to knowe you, hath made mee so confident in your goodnesse, yet I dare hope for your Lops pardon. [46]

What had led Hyde, a determined opponent of Catholic influence within the royalist cause, to visit an English convent, encouraging an English nun to hope for his aid? Sister Clementia (born Anne Cary) was the daughter of a notorious Catholic convert, Elizabeth Tanfield Cary, Viscountess Falkland, the author of the first original play to be published in England (*The Tragedie of Mariam, the Faire Queene of Jewry*, 1613), and one of four Cary sisters who were nuns at Cambrai. [47] More importantly for Hyde, she was the sister of Lucius Cary, Viscount Falkland, from 1633, a dear friend of Hyde's. Falkland rode to his death at the battle of Newbury in 1643, prompting a well-known, moving memorial from Hyde:

> In this unhappy battle was slain the lord viscount Falkland: a person of such prodigious parts of learning and knowledge, of that inimitable sweetness and delight in conversation, of so flowing and obliging a humanity and goodness to mankind, and of that primitive simplicity and integrity of life, that if there were no other brand upon this odious and accursed civil war than that single loss, it must be the most infamous and execrable to all posterity. [48]

---

[45]   Bodleian Library, Clarendon MS 39, fol. 75r, 4 March 1650, 'from the English Closyter in Cambray'.

[46]   For Hyde's determined anti-Catholicism expressed around the same time as Sister Clementia's letter, see Clarendon MS 39, fols 10r–v (Hyde to Nicholas, 3 January 1650); fol. 111r (Hyde to Lady Morton, 18 March 1650).

[47]   Elizabeth Cary, the Lady Falkland, *The Tragedy of Mariam, the Fair Queen of Jewry, with the Lady Falkland her Life by One of her Daughters*, ed. Barry Weller and Margaret W. Ferguson (Berkeley and Los Angeles: University of California Presses, 1994), pp. 180–81; 'Records of the Abbey of our Lady of Consolation at Cambrai, 1620–1793', *Miscellanea*, VIII (Publications of the Catholic Record Society, XIII, 1913), 44–5. Lucy Cary (1619–November 1650) and Mary Cary (1622–93) entered the convent in August 1638; Elizabeth Cary (1617–83) followed in October 1638 and Anne (1615–71) in March 1639.

[48]   Edward Hyde, first Earl of Clarendon, *The History of the Rebellion and Civil Wars in England*, ed. W. Dunn Macray, 6 vols (Oxford: Clarendon Press, 1888), iii, 179.

Hyde's friend had remained a Protestant, but his mother's Catholicism had prompted permanent separation from her husband Henry, Viscount Falkland, Lord Deputy of Ireland, a public scandal, and the conversion of four of her five daughters along with her two younger sons. These children came to 'acknowledge she was their mother in faith as well as in nature', as one of the daughters (probably Lucy) wrote in the life of Elizabeth Cary. The Catholic siblings, like the Cavendishes, made up a close-knit group with literary interests. The life of their mother was probably originally composed before August 1645, with corrections made by another sister and their brother Patrick around the time that Hyde visited the sisters.[49] Religious conflict had shattered this family before the civil war. Despite poverty and harassment, Elizabeth had arranged the abduction of her younger boys from their brother's Protestant household in 1636, and had them sent to the house of the Benedictine fathers in Paris. By the time of her death in 1639, four daughters had become nuns. When summoned before the Privy Council to answer for her actions she was unapologetic, acknowledging that she had:

> sent for her children and had disposed of them as she thought good; and, though she had been forced to fetch them away from their brother's secretly, she had in that done nothing contrary to the law, since she could not be said to have stolen that which was her own, her son having no pretense to right to keep his brothers from her against her will and theirs, having never been committed to him neither by the state, nor their father; that she had often warned him she would do thus, if he would not remove them from under Mr Chillinworth, whom she would not have have the guidance of her children.[50]

Sister Clementia was writing to Hyde on behalf of one of her Catholic brothers, Patrick, who had fallen on hard times in Brussels, where 'hee lives onely upon hopes'. She asked Hyde to help him 'to kisse the kings hand at Breda' and to obtain a post with Charles or in another continental court. The letter implied criticism of Lucius, Viscount Falkland while simultaneously milking Hyde's well-known attachment to him. Falkland and his friends might have done more for Patrick but their 'displeasure hee highly incurred, by being as hee is, they being all great Heretickes (if yor Lordship will give mee leave to call yr Religion so'. On the other hand, 'I will assure you hee is very like my Brother Falkland, & in my opinion & in that of all those that knowe him, hee is equall to him in all kinds'. Patrick would sacrifice himself in the king's service as 'willingly as

---

[49] Some scholars think Anne Clementia was the main author but Weller, Ferguson, and Wolfe agree that Lucy is the most likely, with Mary and Patrick also involved: Cary, *The Tragedy of Mariam*, pp. 51–3; Heather Wolfe, 'The Scribal Hands and Dating of *Lady Falkland: Her Life*', in *Writings by Early Modern Women* (*English Manuscript Studies 1000– 1700*, 9, 2000), ed. Peter Beal and Margaret J.M. Ezell, pp. 187–217 (pp. 191–5, 203–4).

[50] Cary, *Tragedy of Mariam*, p. 258. Chillingworth, a close associate of Lucius Cary, had been for a time a Catholic. He acted as tutor to the younger Cary sons, and Elizabeth regarded him as deceitful.

my two other Brothers did theirs'.[51] An obituary notice twenty years later claimed Sister Clementia shunned 'frequent visits & longe discourses at the grate. And for the space of thirty years used al possible means to promot prayer, Retirement and whatsoever was requised towards the gaining of religious perfection'. Nonetheless Sister Clementia revealed herself as a skilled lobbyist here and in the following year when she mobilized the support of old mistress Henrietta Maria for a new foundation at Paris.[52] Patrick himself followed up his sister's letter with an eloquent narrative that also stressed the Falkland connection. He was confident that Hyde wanted to 'conserve fresh the memory of my Brother Falkland, but allsoe to extend your affection and favour to those who had any relation unto him'. Patrick, an enthusiastic poet, wanted 'to make my selfe lesse a stranger to you, to entertayne you with a kind of Romance and that out of itt you may gather what kind of employment I am fitted for'. Patrick explained how the death of his patron, the last Pope, combined with war and floods in Italy had removed the pension that was his livelihood, reducing him to penury. In one Abbey which paid him an annuity, '300 banditts had made their nest not onely in the troubles but almost ever since'.[53]

The author of the *Life* of Lady Cary did not openly criticize her eldest brother, describing him as a good son, but she admitted that mother and son remained 'at much difference about the stealing away of her little sons', although they were reconciled before her death.[54] In his *History of the Rebellion*, Edward Hyde was more critical, condemning the

> many attempts made upon him [Lucius Cary] by the instigation of his mother (who was a lady of another persuasion in religion, and of a most masculine understanding, allayed with the passion and infirmities of her own sex) to pervert him in his piety to the Church of England and to reconcile him to that of Rome.

Falkland, according to Hyde, had dealt with his Catholic disputants with 'all possible civility' but

> this charity towards them was much lessened, and any correspondence with them quite declined, when by sinister arts they had corrupted his two younger brothers, being both children and stolen them from his house and transported them beyond seas, and perverted his sisters.[55]

---

[51]   Clarendon MS 39, fol. 75–6. Lucius Cary's younger brother Laurence had also died in the civil war.

[52]   'The English Benedictine Nuns of the Convent of Our Blessed Lady of Good Hope in Paris', *Miscellanea*, VII (Catholic Record Society, IX, 1911), 341–2. Clementia/Anne returned to Cambrai after a year establishing the new house in Paris and died in April 1671.

[53]   Clarendon MS 39, fol. 92v–93v (Patrick Cary to Edward Hyde, 14 March 1650); for Patrick see *ODNB*; Wolfe, 'Scribal Hands and Dating', pp. 203–4; Cary, *Tragedy of Mariam*, p. 267; Veronica Delany (ed.), *The Poems of Patrick Cary* (Oxford: Clarendon Press, 1978).

[54]   Cary, *Tragedy of Mariam*, pp. 258, 263–4.

[55]   Hyde, *History of the Rebellion*, iii, 180–81.

Patrick treated his religion in an instrumental fashion: 'Being made in secret of my mother's religion for I knew noe other distinction then betweene the Catholicke and the Protestant one but that my Mother was of that, my Father of this'. His sister was more forthright, openly condemning Protestants as heretics, and when Patrick (briefly) entered the 'cloister' at Douai, Sister Clementia regretted that she could not support Hyde's attempts to dissuade him, for that would be to disobey 'their common master'.[56] Despite this complex history, despite Hyde's opposition to Catholic influence in royalist circles, and despite the darker judgements in more considered literary works, the Carys' appeals to Hyde were remarkably successful. Political defeat and shared exile (the Carys' voluntary and Hyde's involuntary) reunited family and friends torn apart by religious divisions, themselves figured as family conflicts between husband and wife, heir and younger siblings. The memory of his dead friend inspired Hyde to visit his sisters in their convent and to do what he could for Patrick. Hyde declared to Patrick that

> you may very justly believe me when I tell you that since the unspeakable losse of your excellent Brother, I have rarely felt soe great as pleasure as the first sight of your Name. [...] When I had the honor to see your Sisters at Cambray, I carried great joy with me into France.

Hyde defended his friend's actions, confident that 'a Person of that incomparable Virtue, who would not have done an unjust thing to have procured the Peace of his Country, which he desired with the greatest passion imaginable, would have proved an unkinde Brother [...] if he had lived, you had heard from very effectively'.[57] As Falkland was no longer able to care for his brother, Hyde did his best to step in, recommending him, without success, for posts in Spain, Rome and the Spanish Netherlands. Patrick's fleeting resolve to enter the cloister alarmed Hyde more than his actual Catholicism, for, with the death of a nephew, it meant the end of the Falkland line. In the end Patrick Cary did abandon the religious life and his Catholicism. He returned to England, married a Protestant and died in Dublin in 1657.[58]

VI

Long after Hyde and other royalists returned home to England, Anne/Clementia and her surviving sisters continued in their apparently uneventful life at Cambrai. The Restoration brought difficult readjustments for the Cavendish family. In October 1659 Newcastle's heir Charles, Viscount Mansfield, died, prompting a series of anxious letters to his second son Henry, about the estates. Newcastle urged Henry to 'leave your Dove Cote wher you are & live at Well[beck]'. His main obsession,

---

[56]   Clarendon MS 39, fol. 92v; *CCISP*, ii, 63, Sister Clementia to Hyde, 5 June 1650.

[57]   Clarendon MS 39, fol. 160r (Hyde to Patrick Cary, 25 April 1650).

[58]   *CCISP*, ii, 47 (Hyde to Sir Toby Matthew); 55 (Hyde to Sister Clementia); 59 (Hyde to Patrick Cary); 77 (Hyde to Sister Clementia); 95 (Hyde to Patrick Cary).

however, was with the recovery of the 'goods' in Welbeck and Bolsover from Mansfield's widow (once it was confirmed that she was not pregnant). Detailed instructions jostle with elaborate professions of goodwill on his and his wife's behalf, and an unmistakable air of dependency, or even subservience. Henry was to get the goods valued and then buy them back, he was to 'bee vereye Erneste with your father in Lawe to advise & helpe you in Itt'. He was to be cautious how he arranged his sister-in-law's jointure but the final decisions had to be Henry's: 'I will tell you my opinion & then leave itt to your Judgment […] pray thinke of itt & take your owne waye'.[59] All this, Newcastle insisted, was for Henry's own benefit: 'My Intention is butt to save them for you, for I protest that is all the designe my wife & I have for that business, for beleve mee she is as kinde to you as shee was to your Brother & so good a wife as shee is all for my fameleye'. He and his wife 'give of our Intereste upp unto you wholeye & totaleye'. Newcastle was also a supplicant to Henry for the continuation of the allowance of £500 each quarter sent to Antwerp from the Cavendish estates: 'I thanke you for settling my subsistance', he wrote, for 'I am dayley & Infenitlye tortured with my Creditors'.[60]

Newcastle promised Henry, 'if it please God I am bleste with that happiness to see you believe Itt will be manye thousand poundes a yeare the better for you then if I should dye before', and Henry in turn raised the allowance to £600 a quarter.[61] Here the father was the dependent, but the Restoration precisely reversed the relationship. Politically, the restoration of the king was welcome to Henry, now Lord Mansfield, but its more intimate implications were rather different. From being the effective head of the family, with his own, independent political networks, Henry now became again dependent on his father, living on a similar quarterly allowance, albeit a very generous one. The promises of family harmony suggested in the exile publications and correspondence evaporated once the Cavendishes were reunited in England. Henry and his sisters resented their father's grandiose rebuilding projects, his generous provision for Margaret and plans to recover from civil war depredations through ruthless exploitation of the woods on the Cavendish estates. They were particularly contemptuous of the influence of Francis Topp, the Antwerp merchant who had married Margaret Cavendish's waiting woman and had returned to England with them as their chief business adviser: 'hee intends non of my Lords Chilldern any good', wrote Jane Cheyne to her sister-in-law in 1668.[62]

Women, younger brothers and other 'dependents' took major responsibility for the lobbying and compromises through which exile and defiance was underwritten. In most families the prominence of normally subordinate figures was necessary and tactical but it had inevitable consequences for the authority of elder brothers,

---

[59]   Add. MS 70499, fols 351–2, 353, 355–6 (Newcastle to Henry, now Lord Mansfield, 22, 25 October and 15 November 1659).

[60]   *Ibid.,* fols 351–2, 353.

[61]   *Ibid.,* fols 356r, 357 (5 November 1659).

[62]   Whitaker, *Mad Madge*, pp. 277–81, 329–32; Portland MS, PW1/90.

husbands and fathers. The impact of exile and religious or political differences on gendered hierarchies and familial relationships was complex and varied. The Cary sisters could appeal to Hyde for help precisely because profound divisions over religion could be effaced by shared memories of their dead brother and shared pleasure at reunion in a foreign land. It was now forgotten that the sisters had been estranged from Lucius Cary, whom Hyde had loved. More commonly, however, accustomed relationships of authority and hierarchy were disturbed by exile. Within the royal family itself, the king's pre-eminence was acknowledged in theory but qualified in practice by the independent material, cultural and political resources of his sister and his aunt. The wives and daughters of other royalist exiles achieved some autonomy through their participation in the networks developed within the female-headed courts of Elizabeth and Mary Stuart. In the case of the Cavendishes, geographical separation and the political compromises of Newcastle's children with Cromwellian England intensified the inevitable tensions between a young stepmother and adult stepchildren. Margaret Cavendish, as we know, was the first Englishwoman to publish an account of her own life in print, and asked

> Why hath this lady writ her own life? Since none cares to know whose daughter she was, or whose wife she is, or how she was bred or what fortunes she had, or how she lived or what humour or disposition she was of?

Part of the answer she gave to her own question evoked the anxieties of a second wife:

> lest after-Ages should mistake, in not knowing I was daughter to one Master Lucas of St Johns near Colchester, in Essex, second wife to the Lord Marquis of Newcastle; for my Lord having had two Wives, I might easily have been mistaken, especially if I should dye and My Lord Marry again.[63]

Literary and historical preoccupations have of course ensured that it is Elizabeth Basset Cavendish, not Margaret Lucas Cavendish, who has been forgotten, but a full understanding of the experience of exile requires us to pay more attention to her and her children. For everyone – for Hyde and Nicolas as well as for the Carys, Stuarts and Cavendishes – family ties, imagined and real, were essential resources for the survival of exile, but those familial relationships had to be continually renegotiated precisely because of the pressures of distance and political eclipse that exile involved.

---

[63]   Margaret Cavendish, 'A True Relation of my Birth, Breeding and Life', in *Natures Pictures* (1656), pp. 368–91 (pp. 390–91).

Chapter 3

A Broken Broker in Antwerp: William Aylesbury and the Duke of Buckingham's Goods, 1648–1650

Katrien Daemen-de Gelder and J.P. Vander Motten

I

I have only the one sute yᵗ now is on my back and some credit for my belly, which I will streatch out to yᵉ last ragg and bit with this comfort yᵗ it is for my King and masters service, whose person and cause I will never desert whilst I can wagg nose, toes, or finguers end; and soe I beseeche you assure his Maᵗʸ with my humblest duty from my Secretaryes as well as his faythfullest and most affectionat humble servant.[1]

The years of the civil wars and Interregnum were a period of distress and anxiety for most royalists, especially those who, like the courtier and diplomat George Goring, first Earl of Norwich (1585–1663), followed the Stuarts into exile. Deprived of their principal sources of income and often burdened with the care of an extended family and large household, they suffered many hardships – material and emotional. Their memoirs and correspondence, as well as the notarial and judicial records relating to their continental lives, bear witness to their widespread poverty and desperate circumstances, but also enlarge on their basic survival skills. Expatriates and exiles alike turned for financial backing to all who supported, closely or remotely, the Stuart cause: they drew heavily upon each other and negotiated various loans from like-minded relatives and contacts on both sides of the Channel.[2] When necessity demanded, they even pawned or sold the treasured possessions they had managed to secure before leaving their native country.

An interesting case in point is the well-documented transaction of a substantial part of the Buckingham art collection in Antwerp in the late 1640s and early 1650s.[3] Although the 16 chests of 'peintures, tableaux, joyaux et pierreries'

---

[1] 'George Goring to Edward Nicholas, 1 June 1655', *The Nicholas Papers: Correspondence of Sir Edward Nicholas, Secretary of State*, ed. G.F. Warner, 4 vols (London: Camden Society, 1886–1920), ii (1892), Jan. 1653–June 1655, pp. 317–21 (p. 321).

[2] See also Geoffrey Smith, *The Cavaliers in Exile, 1640–1660* (Basingstoke and New York: Palgrave, 2003), pp. 93–114.

[3] Philip McEvansoneya, 'The Sequestration and Dispersal of the Buckingham Collection', *Journal of the History of Collections* 8 (1996), 2: 133–54; McEvansoneya, 'An

[paintings, jewels and precious stones] taken from York House, where the first Duke of Buckingham (1592–1628) had displayed his taste in art, may initially have been sent overseas as a precautionary measure against future seizure, their pawning and eventual sale yielded a considerable sum of money which was used to pay back (at least partially) the long-standing debts of George Villiers, second Duke of Buckingham (1628–87), and his late brother, and to purchase arms and munitions.[4] This historical undertaking was orchestrated by a complex network of British royalists, expatriate merchants, and British as well as continental art dealers and collectors, all of whom (it seems) were carefully chosen either for their proximity to the Buckingham family, their loyalty to the English monarchy, their financial solvency or informed connoisseurship of art.

The collection's principal broker was William Aylesbury (bap. 1612–1656).[5] His connection with the Buckingham family dated back to the time of his father, Sir Thomas Aylesbury (1579/80–1658), who in one of his many capacities had acted as secretary to the first Duke.[6] At the invitation of Charles I, William in 1644 became governor to the second Duke and his brother, Lord Francis (1629–48), an appointment which reflected his closeness both to the Villiers and to the king.[7] In 1645–46 Aylesbury took the young men on a continental tour, journeying in style through France and Italy, while simultaneously incurring large debts.[8] Upon their

---

Unpublished Inventory of the Hamilton Collection in the 1620s and the Duke of Buckingham's Pictures', *The Burlington Magazine*, 134 (1992), 1073: 524–26; and McEvansoneya, 'A Note on the Duke of Buckingham's Inventory', *The Burlington Magazine* 128 (1986), 1001: 607. See also Randall Davies, 'An Inventory of the Duke of Buckingham's Pictures, etc. at York House in 1635', *The Burlington Magazine for Connoisseurs* 10 (1907), 48: 376–82.

[4]   The prospect of new funds – Buckingham's commodities were shipped from Amsterdam to Antwerp in the summer of 1648 – encouraged the royalists to enquire about the possibility of buying weapons. See letters written to Aylesbury on 29 June 1648 and 30 July 1648 by Robert Sidney and Sir Edward Brett (1607/8–1682/3), respectively; *CCISP*, i (1872), to January 1649, nos. 2823 and 2848.

[5]   Sidney Lee, 'Aylesbury, William (*bap.* 1612–1656)', rev. Sean Kelsey, *ODNB*, online edn, accessed 7 February 2008 [http://www.oxforddnb.com/view/article/931]. John Stoye devoted a chapter to Aylesbury in his *English Travellers Abroad 1604–1667* (1952; New York: Octagon Books, 1968), pp. 297–322. Aylesbury fits the general profile of the early modern agent as defined by Keblusek in her Introduction to *Your Humble Servant: Agents in Early Modern Europe*, ed. Hans Cools et al. (Hilversum: Verloren, 2006), pp. 9–15.

[6]   Colin Alsbury, 'Aylesbury, Sir Thomas, baronet (1579/80–1658)', *ODNB*, online edn, accessed 7 February 2008 [http://www.oxforddnb.com/view/article/929].

[7]   According to the address 'To the Reader', prefacing Aylesbury and Sir Charles Cotterell's *History of the Civil Wars of France* (London, 1647), Charles I, 'by whose command, at Oxford, this translation was continued and finished (though not begun) read it there with such eagerness, that no diligence could write it out fair, so fast as he daily called for it; wishing he had had it some years sooner, out of a belief, that being forewarned thereby, he might have prevented many of those mischiefs we then groaned under; […].' (no signature).

[8]   See Evelyn MSS in Christ Church Library, Oxford, as referred to by Stoye, *English Travellers*, p. 302. Aylesbury had resided and travelled on the continent before. A member

return, the brothers eagerly took up arms in the second civil war and joined Henry Rich, first Earl of Holland (bap. 1590–1649), at the head of a cavalry regiment at Kingston, in Surrey. On 7 July 1648 Francis Villiers was killed during an incursion into parliamentarian territory, and only days later George, having been intercepted at St Neots in Huntingdonshire, fled to the continent.[9] Aylesbury had preceded his patron, travelling between London, The Hague, Amsterdam, Antwerp and Brussels for the purpose of coordinating the shipment and storage as well as the pawning and sale of Buckingham's valuables. Having first been taken to Amsterdam in the beginning of 1648, these commodities were – on the suggestion of Stephen Goffe (1605–1681), an exiled royalist divine and informer – transported to Antwerp in the course of the summer: 'without exception Antwerpe will afford many chapmen and the Archduke's good success in Flandre will make him prodigal in these curiosities. I should therefore advise the removal of all your cases thither with the first'.[10]

It should be noted that Goffe was then staying in the Netherlands, having been sent there by Queen Henrietta Maria to borrow money on the security of the crown jewels.[11] His role in the dispersal of Buckingham's art collection was more than advisory, as in April 1649 he was prohibited by the latter from selling 'any of the Pictures or Agatts' to repay his debts to Henry, Lord Jermyn (bap. 1605–84), 'for though Doctor Goffe's power be very large, I [Buckingham] encourage him not to make sale of any of my things which he promised me faithfully'.[12] In the course of December 1649 Goffe witnessed in Antwerp three notarial acts: the first, dated 24 December, concerned the sale of 11 of Buckingham's paintings to the Antwerp merchant Marcelis Liebrechts the younger; the second, dated 28 December, recorded an outstanding financial obligation of Francis Villiers to Pierre Robert, 'gentilhomme franchoys' [French gentleman]; and the third, also dated 28 December, included Aylesbury's testimony about an ebony cabinet to be restored to Robert, its rightful

---

of the household of Robert Sidney, second Earl of Leicester (1595–1677), ambassador extraordinary to Paris, he lived in France from the second half of the 1630s onwards. He became tutor to Robert, one of the Earl's sons, and took him on a tour of Italy in the early 1640s. Aylesbury returned to England in the course of 1644.

[9]   Bruce Yardley, 'Villiers, George, second duke of Buckingham (1628–1687)', *ODNB*, online edn, accessed 7 Feb. 2008 [http://www.oxforddnb.com/view/article/28294].

[10]   Bodleian Library, Clarendon MS 31, fol 131r, as quoted by McEvansoneya, 'Sequestration and Dispersal', 138. Thompson Cooper, 'Goffe, Stephen (1605–1681)', rev. Jerome Bertram, *ODNB*, online edn, accessed 8 Feb. 2008 [http://www.oxforddnb.com/view/article/10901]. Antwerp was at the time one of the principal European art centres. See Filip Vermeylen, 'The Art of the Dealer. Marketing Paintings in Early Modern Antwerp', in *Your Humble Servant*, ed. Cools et al., pp. 109–19.

[11]   Jens Engberg, 'Royalist Finances during the English Civil War, 1642–1646', *Scandinavian Economic History Review*, 14 (1966), 73–96.

[12]   Bodleian Library, Clarendon MS 37, fol. 76r, as quoted by McEvansoneya, 'Sequestration and Dispersal', 153. See also Erik Duverger, ed., *Antwerpse Kunstinventarissen uit de Zeventiende Eeuw*, Vol. 5: *1642–1649* (Brussels: Koninklijke Academie voor Wetenschappen, Letteren en Schone Kunsten van België, 1991), no. 1553.

owner, in July 1650.[13] Goffe, brother of the regicide William Goffe, whose own exile is explored in the penultimate chapter of this volume, probably owed his continuous involvement in these matters – which extended beyond 1649 – to his profound knowledge of Netherlandish culture as well as his closeness to the Buckinghams and their adoptive family – Goffe was one of Charles I's trusted chaplains.[14]

The fate of the Duke's art collection was closely (and nervously) watched by a number of people who either tried to recover money owed to them by the ducal family or hoped to procure future financial support. Among them were, for example, Endymion Porter (1587–1649) and Hugh May (*bap.* 1621–84), 'one of the outstanding English architects of the seventeenth century'.[15]

Porter was a loyal servant of Charles I and protégé of the first and second Dukes of Buckingham, to whom he was related by marriage.[16] Having lost all faith in the Stuart cause, he had left his native country in July 1645, and settled down successively in France and the Southern and Northern Netherlands. The once-celebrated and prosperous Maecenas – Porter was a poet and patron of poets, an avid collector of paintings and a close friend of Rubens and Van Dijck – faced total ruin when as a result of his royalist sympathies most of his grants were revoked and a considerable part of his property confiscated. That he was officially appointed on 29 June 1648 – conjointly with William Aylesbury – as Buckingham's procurator, authorized to manage his valuable goods, not only testifies to his considerable abilities as an agent and art dealer but also strongly suggests a ducal promise of financial relief in recognition of past and/or present services.[17]

The exact nature of Porter's involvement with the collection, however, remains uncertain, as his name appears only twice in the surviving documents and letters related to its dispersal.[18] Porter returned to England in early 1649 and died in London in August of that same year. Employed in the service of Buckingham, Hugh May apparently assisted with the pawning and sale of the collection: several deeds prepared by the Antwerp notaries, Le Rousseau and Ghysberti, name him as witness.[19]

---

[13]   *Antwerpse Kunstinventarissen*, ed. Duverger, vi, nos. 1596, 1598 and 1599.

[14]   That Goffe was fully acquainted with Buckingham's financial hardship can be gathered from several of his letters, included in the Rousham MS and quoted by McEvansoneya, 'Sequestration and Dispersal', 149–51. As Goffe continued to keep Jermyn informed about the fate of the collection, we may assume that his involvement was also driven by loyalty to Jermyn. Two of the above acts were witnessed by the ardent royalist Tobias Rustat (*bap.* 1608–94), a member of Buckingham's household, who had followed his patron to the continent in 1648.

[15]   John Bold, 'May, Hugh (*bap.* 1621, *d.* 1684)', *ODNB*, online edn, accessed 15 Feb. 2008 [http://www.oxforddnb.com/view/article/37749].

[16]   Ronald G. Asch, 'Porter, Endymion (1587–1649)', *ODNB*, online edn, accessed 8 Feb. 2008 [http://www.oxforddnb.com/view/article/22562].

[17]   *Antwerpse Kunstinventarissen*, ed. Duverger, v, no. 1518.

[18]   *Ibid.*, v, no. 1518; and *CCISP*, i, no. 2859.

[19]   *Antwerpse Kunstinventarissen*, ed. Duverger, v, no. 1535, and vi, nos. 1594 and 1596. Some deeds were signed by John May, who may well have been an elder brother of Hugh. See *Antwerpse Kunstinventarissen*, ed. Duverger, vi, nos. 1632 and 1633.

His involvement should also be seen in the light of Buckingham's unsettled debt to him: in a notarial document of 24 December 1649 it was recorded that May was owed 10,000 florins (guilders) and entitled to a yearly pension of 1,000 florins.[20]

II

The pivotal figure in the network dependent on the sale of Buckingham's commodities was William Aylesbury. Initially, he shared with Porter 'entière authorité et charge expresse de pouvoir vendre, engager et transporter toutes et chascunes peintures, tableaux, joyaux et pierreries'[21] [full authority and the express duty to sell, pawn and move all and any paintings, jewels and precious stones], but from 12 December 1648 onwards, shortly before Porter left, he was given sole power, based on a procuration dating back to Buckingham's minority, to pawn several of the latter's paintings to Leonel Corham and François Wouters (1612–59):

> Comparust en personne Son Excellence le Ducq de Buckingam se trouvant présentement en ceste ville d'Anvers et a dict et déclairé comme déclaire par cestes comme ainsy soit que Guilliaume Alytesbury en vertu de la procure à luy donnée par ledit Seigneur comparant au temps de sa minoreunité at engagé aux Sieurs Leonel Corham et Franchois Wouters diverses précieuses peintures, agats, pierreries et autres semblables raritez jusques à la somme de trente mille florins avecq promesse de constituer et hypoticquer rente à raison du denier seize sur biens immeubles endéans l'an, ou bien de restituer ladicte somme empruntée avecq l'intérest à huict pour cent, ou a faute de ce que lesdicts Corham et Wouters pourroient les dictes peintures et autres curiositez faire vendre à cry publicquement sans estre tenu à aultre debvoir judiciare, suivant l'instrument en passé pardevant le notaire Gisberti et tesmoings le douziesme de décembre XVIc quarante-huict.[22]

> [Having appeared before us, his Excellency the duke of Buckingham now residing in this city of Antwerp, has declared that William Aylesbury by vertue of a procuration given to him by the said duke at the time of his minority, has pawned to Leonel Corham and François Wouters several valuable paintings, agates, gems and similar precious curiosities to the value of 30,000 florins, with the promise of mortgaging immovables at the rate of 'denier seize' [i.e. 6,25 %] within a year, or to restitute the said sum at the rate of 8 per cent. Failing these, Corham and Wouters will be authorised to have the said paintings and other curiosities publically sold without any other liabilities, according to the act certified by notary public Gisberti and witnesses on 12 December 1648.]

---

[20] *Ibid.*, vi, no. 1597.

[21] *Ibid.*, v, no. 1518.

[22] *Ibid.*, v, no. 1535.

Corham and Wouters, to whom the commodities were given as security for a loan of 30,000 florins, were Antwerp-based dealers. The former was a close relative of Justus Collimore, in whose Antwerp house the Buckingham collection was stored.[23] In 1649 two of Buckingham's paintings by Rubens were pawned to Collimore, and on several occasions he witnessed notarial documents relating to the collection.[24] Collimore was no stranger to the royalists: a contract was drawn up in February 1645 between him and the Lord High Treasurer, Francis Cottington (1579?–1652), for the supply of '1000 barrels of powder, 30 tons of brimstone, and 200 or 300 tons of saltpetre, at some of the King's magazines'.[25] In the 1630s François Wouters had served as court painter to the Emperor Ferdinand II in Vienna and, from 1637, to Charles I in England. By 1641 he had returned to Antwerp, where he contributed to the valuation of Rubens' collection of paintings.[26] It can have been no coincidence that his employment at the court of Archduke Leopold Wilhelm, Governor General of the Spanish Netherlands from 1647 to 1656, and a major patron of the arts, concurred with his involvement with the sale of the Buckingham collection: Buckingham and his representatives (on Goffe's advice) considered the Archduke an important potential buyer from the outset.

The same pawn agreement was repeated in The Hague on 20 April 1649, with a new clause added:

> I William Aylesbury ... haveing full powre to dispose of all the pictures & agatts and medals belonging to the ... Duke of Buck: & now in the house of Mr Justus Collimar of Antwerpe merchant being engaged for the sum of thirty thousand guilders to Mr John and Mr. Lionel Coram and Mr Thomas Woulters of Antwerpe, with these conditions that if within the space of one yeare after the date of the said agreement, the said summe of thirty thousand bee not payd, then soem of the said pictures and Agatts beeing sold as will satisfye the debt of the above mentioned John and Lionel Coram and Tho: Woulters, the remainder are to be restored to mee William Aylesbury. Therefore I do by this present writeing declare that by the virtue of the said procuration I doe engage the remainder of the said Pictures and Agatts to Lietnt Coll: Robert Sidney in consideration of a bond hee is entered into for my personall appearance in the Court of Holland to answere to the suite of Charles Valois for the sum of five thousand ninety and eight guilders, within 3 months after the Date hereof. And I doe further promise and oblige my selfe that within the space of 15 dayes after the date here of I will cause a more formall act to be made according to the stile of the Court of Antwerp where the said pictures and Agatts doe now remaine. Furthermore I doe

---

[23]   *Ibid.*, v, no. 1553.

[24]   *Ibid.*, v, no. 1559, and vi, nos. 1587, 1621, 1643, 1644, and 1651.

[25]   *CClSP*, i, no. 1823. Included is also an 'Account of moneys paid by Collimar on the King's account'. See *Ibid.*, i, no. 1844, for an 'Account of several sums paid Mr. Justus Collimar out of the excise of this city [Bristol]; extending from Feb. 20 to March 26 (1645), and amounting to 1324*l.* 1*s.* 6¼*d.*'

[26]   Hans Vlieghe, *Flemish Art and Architecture, 1585–1700* (New Haven: Yale University Press, 1998), p. 111.

declare that the sayd debt of 5098 guilders is the true and lawful debt of George D: of Buckingham, and I doe here by entitle and make over to Lietnt Coll: Robert Sidney all my right to claim the saide debt upon the Accompt Audited by Mr Drury Burton and signed all allowed by his grace the D: of Buck: and his Brother the Lo: Fr: Villiers.[27]

Signed by Aylesbury in the presence of Sir Roger Pratt (*bap.* 1620–85) – another Restoration architect who spent time on the continent in proximity to Buckingham – this document introduced a further party asserting his right to the Duke's property. In return for some of the paintings, Robert Sidney, Aylesbury's former pupil, had agreed to take upon himself Buckingham's debt to Charles Vallois, a French merchant from whom the Duke and his late brother had borrowed in 1645 'la somme de cincq mille noeuff cent quatrevingt florins argentz de France' [the sum of 5980 French florins] to fund their continental tour.[28] Despite the particular provision in the Hague contract that 'a more formal act' was to be drawn up according to 'the stile of the Court of Antwerp', this arrangement was never formalized in the Southern Netherlands. Instead, a deed was drawn up by notary Ghysberti on 30 April 1649, recording Buckingham's disinclination to relinquish his goods. Having already loosened Goffe's firm grip on his art collection, Buckingham now bade Aylesbury instruct Corham and Wouters 'de ne laisser transporter dehors leurs mains lesdicts peintures et joyaulx, pour ce que lesdicts peintures et joyaulx à luy comparant pour ledict Son Excellence sont mis en ses mains pour hipotèque de ladicte debte'[29] [not to let the said paintings and precious stones pass out of their hands, as they have been entrusted to him (i.e., Aylesbury) by his Excellency as a mortgage for the said debt].

In the same document were set down Buckingham's outstanding debts to Vallois (without any mention of Robert Sidney's involvement) as well as to Aylesbury:

L'an XVIcXLIX le dernier d'avril comparut etc. Monsieur Willem Aylesbury gentilhomme anglois présentement en ceste dicte ville à moy notaire bien cognu, comme ayant procure de Son Excellence le duc de Buckingam passé soubz sa signature et cachet le XXIX de juing XVIc quarante-huict et en ladicte qualité at dict et déclaré que ledict Son Excellence doibt à luij comparant la somme de

---

[27] Bodleian Library, Oxford, Clarendon MS 37, fol. 77, as quoted by McEvansoneya, 'Sequestration and Dispersal', 148. As McEvansoneya pointed out, this is the sole document that mentions 'Thomas Woulters'. The Antwerp records refer to Franchois [François] Wouters. John Corham, who is included only in the Hague agreement, may be the English merchant in Antwerp referred to in the Trumbull Papers, BL, Add. MS 72280. He was in all likelihood a relative of Leonel.

[28] *Antwerpse Kunstinventarissen*, ed. Duverger, v, no. 1554. See also n. 8. *CCISP*, i, nos. 2836 and 2884. Both items refer to letters from Vallois to Aylesbury, enlarging on the former's impoverished state. Vallois had also worked for Buckingham in London. See Stoye, *English Travellers*, p. 313.

[29] *Antwerpse Kunstinventarissen*, ed. Duverger, v, no. 1553.

soisante mil florins à cause des deniers furnies en diverses temps pour service dudict Son Excellence et feu son frère.[30]

[On 30 April 1649 Mr. William Aylesbury, English gentleman now residing in this city, appeared before me notary public, having a procuration from his Excellency the duke of Buckingham, signed and sealed on 29 June 1648, and in this capacity has declared that his Excellency owes him the claimant the sum of 60,000 florins in repayment of moneys spent at various times in the service of the said duke and his late brother.]

Although Buckingham's restrictions were revoked on 16 December 1649, Aylesbury seemed sufficiently alarmed by his patron's heavy burden of debt (and his reluctance to pay back some of his creditors) to have the dazzling sum of 60,000 florins owed to him registered. Aylesbury's private finances were a shambles: ever since the early 1640s he had been plagued by debts and had repeatedly begged for money, a situation worsened by his patron's failure to meet his financial obligations.[31] For some reason Buckingham did not consider the compensation of his agent a priority. Whereas he pledged or even sold paintings with the intention of recompensing Vallois and May, contemporary records contain no traces of reimbursement of Aylesbury.[32]

During the remainder of 1649 Aylesbury continued to promote Buckingham's interests. On 8 May he deposited several of Buckingham's paintings with the Antwerp merchant Salomon Cock as security for a loan of 324 pounds; six days later he sold Cock eleven paintings, including several by Rubens, for 1,500 florins, with the stipulation that if the money were paid back with interest within one year, the paintings would have to be returned to their seller.[33] At the end of May two more paintings were sold to Marcelis Liebrechts the younger for 600 florins. Again, this was:

à condition que d'aujourd'huy date de cestes en un an prochain ledict Monsieur Alesburij ou ayant son ordre pourra lever et tirer dhors les mains dudict Sieur

---

[30]   *Ibid.*, v, no. 1553. It is not certain, however, that Buckingham paid Vallois all of what was due. By a deed of 18 February 1650 Vallois authorized Sir Joseph Ash to receive the money the Villiers brothers still owed him. Nearly three months later Buckingham promised to settle the remainder of his debts with Vallois. *Ibid.*, vi, nos, 1606 and 1624.

[31]   Stoye, *English Travellers*, pp. 299, 301, 302, and 304. His father's property having been confiscated in the second half of the 1640s, Aylesbury did not have a family fortune to fall back on.

[32]   *Antwerpse Kunstinventarissen*, ed. Duverger, vi, no. 1597. Also in this respect, Aylesbury meets the profile of the early modern agent: 'Agents asking, begging, even threatening their employers in (often vain) attempts to get hold of their money is a *leitmotiv* familiar to anyone reading their correspondence.' (Keblusek, 'Introduction. Profiling the Early Modern Agent', in *Your Humble Servant*, ed. Cools et al., p. 13.)

[33]   *Antwerpse Kunstinventarissen*, ed. Duverger, v, nos. 1557 and 1559. One of Rubens's patrons was the wealthy Antwerp citizen Jeremias Cock, who was almost certainly related to Salomon.

Liebrechts lesdicts deux peintures en luy payant ladicte somme de six cent florins avecq une cortosie de trente et sept florins et dix pattars.[34]

[on condition that within one year from today Mr. Aylesbury will recover the said two paintings from Mr. Liebrechts, paying him the said sum of 600 florins with an interest of 37 florins and 10 'pattars'.]

Later that year Liebrechts was also offered the same 11 paintings that had been sold to Cock on 14 May; this time, however, in exchange for 2,600 florins, with the period of reimbursement limited to six months.[35]

Undoubtedly realizing that he would not be able to restitute Corham and Wouters by May 1650, Buckingham on 24 December 1649 sold 'toutes les peintures, agats et aultres choses et raritez qui sont engagez à Leonel Corham et Franchois Wouters' [all the paintings, agates and other objects and curiosities pawned to Leonel Corham and François Wouters] to William Widdrington (1610–51). By way of compensation the latter was expected to refund the Antwerp dealers and pay Hugh May 'la somme de dix mille florins au mois de juing de ladicte année seize cent et cincquante et pardessus ce de payer une pension annuelle audict Sieur Hugo May de mille florins par an durant la vie dudict Sieur May'[36] [in June 1650 the sum of 10,000 florins as well as an annual pension of 1,000 florins until his death]. Not only did this strategy allow Buckingham to reduce his financial worries, it also prevented the dispersal of the collection, while at the same time guaranteeing its English ownership. Not otherwise known as a keen art collector, Widdrington, a devoted Stuart supporter, may have been brought into the project for his loyalty and sense of duty, as well as for his capital resources – even though his coalmines had been sold and his estates confiscated in the later part of the 1640s. That after the transaction Buckingham was still allowed to exert at least some control over the commodities that were officially no longer his indicates that Widdrington anticipated benefiting – financially or otherwise – from his cooperation with the Duke.

After 24 December 1649 the pawning and sale of the goods continued as before, albeit with markedly decreased involvement on Aylesbury's part. (Was it mere coincidence that as soon as Widdrington came forward, Aylesbury's career as Buckingham's agent began to wane?) Negotiations in which Aylesbury apparently had no part were entered into with Archduke Leopold Wilhelm and his representatives. In the summer of 1650 some of Buckingham's valuables were brought to Brussels for close examination by the Archduke, while others were inspected at the lodgings of the count of Ursel by the Flemish painters Gerard Seghers (1591–1651) and Cornelis Schut (1597–1655).[37] In July and August

---

[34]   *Ibid.*, v, no. 1561.

[35]   *Ibid.*, v, nos. 1557, 1559 and 1561, and vi, no. 1596.

[36]   Martyn Bennett, 'Widdrington, William, first Baron Widdrington (1610–1651)', *ODNB*, online edn, accessed 18 Feb 2008 [http://www.oxforddnb.com/view/article/29359]; *Antwerpse Kunstinventarissen*, ed. Duverger, vi, no. 1597.

[37]   *Antwerpse Kunstinventarissen*, ed. Duverger, vi, nos. 1632 and 1645.

deeds were issued registering the sale of a considerable number of paintings to the Archduke, including several of the 190 which had been sold to Widdrington.[38]

Aylesbury's final engagement in brokerage activities seems to have been his participation in the organizing of an auction, which took place some time before May 1650.[39] The paintings put on sale were almost certainly those 'redeemed from Brussels', i.e., not sold to the Archduke.[40] Although 'of no great valew', their purchase prices were forced up by 'parties' bidding for 'my Ld Dukes advantage', as a result of which the items remained unsold and were returned to Aylesbury.[41] Around the same time, Buckingham replaced his agent with the trio of Sir Charles Cotterell (1615–1701), William Frizell and Pierre Robert, a move possibly informed by a growing distrust of Aylesbury's management and accounting methods.[42] In the instructions to Robert of 26 May 1650, it was carefully pointed out that the

> blanks which are put into your hands must be employed for the uses following and no other, viz: to call Mr. Alesbury to account for the two debts of £200 a peice, using therein such persons as you shall find fittest, allowing them such rewards out of them as you shall agree. [...] To take Alesbury's account for £2000 in England.[43]

Although the specific nature of these debts is not marked, it is obvious that Buckingham questioned Aylesbury's integrity (or pretended to do so in order to get rid of him), and was prepared to take harsh measures against him. When the Duke followed Charles II to Scotland, he gave Goffe, his advisor in Paris, direct orders as to how to deal with his former servant during his absence:

> Besides the real debts I assure you my Lord Duke was in some apprehension that Mr Aylesbury (knowing his Graces fast engagement in Scotland) might renew again some suit for his pretended debts, for prevention of which I may let you

---

[38]   *Ibid.*, vi, nos. 1632, 1642, and 1654.

[39]   'Gough to Cotterell, 18 November [1650]' (Rousham MS), as quoted by McEvansoneya, 'Sequestration and Dispersal', 151.

[40]   'Gough to Cotterell, 4 November [1650]' (Rousham MS), *Ibid.*, pp. 150–51.

[41]   'Gough to Cotterell, 18 November [1650]' (Rousham MS), *Ibid.*, p. 151.

[42]   Roderick Clayton, 'Cotterell, Sir Charles (1615–1701)', *ODNB*, online edn, accessed 15 Feb 2008 [http://www.oxforddnb.com/view/article/6397]; and Brian Reade, 'William Frizell and the Royal Collection', *The Burlington Magazine for Connoisseurs* 89 (1949) 528: 70–75. Cotterell also represented Widdrington in contacts with Leopold Wilhelm (*Antwerpse Kunstinventarissen*, ed. Duverger, vi, nos. 1633, 1636, 1643, 1644, and 1649). Robert was a former servant of Randal MacDonnell, Marquess of Antrim (1609–83) and his consort Katherine Manners (1603?–49), Buckingham's mother. See also Stoye, *English Travellers*, pp. 309–11.

[43]   Excerpt from the 'Instructions for my servant P. Roberts going into England. 26 May 1650 o.s. ...', as quoted by Stoye, *English Travellers*, pp. 319–20. The final phrase suggests that Aylesbury was to be called to account for having spent money without Buckingham's approval.

know that I am instructed with full powers to arrest him if he, coming over on this side of the sea, gives the least cause to suspect him.[44]

In early 1650 Aylesbury had absconded to England, his disappearance most likely dictated by the deterioration of his relationship with Buckingham and his bankruptcy.

III

In the City Archives of Antwerp are preserved four hitherto unnoticed records – one dated 1649, the others 1650 – attesting to Aylesbury's impoverished state: three documents concern money he owed to Antwerp lenders, the fourth itemizes the possessions that were retrieved from his Antwerp home and sold to cover his debts.[45] The 1649 date on the first document probably refers to its attached obligation payable to Ambrose Mather, from whom Aylesbury, on 20 December 1649, had borrowed 325 guilders:

Ick be kenne ontfanghen te hebben van Ambrosio Mather den somme van drijhunderd twentich fijve guldens currant gelt die ick bij desen obligere mijne selve wedrom te betaele aen hem op den Eersten dach februaris nast volghende den datum deser in Antwerpe den 20 dach. Decmber 1649

William Aylsburije

Oock twalve guldens meere te betaele den selfsten tijte
ghetuijghen hiervan Nichola metchaut[46]

[I declare having received from Ambrosio Mather the sum of 325 guilders of acceptable currency which I hereby promise to return to him on the first day of next February, Antwerp 20 December 1649. William Aylesbury. Also 12 more guilders to be paid on the same day. Witnessed by Nichola Metchaut.]

Edward Hyde's name appears at the bottom of this document, which may suggest that Aylesbury intended to forward it to his brother-in-law. By mid-May 1649 Alyesbury had brought over from England his father and mother, both his sisters (one of whom, Frances [d. 1667]), was married to Hyde [1609–74]), and his friends Sir Charles and Lady Cotterell (1614–c. 1657).[47] He had made an agreement with Hyde to support both

---

[44]   'Goffe to Cotterell, 18 November 1650', as quoted by Stoye, *English Travellers*, p. 320.

[45]   We are indebted to the Stadsarchief Antwerpen (City Archives, Antwerp) for permission to reproduce these documents. The original spelling and punctuation have been preserved.

[46]   Stadsarchief Antwerpen, GF 188/2.

[47]   Hyde wrote to Aylesbury on 3 January 1650 enquiring about his whereabouts: 'My William […], if you will write nothing else, nor ever again after this tyme, at least tell me what is the reason of this strange, peremptory, unkind silence.' Clarendon MS 129, fol. 27; see Stoye, *English Travellers*, pp. 316–17.

families for one year on condition that Hyde took upon himself the same responsibility the following year. Eagerly complying with Aylesbury's request, Hyde promised 'to discharge the 2nd year for the whole company (which I doubt not I should be able to do) but if I lyve will likewise reimburse you for what you lay out in the first year.'[48] The loan of 325 guilders may thus have been raised to cover expenses specifically made to support the continental residence of the Aylesburys and Cotterells.

The covering document addressed to 'mijne Heere M Tomass advocate' [To my Lord M Tomass lawyer] is a copy – in abbreviated form – of the second document, an 'Extract tuyt het Arrestboeck mijns heeren des Amptmans der Stadt Ant^{pen}' [excerpt from the Antwerp baillif's register of arrests] dated 27 May 1650, and concludes with the phrase 'given this to pcuruer [procureur = attorney?] Johnsons den 22 maij to make the arrest als boven [as above]'. The date of 22 May refers to 1650 rather than 1649, as Aylesbury had left Antwerp for good by then. Soon afterwards, legal action was taken by Mather. To retrieve the money owed to him, he insisted on the sale of his borrower's personal belongings, which had been left behind in 'den Swerten Arent op de Caport brugghe' [The Black Eagle on Cowgate Bridge], the house Aylesbury shared with his father, Lady Hyde and Jan Hoff:

Ambrosius Mather woonende inden Morijaen op den Caport brugghe binnen desen Stadt heeft begheirt beseten te hebben onder Sr Thomas Ayelburije ende onder de huysvrouwe van Sr Eduart Hijde mitsgaders onder Joannes hoff alle drij woonende int huijs den swerten Arent op de Caport brugghe alhier alle alsulcke goederen meubelen cleederen. lijnwaet husraet ofte eenigherhande effecten als sij lieden oft yemandt van hun. is onder hebbende ofte inde voorß huijsen den swerten Arent sijn berustende de welcken toe commen aen Willem Aijlesburij. Ende int besunder op alsulcken tappijten aldaer wesende ende hanghende op de boven camer aen den straeten daer de voorß Willem Ayleburij curts voor sijn vertreck plachten te slaepen mitsgaders op desselffs bedden roodt behanghsel ende toe behoerten ende een cabinett met laeijkens dwelcke den selves in t voorß heeft gelaeten. ende daerenboven op een twee oft meer kistiens met lij^{n}waet cleederen ende anderen dingen die daerin souden mogen wesen staende op de middelste camer boven aenden straeten oft elders inden voorß huijse de voorß Willem Aylesburij ooc toecomende. Alles om daer aan te verhaelen de somme van drij hondert vijffentwintich gulen mitsgaders de som[m]e van twelve ende noch van tweentwintich guldens ende 4 stij.[49]

[Ambrosius Mather, living at the sign of the Moor, on Cowgate Bridge in this City, has requested to be put in possession, under (in the days of) Sir Thomas Aylesbury, Sir Edward Hyde's wife and Johan Hoff, all three living at the Black Eagle on Cowgate Bridge, of all such goods, furniture, clothes, linen, household effects or any items owned by them together or severally, or remaining in the aforementioned house the Black Eagle and belonging to William Aylesbury. And especially all tapestries in the upper room on the street-side of that house, where

---

[48]   *CClSP*, ii, no. 18.
[49]   Stadsarchief Antwerpen, GF 188/2.

William Aylesbury aforesaid used to sleep shortly before his departure, as well as his red bedcovers and bedclothes, and a linen-cabinet which he left behind there, and also one, two, or more chests containing linen clothing and any other objects, now in the upstairs middle room on the street-side or elsewhere in the house, also belonging to William Aylesbury. All of this in order to recover the sum of 325 guilders as well as a sum of 12 guilders and of 22 guilders and 4 stivers.]

The record dated 22 May was undoubtedly intended for English use, whereas the excerpt from the Antwerp 'Arrestboeck' of 27 May 1650 registers the court case brought against Aylesbury in Antwerp.

The third document sets down Aylesbury's debts to Jan Hoff. Like Mather, Hoff had witnessed several notarial acts passed between 30 April 1649 and 22 August 1650 regulating the sale of Buckingham's paintings.[50] In the register of arrests the creditor announced his intention to dispose of certain pieces of furniture which his former housemate had left in his possession, thus hoping to recoup a loan of 334 guilders as well as the sum of 556 guilders and 6 stivers. The matter was presented to the Antwerp High Court of Justice and a summons delivered on 21 June 1650 to Aylesbury's father, who accepted it on behalf of his son.

According to the extract from the Antwerp book of sale, the fourth document, Aylesbury's moveable goods, were sold on 5 and 6 August 1650, the culmination of legal action taken by his creditors.[51] The five-and-a-half-page list comprises items as varied as a pair of new Spanish leather boots, four books by Titus Livy and others, a dirty shirt, a pair of linen drawers, a pair of grey English stockings, and an inlaid table, as well as numerous paintings. The large number of personal belongings, ranging from underwear, shoes and cloaks to books and furniture, suggests that Aylesbury left Antwerp in great haste. Fleeing from his creditors (and Buckingham?), he may have had no choice but to forsake his more valuable commodities. He possibly intended them as capital to help his family repay his debts: of the total amount of 919 guilders 5 stivers raised, the larger part was derived from the sale of 18 paintings.[52]

IV

Unable or unwilling to fall back on a royalist network as yet in the making, Aylesbury's only expedient was to take flight to England and make his peace with

---

[50] Stadsarchief Antwerpen, GF 188/2; *Antwerpse Kunstinventarissen*, ed. Duverger, v, nos. 1553 and 1561, and vi, nos. 1649 and 1650.

[51] Stadsarchief Antwerpen, GF 188/2.

[52] This list interestingly identifies most of the buyers: Augustijn Thijssens, for example, bought a landscape painting on panel no. 10 for 10 guilders and 13 stivers. Although it is not clear which Augustijn Thyssens is referred to – the elder (1597–1692) or the younger (1623–75) – both played a prominent part in the contemporary Antwerp art scene. Thijssens sr was an art dealer, his son a painter. Among the buyers was also the portrait painter Pauwel Flocquet (d. 1667), who purchased amongst other things a gilt-framed portrait on canvas of an English earl for 10 guilders and 10 stivers.

parliament. As the reward for his position as a broker had turned out to be a purely nominal one, insufficiently substantial to shoulder the extra burden of supporting his family and friends, his private debts had forced him into irreversible poverty. And so, his once promising career in the service of one of the century's most influential patrons had been cut short. Perhaps Buckingham had been right to suspect him of mismanagement, but Aylesbury's disillusionment with his treatment at the hands of a parsimonious patron would have run equally deep. Back in England, for a number of years he lived a precarious life, subsisting on the generosity of his friends, until early in 1656 he once again exchanged his native country for foreign soil. His final years, indeed, would have passed into complete oblivion had it not been for his appointment as secretary to Major-General Robert Sedgwick (*bap.* 1613–56), Commander-in-Chief of the English forces in America and one of the commissioners for civil government of Jamaica.[53] Shortly after Sedgwick's decease in May 1656, Aylesbury begged the support of John Thurloe, Cromwell's Secretary of State, advertising himself as a faithful and conscientious servant of the English Republic. Possibly alluding to his hapless service under Buckingham, he gave expression to his enthusiasm 'to discharge that trust [that] is reposed in me by my imploy, without any private ends or interest.' Some six months into his term of office, Aylesbury's death on 24 August 1656 was reported in a letter from Jamaica, describing the onetime disgraced broker as a respected military advisor, a 'man well versed in the weighty affairs of state, … for the want of which we shall have more and more to grieve'.[54]

The four Antwerp documents of 1649–50, which have gone unnoticed in Stoye and McEvansoneya, shed an interesting light on the concluding stage of Aylesbury's life as an expatriate in the Southern Netherlands. Despite his close relations with more affluent royalists, personal and professional problems, including long-standing financial ones, forced him to fall back on the time-honoured survival strategy of borrowing money, in his case primarily from local lenders – all to no avail, however.[55] Aylesbury's example goes to show that even in the context of an expatriate (and by extension, exile) community, the quality of the patron-client relationship strongly determined the course of an individual's career and the lives of his dependents. Buckingham's agent may have failed to anticipate his eventual replacement, and, unlike other members of this community, he appears to have lacked the resourcefulness to strike out in different directions and secure alternative sponsorship.[56]

---

[53]   Richard P. Gildrie, 'Sedgwick, Robert (*bap.* 1613, *d.* 1656)', *ODNB*, online edn, accessed 22 Feb 2008 [http://www.oxforddnb.com/view/article/25017].

[54]   *TSP*, v, 154–5, 374.

[55]   Margaret Cavendish, *The Life of the Thrice Noble, High, and Puissant Prince William Cavendishe, Duke, Marquess, and Earl of Newcastle* (London, 1675), p. 82.

[56]   J.P. Vander Motten and Katrien Daemen-de Gelder, '"Les plus rudes chocs de la fortune": Willem Frederik, stadholder of Friesland (1613–1664), Thomas Killigrew (1612–1683) and Patronage in Exile', *Anglia: Journal of English Philology*, 127 (2009), 65–90.

Chapter 4

A Tortoise in the Shell: Royalist and Anglican Experience of Exile in the 1650s

Marika Keblusek

I

On 30 April 1654, the Anglican divine Henry Hammond presented a plan to Gilbert Sheldon:

> Let me mention to you an hasty undigested phansy of mine suggested to me by reading the Conclusion of BP Bramhalls excellent booke of Schisme p. 276. 277. It is this. What if you & Dr Henchman and I should endeavour to raise £ 600 per ann: (each of us gaining subscriptions for £ 200) for 7 yeares, to maintain a society of 20 Exiled scollers, and when we discern ye thing feesible communicate it to BP Bramhall, & require of him a Catalogue of 20 such, whose wants & desires of such a recess in some convenient place (by him to be thought of also) might make it a fit charyty to recommend to pious persons. Next if this be not unreasonable to be endeavourd, then tell me whether it must be privately carryed, or may be publickly avoied, & what els you can think of to perfect & forme this suddein rude conceit.[1]

Hammond contemplated this scheme, which was never realized, after finishing his reading of John Bramhall's *Just vindication of the Church of England, from the unjust aspersion of criminal schism* (London, 1654), in which the exiled Bishop of Derry had plainly outlined the wretched state of refugee partisans of the House of Stuart and the Church of England:

> They who have composed minds, free from distracting cares, and means to maintain them, and friends to assist them, and their books and notes by them, do little imagine with what difficulties poor Exiles struggle, whose minds are more intent on what they should eat to morrow, then what they should write, being chased as Vagabonds into the merciless world to beg relief of strangers.[2]

---

[1] BL, Harleian MS 6942, fol. 18. Victor D. Sutch, *Gilbert Sheldon: Architect of Anglican Survival* (The Hague: Nijhoff, 1973), p. 41, mentions the 'Charitable Uses Fund', established by Sheldon and Hammond. Whether the project was actually realized remains unclear.

[2] John Bramhall, *A just vindication of the Church of England, from the unjust aspersion of criminal schism* (The Hague, 1654), p. 276.

Writing and reading, so Bramhall implied, could be the exile's strategy for survival; although, being chased out of one's own world, one not always had the means and tools to do so – one's library, study, peace of mind.

Indeed, the world of the book quickly became a safe haven for disenfranchised royalists; a quiet place 'to outlive the storm', as Edward Hyde had phrased it in a letter to Edward Nicholas.[3] For many refugees, books formed an essential part of their now-scattered lives – a means of information, confirmation, recreation and comfort. Literary and intellectual activity proved a beneficial way to bide their time. One author referred to his writings as the 'green, and *sowre* fruits of exile', while another simply stated that 'banished men find very little business besides books'.[4] Among the exiles we find poets like John Denham, William Davenant, Edmund Waller, Richard Fanshawe, Richard Flecknoe and Abraham Cowley; playwrights like Thomas Killigrew, William Cavendish and William Lower; philosophers like Thomas Hobbes, Charles Cavendish and Margaret Lucas Cavendish; apologists of the Church of England, like John Bramhall, George Morley, John Cosin, Isaac Basire, Richard Watson and Robert Creighton; and historical and political authors like Thomas Ross, Christopher, Lord Hatton and Edward Hyde – to name but a few.

Numerous passages in royalist correspondence, memoirs, dedications and forewords refer to the practices of writing, reading, book buying, sharing, borrowing, selling and collecting; to the exchange of information on the latest editions, newssheets and pamphlets; to the availability and prices of certain titles, and to logistical details of book sending and transportation. These remarks all emphasize the meaning and status of the printed word within the émigré world. Mapping out this exile book culture – the production, distribution and consumption of texts – is crucial to the reconstruction of social, political, intellectual and cultural networks on the continent, to the understanding of royalist and Anglican thinking, and to the appreciation of the exile experience as a whole.[5]

II

Despite the hardships that John Bramhall had mentioned, and which had caused Hammond to come up with the plans for his charity, many exiles managed to build libraries abroad, thus replenishing, or replacing, the books they had had to leave behind in Britain. Bishop John Cosin amassed a substantial number of

---

[3]   Bodleian Library, Clarendon MS 47, fol. 362 (Edward Hyde, Paris, to Edward Nicholas, 6 February 1653/4)

[4]   John Quarles, *Fons lachrymarum, or, A fountain of teares* (London, 1648), fol. A4v; Gervase Holles, *Memorials of the Holles Family, 1493–1665*, ed. A.C. Wood (London: Royal Historical Society, 1937), p. 2.

[5]   Much of this essay is based on research undertaken for my *Minds of Winter: Book Culture and Literary Life of Royalist Exiles in the Netherlands, 1642–1660* (Leiden: Brill, forthcoming).

French books and pamphlets during his years in Paris.[6] Continental imprints in the library of George Morley (now part of Winchester Cathedral Library) reveal his active interest in books during his time abroad – despite his lack of funds. In his notebooks, the former royalist officer Richard Symonds frequently mentioned purchasing manuscripts, prints and books during his travels in Italy between 1649 and 1652.[7] In Paris, Christopher, Lord Hatton received numerous book trunks from his agent Peter Gunning in London, filled with the specific editions he had ordered for his historical and political studies. The preserved accounts of his acquisitions at various Paris bookshops show his enthusiasm for continental titles. Many of Hatton's purchases can be related to his studies in collaboration with John Cosin in Paris in the 1640s, the result of which, they hoped, would prove the historical and theological legitimacy of the royalist cause.[8] Similarly, Edward Hyde's extensive book-buying sprees were inspired by his own literary projects, and several historians have shown that Hyde's reading was closely connected to his own writings, notably his *History of the Rebellion*. John Evelyn, en route to the continent in the 1640s, bought many books, prints and other cultural artefacts in Italian and French bookshops; in 1651–52 he almost succeeded in buying the better part of the library which John Cosin had been forced to leave behind in England.

In Evelyn's case, the wealth of documentation on his library enables scholars to reconstruct his exile acquisitions in great detail.[9] Unfortunately, lack of documentation in the case of almost all other royalist book collectors makes it difficult to determine what parts of their libraries date back to their exile years. Some refugees, notably Anglican divines like George Morley, John Cosin and Robert Creighton, bequeathed their books to institutional and ecclesiastical collections – the cathedral libraries of Winchester, Durham and Bath & Wells – but without specified lists or catalogues it is virtually impossible to reconstruct their exile collections. Fortunately, however, both the extant catalogue and lending administration of Michael Honywood's library, a vast collection built up during his 17 years of exile in the Dutch Republic, testify to the wide-ranging interest of the royalist community in the printed word. Honywood's 'Utrecht' library grew to be a cultural centre where royalists and Anglicans could meet, talk, and

---

[6]   E. Dubois, 'La bibliothèque de l'évêque Cosin à Durham et sa collection des livres français de théologie et de spiritualité protestantes des XVIe et XVIIe siècles', *Bulletin de la Société de l'Histoire du Protestantisme Français*, 128 (1982), 173–88; A.I. Doyle, 'John Cosin (1595–1672) as a Library Maker', *The Book Collector*, 40 (1991), 335–57.

[7]   O. Millar, 'An Exile in Paris: the Notebooks of Richard Symonds', in *Studies in Renaissance and Baroque Art presented to Anthony Blunt*, ed. Michael Kitson and John Shearman (London and New York: Phaidon, 1967), pp. 157–64.

[8]   A scrapbook containing letters, receipts and clippings chronicling Hatton's purchases of books during his exile (covering the period 1648–50) is in the Bodleian Library, Bodley MS 878. A detailed analysis of this scrapbook can be found in Keblusek, *Minds of Winter*.

[9]   Guy de la Bédoyère, 'John Evelyn's Library Catalogue', *The Book Collector*, 43 (1994), 529–48; Michael Hunter, 'John Evelyn in the 1650s: A Virtuoso in Quest of a Role', in de la Bédoyère, *Science and the Shape of Orthodoxy* (Woodbridge: Boydell, 1995), pp. 66–98.

discuss books and current affairs – indeed much resembling the social function of bookshops and, later, coffee-houses as centres of information exchange.[10] John Bramhall impressed upon his readers the importance of this collection to the exile community when he explained, in an introductory note to one of his books, that without the library of his 'kind friend Mr Michael Honywood' he could not have completed his writings.[11] Like Morley and Creighton, Honywood brought these books and manuscripts back home with him after the Restoration, and they now form the nucleus of the collection in Lincoln Cathedral Library.[12]

A lack of books was a recurrent lament in exile correspondence, and indeed, exchange and communal use of texts were common practice among Bramhall, Honywood and their fellow sufferers. In his preface to *The Table, or, The Modereration* (The Hague, 1649), Joseph Arnway, an exile living in The Hague, reminded his reading public of how he had been forced to write without 'all Bookes and Papers', in 'want of friends to advize, of necessaries to use, of quietnesse to sit or study'.[13] Robert Creighton, ejected Canon of Wells and former royal chaplain to both Charles I and the Prince of Wales, similarly envied 'the Roman Catholic happiness that when they are about any work [they] are so well furnished with amanuenses, books and all other utensils and necessities'.[14] His own much-needed books and papers, meanwhile, had been lost when they were shipped from Brussels to his new lodgings in Utrecht. 'I am a man very unhappy in books', he wrote in a

---

[10] Royalist news, for that matter, was also distributed and discussed in the Hague bookshop of the royalist printer Samuel Browne, which established a firm reputation as a royalist meeting point – well known within the exile community, but equally notorious in England. A parliamentary spy, reporting weekly from The Hague and Leiden, noted in 1651 how he had heard the latest rumours 'at Brown's shop, where is daily a little Exchange held, of Romance [i.e. royalist] news', in which the 'bold Bookseller' took an active part; *Mercurius Politicus* 39, 637 (5 March 1651). In 1655, the royalist officer Peter Mews discussed pamphlets on current European and English affairs in Browne's bookshop; BL Eg MS 2535, fol. 239r ('757' [Peter Mews], The Hague, to Edward Nicholas, Cologne, Friday 4 June 1655). For bookshops as centres of scholarly discourse, see P.G. Hoftijzer, 'Between Mercury and Minerva: Dutch Printing Offices and Bookshops as Intermediaries in Scholarly Seventeenth-century Communication', in *Commercium litterarium 1600–1750: la communication dans la république des lettres: forms of communication in the republic of letters*, ed. Hans Bots and Françoise Waquet (Amsterdam: APA-Holland University Press, 1994), pp. 119–29. For two pertinent and recent studies of the role of coffee-houses, see Brian Cowan, *The Social Life of Coffee: The Emergence of the British Coffeehouse* (London and New Haven: Yale University Press, 2005) and Markman Ellis, *Eighteenth-Century Coffee-House Culture* (London: Pickering & Chatto, 2006).

[11] John Bramhall, *The Church of England Defended ...* (London, 1659), fol. 2v.

[12] A study of Michael Honywood's exile library is in preparation; Marika Keblusek, *Honywood in Holland*.

[13] John Arnway, *The Tablet, or, the Moderation*, 2nd ed. (The Hague, 1649), fols A3–A4.

[14] Bodleian Library, Oxford, MS Clarendon 59, fol. 387 (Creighton to Hyde, 12 January 1659).

letter to Edward Hyde, 'though no man loves them better'.[15] Scholarly hardships are, of course, a common notion in exile literature and reflections on writing; indeed, they may, albeit implicitly, have spurred some authors into writing, who had little else to do but to produce 'fruits of exile'. For those whose swords had been taken, the pen was the only weapon left.[16]

Like Bramhall, Robert Creighton could, and did, make use of Michael Honywood's outstanding library, where he borrowed the theological books and classical editions he needed for his own projects as well as for his work as tutor to Edmund ('Mun') Verney, son of a well-known royalist.[17] The writings of Creighton, Bramhall and their friends and fellow exiles formed part of an ongoing literary effort to keep the Anglican spirit alive, as Bramhall himself testified in print:

> Since I came into exile these sixteen years, where have my weak endeavours ever been wanting to the Church of England? Who had more disputes with their seculars and regulars of all sorts, French, Italian, Dutch, English, in word, in writing, to maintain the honour of the Church of England?[18]

Ejected from their livings and universities, the Anglican exiles in particular formed a close-knit community, collaborating on intellectual projects, assisting each other financially and logistically, travelling together, exchanging and sharing materials and books.

III

Yet these exiles were not the only group who felt forced to escape into a self-constructed universe of paper and words. In Britain, royalists and Anglican clergy could be found living quietly in retirement, writing and reading, keeping in close touch with each other and their fellow sufferers across the seas. Having withdrawn themselves from public life, churchmen like Gilbert Sheldon, Henry Hammond,

---

[15] *Ibid.*, fols 2–3 (Creighton to Hyde, 1/10/1658).

[16] For classic and modern examples of the many exiles who experienced the urgency of writing (Cicero, Dante, exiles from Nazi Germany) see Jo-Marie Claassen, *Displaced Persons: The Literature of Exile from Cicero to Boethius* (Madison: The University of Wisconsin Press, 1999); Caren Kaplan, *Questions of Travel: Postmodern Discourse of Displacement* (Durham: Duke University Press, 1996).

[17] BL, MS Verney Papers (microfilm); Lincoln Cathedral Library, MS 276, fols 46v, 50r, 53r, 54v (Creighton's book borrowings).

[18] John Bramhall, *The Works of the most Reverend Father in God, John Bramhall ... With a life of the author, and a collection of his letters*, 5 vols (Oxford: J.H. Parker, 1843–45), iii, 540. See also Robert S. Bosher, *The Making of the Restoration Settlement: The Influence of the Laudians 1649–1662*, rev. reprint (Westminster, 1957), p. 66.

Brian Duppa and others thought of themselves as living in exile, too.[19] They, too, felt displaced, and had now retreated into the countryside, into the safe haven of their houses and studies. There, they could endure the political storms, living, as they were, in a state of mental, spiritual, 'inner' exile. In 1650, Brian Duppa described himself as an anchorite, having confined 'my self within my own walls'. Two years later he told a friend: 'I secure my self the same way as the tortoise does, by not going out of my shell.' And, in a similar vein, three years later:

> I am likely now (especially this winter time) to gett into the chimny corner, where telling sad stories past, and divining evils that are to come, I shall have left nothing to do but keep my self to a constant way in my devotions.[20]

Books and papers were of the utmost importance to successfully retreat into this internal world of patience and endurance, a world tinged with nostalgia. Indeed, printed texts had become even more crucial now that the Church of England had been forced to go underground:

> Certainly there was never more need of the press, than when the pulpits [...] are shut up. Let all good sons of the Church go on in their duty, and when they can no longer preach to the ears of men, let them preach for their eyes.[21]

According to Duppa, the survival of the Church of England solely depended on the printed word.

There is, of course, a parallel to be drawn here with the growth in published drama and in the culture of play-reading after the closing of the (public) theatres in 1642. John Denham, in his 'Prologue to His Majesty' – one of many publications celebrating the return of the king in 1660 – welcomed Charles II back to the theatre, 'this place/Which *Majesty* so oft was wont to grace/Before our exile'.[22] Referring to the puritan ban, during the 1640s and 1650s, of recreational pastimes staged either in the field or the theatre, Denham described those restrictive decades as a time when those who 'would have no KING, would have no Play'. Thus, both suppressed, 'the *Laurel* and the *Crown* together went,/Had the same *Foes* and the same *Banishment*'. The banishment Denham referred to meant, first, a

---

[19]   John Spurr, *The Restoration Church of England, 1646–1689* (New Haven and London: Yale University Press, 1991), pp. 21–2, does not refer to this practice of retirement as 'exile', but signals it nevertheless as an important feature of Anglican culture in the 1650s.

[20]   *The Correspondence of Bishop Brian Duppa and Sir Justinian Isham 1650–1660*, ed. Gyles Isham (Northampton: Publications of the Northamptonshire Record Society, 17, 1951), p. 12 (Duppa to Isham, 7 August 1650), p. 52 (Duppa to Isham, 20 January 1652), p. 99 (Duppa to Isham, 24 October 1654).

[21]   Bodleian Library, MS Tanner 52, fol. 207 (Duppa to Anthony Farindon, 1654).

[22]   John Denham, *Poetical Works*, ed. Theodore H. Banks (New Haven and London: Yale University Press, 1928), p. 94. The 'Prologue' was published, as a single broadsheet, in November 1660, on the occasion of a drama production General Monck had staged for Charles II. See *Dictionary of National Biography* (1888), 'John Denham'.

physical one, a displacement of persons and court. Yet he also alluded to a more general *sense* of exile prevalent during the Commonwealth, a sense of retreat and withdrawal expressed in numerous poems of the period: the retreat from active, public life into a quiet existence in the countryside; the passing of time in literary celebrations of nature, friendship and (ceremonial) pastimes;[23] the withdrawal into what has been termed 'a neo-stoic or epicurean horticulture of the mind'; and even, in some cases, the solitary 'exile' of the imprisoned and incarcerated.[24] Here, again, writing and reading were the preferred means of survival, comfort and recreation in a life of retirement – whether voluntary or enforced.

Much scholarly work has been done on the 'retirement' poetry of authors such as Henry Vaughan, Richard Lovelace, Mildmay Fane, and others.[25] In some of their poems, the distinction between physical and spiritual exile is a theme in itself. Significantly, the actual removal of one's body from British soil is judged to be a far easier option than passively suffering for one's cause in the hidden corners of Cromwellian Britain. Henry Vaughan, for example, felt that 'Who sits at home too bears a loade/Greater than those that gad abroad'.[26] Apart from precluding royalists from taking an active part in the politics of the displaced court, passivity at home was perceived to be a burden because it brought with it notions of extreme boredom, of excess of time. (As we have seen, many of the exiles who had chosen to go abroad complained of the very same things.) Not surprisingly, prison poetry was a popular genre in mid-century cavalier literature, allowing its authors to present themselves as forcedly retired from the world, leading 'reduced' lives.[27] At the same time, being incarcerated also signalled a – formerly – active part taken in the political troubles of the time: active resistance

---

[23]   Izaak Walton, *The Compleate Angler, or, The Contemplative man's recreation* (London, 1653); Taylor Downing and Maggie Millman, *Civil War* (London: Collins & Brown, 1991), p. 158: 'Walton's own reaction to the nation's new masters was to stay out of public life, avoiding public protest, following, however unwillingly, the edicts of the Commonwealth. His was probably a common reaction. Fishing provided an excuse to escape, and it was a pastime in which many sequestered clergy indulged, allowing them the opportunity to talk and complain and dream together'.

[24]   *The English Civil Wars in the Literary Imagination*, ed. Claude J. Summers and Ted-Larry Pebworth (Columbia and London: Missouri Press, 1999), p. 2: 'The celebration of rural retirement, the retreat to private spheres of emotion, and the adoption of stoic attitudes in the face of defeat or disappointment are themselves responses to the turbulent political climate'; James Loxley, *Royalism and Poetry in the English Civil Wars: The Drawn Sword* (Basingstoke: Palgrave, 1997), p. 201.

[25]   For example, Robert Wilcher, *The Writing of Royalism, 1628–1660* (Cambridge: Cambridge University Press, 2001), esp. Chapter 12, 'Coping with defeat and waiting for the King: 1649–1660'.

[26]   Henry Vaughan, 'Misery', in *Silex Scintillans: Sacred Poems and Private Ejaculations*, 2nd edn (London, 1655), pp. 100–101. See also Wilcher, *Writing of Royalism*, pp. 316–17.

[27]   Exemplified by Richard Lovelace in his 'prison letters' to Alathea and Lucasta.

had led to imprisonment, and thus being imprisoned could, and should, be interpreted as an act of resistance itself.[28] Losing one's physical freedom ensured the absolute freedom of one's spiritual liberty.

The obscure cavalier poet Pathericke Jenkyn explicitly linked imprisonment with exile, addressing, in a poetic prison letter, his lost lover Amorea thus:

> We have conquered our fate
> By a suffering Loyaltie.
> We know how to captivate,
> Chain, and bind captivitie.
> Come my dearest come and see
> What it is to have a mind
> Nobly born,
> That can scorn,
> And disdain a Tyrannie [...]
> Come away unto the place,
> Where the Royal slaves do dwell.[29]

Loyalty in suffering helps the poet to overcome his fate and to endure his state as a prisoner or an exile, and at the same time shows his contempt for tyranny. Suffering, in a way, makes him superior. At first sight, Jenkyn's 'suffering loyalty' meant to invoke the poet's experience as a lover separated (exiled) from his beloved. There is a strong political undercurrent here, of course; the notions of suffering and loyalty having a particularly wide resonance in the writings of royalists, notably the exiles among them.

Imprisoned in Durham Castle between 1655 and 1660, Sir John Gibson filled his commonplace book with samples from his reading, with clippings from books and prints he carefully pasted in, and with his own poems and thoughts – all on the theme of the loyal subject suffering for the royal cause. 'A prison is but a retirement', Gibson contemplated, imprisonment giving ample 'opportunitye of serious thoughts to a person, whose spirit is confined, and apt to sit still, and desires no enlargement beyond the cancels of the body till the state of separation calls it foot into a fair liberty'. For Gibson, as for other royalists, being locked up

---

[28] The connection between the literary motives of drinking and imprisonment as political actions in cavalier poetry has been noted by recent critics. See, for example, Lois Potter, *Secret Rites and Secret Writing: Royalist Literature 1641–1660* (Cambridge: Cambridge University Press, 1989), pp. 137–8); see also Marika Keblusek, 'Wine for Comfort: Drinking and the Royalist Exile Experience, 1642–1660', in *A Pleasing Sinne: Drink and Conviviality in Seventeenth-Century England*, ed. Adam Smyth (Woodbridge: Boydell, 2004), pp. 55–68, esp. p. 58.

[29] Pathericke Jenkyn, *Amorea. The Lost Lover. Or, The Idea of Love and Misfortune. Being Poems, Sonets* [sic]*, Songs, Odes, Pastoral, Elegies, Lyrick Poems, and Epigrams. Never before Printed* (London, 1661), p. 9.

for his political and religious beliefs emphasized the righteousness of his cause, and marked him as a fellow exile; a fellow sufferer.[30]

IV

'Suffering' is undoubtedly one of the most frequently used terms to describe the mid-century exile experience, one especially favoured by Anglican refugees, but also widely adopted by others: in prefaces, on title-pages and in correspondence. On the eve of his departure for the continent, the poet John Quarles felt that:

> the worst I can expect to suffer abroad, is but the extremities of Warre; and the best that I can expect at home is but the worst of miseries, if therefore there be a necessity of suffering, I can conceive it to be the best of sufferings to suffer with the best of sufferers.[31]

Exiles (those 'best of sufferers') should be considered to be martyrs, as Edward Hyde later reflected in his essay on patience in adversity:

> We have undergone [our sufferings] out of Piety to God, and Devotion to his Worship; out of Allegiance to our Sovereign Lord the King, and because we would not consent to the Violation of that: out of tender affection to our native Country, and because we would not consent that should be subject to the exorbitant lawless Power of ambitious wicked Men: the suffering for either of which Causes (and we would have it believed we suffer jointly for them all) intitles us justly to the Merit of Martyrdom.[32]

Addressing the royalist congregation in Paris, John Cosin comforted his audience by reminding them that 'it hath been the lot of many a saint of God before us, and of far more worth and dignity than any we are, to be in adversity, to be persecuted, afflicted, tormented, to be robbed of goods and lands and lives, and all'.[33] John Bramhall was 'forced into the fortune of the patriarchs, to leave his country and his charges and seek for safety in a strange land; for so the prophets were used to do, wandering up and down in sheep's clothing'.[34]

---

[30]   BL, Add. MS 37719. On Gibson's notebook, see Potter, *Secret Rites*, pp. 136–7; Adam Smyth, '"Rend and teare in peeces": Textual Fragmentation in Seventeenth-Century England', *Seventeenth Century*, 19 (1) (2004), 36–52.

[31]   John Quarles, *Regale Lectum Miserae, or, a Kingly Bed of Miserie* (s.l. 1649), fols A4r–v.

[32]   'On Patience in Adversity', in Edward Hyde, *Miscellanous Works of the Right Honourable Edward, Earl of Clarendon*, 2nd edn (London, 1751), p. 124.

[33]   Qtd in Elsie E. Duncan-Jones, 'English Exiles in Paris in the 1640s' (unpublished dissertation, University of Cambridge, 1930–31), Chapter II, p. 8.

[34]   Jeremy Taylor, *A sermon preached in Christs-Church, Dublin, July 16, 1663, at the funeral of the most Reverend Father in God John, late Lord Archbishop of Armagh and primate of all Ireland with a succint narrative of his whole life* (London, 1663), pp. 49–50.

Their suffering and persecution linked the exiles directly to the early Christians, and Anglican writers frequently exploited this connection. The Anglican clergyman William Sancroft, for example, who would go into exile in the 1650s, foresaw a sombre future for the Church of England in 1649:

> The doors of that church we frequented will be shut up, and conscientious men will refuse to preach, where they cannot (without danger of a pistol) do what is more necessary, pray according to their duty. For my part, I have given over all thoughts of that exercise in public. In the mean time, there are caves and dens of the earth, and upper rooms and secret chambers for a church in persecution to flee; and there is all our refuge.[35]

In his 1654 treatise, *Of Schisme*, Henry Hammond – who had chosen, like Duppa and Sheldon, to retire in England, but whose work was widely read in the exile community – included a chapter on 'the present Persecution of the Church of *England*, and the advantages sought from thence'. He struck a more optimistic note than Sancroft:

> As yet, Blessed be God, the Church of England is not invisible; It is still preserved in Bishops and in […] multitudes rightly baptized, […] and so that many men cannot any other-wise, then in private families, serve God, after the Church-way […]. The night-meetings of the Primitive Christians in dens and caves are as pertinent to the justifying of our condition, as they can be of any.[36]

In December 1655, Brian Duppa similarly observed how the Church of England had gone underground, persisting in a semi-exilic existence:

> We ar [*sic*] yet suffer'd to offer up the publick prayers and Sacrifice of the Church, though it be under privat roofs […]. When the persecution goes higher, we must be content to go lower, and to serve our God as the antient Christians did, in dens, and caves, and deserts.[37]

Henry Ferne, a popular writer amongst the exiles, pointed out in *Of the division* (1652) that 'it is not a new thing to see a Church under the power of the sword, oppressed by the hand of violence, persecuted, scattered'. True Christians, according to Ferne, had always been persecuted,

> *scattered abroad* […] their meetings […] very close and secret. And so it was often with the Church, during the persecutions of the first 3000 years, often

---

[35]   Henry Cary, *Memorials of the Great Civil War in England*, 2 vols (London: Henry Colburn, 1842), v. 2, pp. 118–19 (William Sancroft to his father, 10 February 1649).

[36]   Henry Hammond, *Of Schisme* (London, 1654), pp. 179–80.

[37]   *Correspondence of Bishop Brian Duppa*, p. 113 (Duppa to Sir Justinian Isham, 16 December 1655).

put to have their meetings before day, and in caves, or secret places: yet so maintained the Communion and being of the Church.[38]

Of course, the association with the early Christians also included Anglican clergy and royalists living in retirement in England, yet it seemed to apply particularly well to the 'physical' exiles, and it greatly contributed to their sense of suffering for the right cause.

V

Royalist and Anglican experience of exile in the 1640s, and especially in the somewhat calmer years of the 1650s, is a theme that has been largely left unexplored by historians and literary critics of the period, with notable exceptions.[39] From this study, it is evident how many exiles sought refuge in the world of print and paper. Involvement with books and intellectual projects was an instrumental, perhaps even therapeutic, means to maintain political, religious and intellectual perspective in hard times. For those men living a life of inner exile, reading and studying was often the only way to engage their mind while waiting for better times to come, enabling them to become part of the active, public life once again. For the Anglicans among them it was the only way to keep the persecuted Church of England alive. Most importantly, whatever the nature of one's exile – voluntary or involuntary, physical or spiritual – it made one belong to a community of fellow sufferers, with all the practical, religious and political significance that this carried.

---

[38] Henry Ferne, *Of the Division between the English and Romish Church upon the Reformation by Way of Answer to the Seeming Plausible Pretences of the Romish party* (London, 1652), fols A6r–A7v. Ferne's sermons and other books were regularly borrowed from Michael Honywood's library.

[39] See, in particular, Geoffrey Smith, *The Cavaliers in Exile, 1640–1660* (Basingstoke and New York: Palgrave, 2003); Christopher D'Addario, *Exile and Journey in Seventeenth-Century Literature* (Cambridge: Cambridge University Press, 2007), pp. 57–86.

Chapter 5
Exile, Apostasy and Anglicanism in the English Revolution

Sarah Mortimer

I

The years of the English Revolution were a dark time for the loyal sons of the Church of England. With church lands sold, episcopacy outlawed and the dwindling number of bishops withdrawing further into solitude, the prospects looked bleak to Henry Hammond, one of Charles I's former chaplains. His friends and allies were abandoning the church of their youth; some embraced the Catholic Church while others remained content to accept whatever religious settlement was imposed upon England. At the nadir of the Church's fortunes, in 1654, Hammond confided his fear to his friend Gilbert Sheldon that, unless things changed, 'it is to little purpose what any write in defence of it [our church]. It will soon be destroyed'.[1] Yet, as I will show in this essay, such pessimism hardly does justice to Hammond's efforts not only to preserve but even to recreate the Church of England. In response to the twin challenges of exile and apostasy, Hammond and his circle began to lay new foundations for the Church, foundations which would be essential to the Anglicanism of the Restoration and beyond. The royalist experience of exile, from England and from the centre of political power, brought new challenges for those who would defend the English Church. As his English friends left their native church, distanced from it geographically and disillusioned with it intellectually, Hammond countered with a new, robust vision of the Church.

Insofar as the English Church was the child of the Tudor Reformations, it was born of king and parliament. And the Church's custody was heavily contested between these two in the 1640s. With parliament's victory on the battlefield, and its *de facto* assumption of sovereignty, it asserted its control over the Church. Early in the war, when parliament was anxious to secure Scottish support, MPs had in 1643 taken the Solemn League and Covenant, which committed them to the 'extirpation of Popery, prelacy' and everything else contrary to the 'power of godliness'.[2] By 1646 they had legislated for a Presbyterian system, albeit one which was only partially implemented, and the following year the sale of bishops' lands was in

---

[1] BL, Harleian MS 6942, fol. 31.
[2] *The Constitutional Documents of the Puritan Revolution, 1625–1660*, ed. S.R. Gardiner, 3rd edn (Oxford: Clarendon Press, 1906), p. 268.

full swing.[3] Under pressure from their Scottish allies and desperate for cash, many English MPs saw little point in preserving episcopacy. The bishops – and their lands – simply could not be retained. The king did not agree to these measures, and these questions of ecclesiology continued to be contentious throughout the peace negotiations of the 1640s.

Charles himself had displayed his support for episcopacy throughout the years of the Personal Rule, and during the first civil war the bishops and the clergy who were committed to maintaining the old structure and form had looked to him.[4] They hoped for safety and salvation through a royalist victory which would reverse parliament's unilateral changes. During the first civil war Charles had not disappointed them; but by the mid-1640s the situation had become much less clear-cut. Charles's support for his bishops began to waver as he was tempted by offers of assistance from the Scottish Presbyterians. It became increasingly clear that he might be willing to sacrifice some or all of the old Church's attributes if this proved necessary to retain his crown.[5] As the king began to consider bargaining over the Church, its dependent status was reinforced. Torn between her warring parents, the Church could exert little authority of her own, let alone lay claim to sacred status. Her human origins seemed to have been laid bare.

With the Church stripped of her sacred mantle, many looked elsewhere for the divine authority and religious certainty which they craved in time of revolution. For Hammond and the royalist Episcopalians, this seemed a particularly dangerous development, for they saw their friends and erstwhile allies drawn either to the Catholic fold or to compromise with Presbyterian or Erastian forms of church government. As the conflict wore on, the attachment to the Church of England which many royalists had displayed in 1642 began to weaken. Exile exacerbated this process, for Englishmen were exposed to an unprecedented range of ecclesiastical and theological choices through their contact with European religious ideas and practices. The intellectual basis of the Church of England seemed, to many, to be no longer sustainable. In response, Hammond and a handful of loyal friends sought to provide a defence of the Church that would satisfy these critics, at home and abroad.

In the halcyon days of the 1630s, Hammond and many others who later became royalists had discussed Biblical criticism and ecclesiastical authority, seeking to base their faith on scripture and reason. Then, the Church of England had

---

³   Elliot Vernon, 'A Ministry of the Gospel: The Presbyterians during the English Revolution', in *Religion in Revolutionary England*, ed. Christopher Durston and Judith Maltby (Manchester: Manchester University Press, 2006), pp. 115–36; G.B. Tatham, 'The Sale of Episcopal Lands during the Civil Wars and Commonwealth', *English Historical Review*, 23 (1908), 91–108.

⁴   David Smith, *Constitutional Royalism and the Search for Settlement, c.1640–1649* (Cambridge: Cambridge University Press, 1994), pp. 102–6.

⁵   John Morrill, 'The Church in England 1642–1649' in *The Nature of the English Revolution* (London: Longman, 1993), pp. 158–60.

seemed attractive, especially as it was presented by the future royalists William Chillingworth and Lucius Cary, Lord Falkland. In the comfort of Falkland's house at Great Tew, Chillingworth had argued that the English Church – like all Protestant churches – rested on the 'Bible only', but his claims began to look rather frayed once civil war broke out.[6] With the breakdown of ecclesiastical authority and censorship, a plethora of scriptural interpretations emerged. Roman certainty and infallibility became increasingly attractive to men anxious for a stable source of truth. This seems to have been especially true for those who left England for Paris, where they found themselves surrounded by Catholics keen to win converts. The Catholic case was strengthened by the intellectual currents these exiles experienced in the French capital, where they encountered a world of Biblical scholarship and erudition more intense than anything they had known in England. The early 1640s saw a flurry of intellectual activity on this score, activity which clearly engaged the attention of the English exiles.[7]

In Paris, theologians and scholars spent much time and energy grappling with the recently published works of the Socinians, for this group threatened to make key Christian doctrines – notably the Trinity – absurd. The central Socinian text was Johannes Crellius's *De Uno Deo Patre*, originally printed in 1631 but made more widely available from the late 1630s in two further editions.[8] Here, Crellius launched a devastating critique of the Trinity, designed to show not only that it could not be found in the scriptures but also that it violated all known rules of logic. In response, divines across Europe sought to show that the doctrine of the Trinity was both coherent and scripturally based. One theologian who showed a particular concern to see Crellius refuted was the Parisian savant, Marin Mersenne, who welcomed many of the royalist exiles into his scholarly circle. Mersenne encouraged his friends, both Catholic and Protestant, to provide an explanation for the Trinity based upon the principles of scripture and reason. He soon found that they, like so many others, struggled with this task.[9]

Not everyone was so distressed by the appearance of Crellius's writing. Jesuits seized on anti-Trinitarian works as evidence of the insufficiency of the scriptural text and the need for ecclesiastical authority to interpret the Bible. In the 1630s, the English Jesuit Edward Knott had taken this line against William Chillingworth, denouncing his high claims for the 'Bible only' as a sure-fire route to anarchy

---

[6]   Hugh Trevor-Roper, 'The Great Tew Circle', in *Catholics, Anglicans and Puritans: Seventeenth-Century Essays* (London and Chicago: Secker & Warburg, 1987), pp. 166–230; William Chillingworth, *The Religion of Protestants A Safe Way to Salvation* (Oxford, 1638).

[7]   See Chapter 1 by Timothy Raylor, this volume.

[8]   It was reprinted with a refutation as J.H. Bisterfeld, *De uno deo, patre, Filio ac Spiritu sancto, mysterium pietatis ...* (Leiden, 1639), and with Johannes Völkel, *De Vera Religione ...* (Rakow [Amsterdam], 1642).

[9]   Many of Mersenne's letters of the period deal with the questions raised by the Socinians. See, for example, *Correspondance du P. Marin Mersenne*, ed. Paul Tannery and Cornelis De Waard, 17 vols (Paris: Éditions du Centre national de la recherche scientifique, 1932–88), ix, 371; x, 719–20, 740–47, 763.

and theological chaos. Chillingworth had ignored such jibes, but once Crellius's explosive arguments were well known, such a strategy was unconvincing. It was Denis Petavius, Professor of Divinity at the flagship Jesuit college of Clairmont, who really made ecclesiastical capital from his opponents' discomfort. In his *Dogmata Theologica*, he showed the diversity of opinion among Church Fathers on the doctrine of the Trinity. He also provided a singularly unconvincing refutation of Crellius, perhaps designed to show that the Socinians' reading of scripture was unanswerable without resort to tradition.[10]

Protestants sought to hold their own, squeezed between the Socinians and the Jesuits, but they feared that some among their own ranks were beginning to defect. They had good cause to fear, and the 1640s saw a number of conversions among the French Huguenot elite. The well known irenicist Theodore Brachet de la Milletière abandoned the Protestant faith in 1645, blaming the Socinians for highlighting the problems with Protestantism.[11] The most notorious case of the European trend towards Catholicism, however, was the great jurist and Biblical scholar, Hugo Grotius. His plans for religious reconciliation – sponsored by Cardinal Richelieu – appeared to the French Protestants to sell the pass to the Catholics, while his Biblical *Annotationes* repeated much Socinian Biblical scholarship.[12]

Catholics pointed to these divisions as evidence of Protestant meltdown, as they began to proselytize among the English community in Paris.[13] There, they gained some notable successes – one of their greatest coups was the conversion in 1646 of Hugh Cressy, friend of Hammond, Chillingworth and Lord Falkland. In the 1630s, Cressy had been a frequent guest at Great Tew, sharing his friends' desire to base his faith upon scripture and reason. He had been as opposed to papal infallibility as any of them, seeing it as unreasonable and unnecessary, yet it was men like Cressy who now seemed most vulnerable to the pull of Catholicism. His time in Paris alerted him to the need for clerical authority, for without this he feared that no answer could be given to the anti-Trinitarians, who based their claims on the Bible alone. Indeed, he recounted how Crellius's work had convinced him that 'if reason be the judge', then the Socinians' argument against the Trinity and

---

[10]   Petavius's discussion of Crellius's *De Uno Deo Patre* can be found in Volume II of *Dogmata Theologica* (Paris, 1644). For the criticisms it attracted, see P. Galter, 'Petau et la preface de son "de trinitate"', *Recherches de science religieuse*, 21 (1931), 462–76.

[11]   R.J.M. van de Schoor, *The Irenic Theology of Théophile Brachet de la Milletière (1588–1665)* (Leiden: Brill, 1995), p. 29.

[12]   On suspicions of Grotius's Catholicism, see Hans Bots and Pierre Leroy, 'Hugo Grotius et la Reunion des Chrétiens: Entre le Savoir et l'Inquietude', *XVIIe Siècle*, 35 (1983), 451–69; Owen provides detailed evidence for Grotius's 'Socinianism' in his *Review of the Annotations of Hugo Grotius* (London, 1656).

[13]   Details of Catholic proselytism can be found in Robert S. Bosher, *The Making of the Restoration Settlement: The Influence of the Laudians 1649–1662* (London: Dacre Press, 1951), pp. 60–67.

incarnation was unanswerable.[14] Any Church which claimed, as the Protestants did, to be based upon the Bible alone could have no grounds to exclude them from communion. He began to conclude that these doctrines needed to be defended using the historical consensus of the Church, the writings of her Fathers and, most importantly, the received interpretations of her clergy and councils.

At the same time, Cressy began to discover the diversity of Catholicism, and he found his spiritual home in the English chapter in Paris. This was a semi-autonomous body, working to distance itself from Rome as far as possible. It was committed to a degree of liberty of conscience, recognizing a relatively broad Catholic framework shaped by the decisions of the church councils and the traditions of antiquity.[15] In the English chapter, Cressy could distance himself from claims of infallibility, arguing that many Catholics considered nothing to be an article of faith except that which was both determined to be such by a General Council and specifically accepted by their own national church. There was no need here for the blind obedience which Cressy had formerly associated with the Roman Church. Exile opened his eyes to the virtues of a Catholicism which provided many of the advantages he had once associated with the Church of England. Cressy's *Exomologesis*, his account of his conversion and of the brand of Catholicism which he found so congenial, was published in 1646. It soon caused a sensation, especially among his old friends in England, who felt a keen sense of betrayal. Not content with abandoning the Church, Cressy also sought to win over others in England and in France, and to strike at the principles of his friends in their darkest hours. Although he remained in touch with his former friends, his apostasy remained a sore point, especially when he criticized the luminaries of Great Tew in the 1670s.[16]

Cressy was not the only fresh convert who emphasized that Gallican Catholicism provided the right combination of certainty and authority. In a letter to Prince Charles of 1653, Milletière argued that the late king's troubles stemmed from the Reformation, when the English Church set herself up anew on the basis of scripture alone. The 'Protestant-Episcopalians', Milletière argued, could not subsist upon these foundations. Only when backed by the Catholic Church and the tradition which it guarded could an ordered and episcopal church exist. Milletière added another dimension to the Catholic argument, for he defended the doctrine of transubstantiation and the ceremonies practiced by Catholics when they adored the host.[17]

---

[14]   P. Brückmann, 'Hugh Cressy', *ODNB*; Hugh Cressy, *Exomologesis; or a faithful narrative of the occasion and motives of the Conversion unto Catholique Unity of Hugh Paulin de Cressy* (Paris, 1647), pp. 483–4. (Cressy refers to the work as *De uno vero deo.*) Details of Cressy's life and faith are scattered through this long book.

[15]   Thomas H. Clancy, 'The Jesuits and the Independents', *Archivum historicum Societatis Iesu*, 40 (1971), 67–90.

[16]   Trevor-Roper, 'The Great Tew Circle', pp. 184–5.

[17]   *The victory of truth for the peace of the Church to the king of Great Britain to invite him to embrace the Roman-Catholick faith by Monsieur de la Militiere, ... with an*

Charles was not persuaded, but the speed with which the English bishops rushed to denounce the Frenchman suggests that some of his arguments hit home, particularly among those already disenchanted with the austere Biblicism they associated with puritanism. Among the French Churches, English men and women could find worship which satisfied their desire for beauty and order; it was a style of worship akin to – but more throroughgoing than – that which they had grown up with in the 1630s. Moreover, they could see the rituals and practices defended within a robust intellectual framework. This may help to suggest why conversion was particularly widespread among those who had experienced the Laudian style at its height, including a clutch of young men educated at Peterhouse, Cambridge. This was deeply distressing for John Cosin, Bishop of Durham and former master of Peterhouse. His son and his son-in-law were both reconciled to the Roman Church in the early 1650s; their aesthetic and religious experiences as undergraduates at Peterhouse may well have preconditioned them.[18]

More mundane considerations also played a part in the religious choices of those who fled to France. For there were powerful forces encouraging them to convert, most notably Queen Henrietta Maria. Another man well known to Hammond, Stephen Goffe, soon followed Cressy's path to Rome, and here we can see the political as well as the intellectual threat which such conversions posed. Both Cressy and Goffe enjoyed Henrietta Maria's favour; Goffe was also close to Henry, Lord Jermyn, one of her principal advisors. With the removal of the Prince of Wales to France and into the arms of his mother, this group looked ideally placed to restore Charles to power, perhaps with the help of Catholic France.[19] Henrietta was also busily, if unsuccessfully, matchmaking between her son and her niece, the French Princess Henriette Anne, hoping to cement any such alliance.[20] Depending on how much support the French provided, there was a possibility that the religious settlement which this would bring might include some degree of toleration for Catholics. And if this did not reach fruition, the Catholics were pursuing a variety of other routes to strengthen their position in England, including negotiations with the Independents and the New Model Army. At the end of his *Exomologesis*, Cressy announced his 'hope for some ease from a Prince of eminent clemency, and from Governours whose Profession is to leave mens consciences to God'.[21]

---

answer thereunto, written by the right reverend John Bramhall, D.D (The Hague, 1653), pp. 17–21, 48–52.

[18]   A. Milton, 'John Cosin', *ODNB*.

[19]   Thompson Cooper, rev. Jerome Bertram, 'Stephen Goffe', *ODNB*; David Scott, *Politics and War in the Three Stuart Kingdoms, 1637–49* (Basingstoke and New York: Palgrave, 2004), p. 121.

[20]   C. Hibbard, 'Henrietta Maria', *ODNB*.

[21]   Clancy, 'The Jesuits'; Jeffrey R. Collins, 'Thomas Hobbes and the Blackloist Conspiracy of 1649', *Historical Journal*, 42 (2002), 305–31; Cressy, *Exomologesis*, p. 653.

All of this opened up the prospect that many more Englishmen would see, with Cressy, the merits of such a church, even without the experience of exile. Those who had once been the Church of England's firmest adherents might find in a modified Catholicism a purer distillation of the religious values they sought. Hammond described in 1646 how many around him had sought 'some Catholick umpire' as a result of the troubles in Britain,[22] and he realized that a subservient English Church was ill-placed to provide one.

II

Cressy's Gallican Catholicism was one vision of England's religious future, but a Presbyterian settlement – under the aegis of the civil magistrate – looked far more likely. Cressy's experiences of life beyond the English Channel had convinced him of the incoherence of pre-war English ecclesiology, but many of his compatriots found grounds both at home and abroad to redefine and recast the Church settlement in a rather different and highly Erastian direction. It was in Paris, among the royalist exile community, that the most influential arguments were heard and formulated. Some urged Charles to give up on his bishops and seek Scottish help; others warned more generally against allowing any form of clerical power, Presbyterian or Episcopal. Although these men wanted to end their own exile and return to England, they were not concerned to bring back an episcopal church with them.

In Paris, the Queen's party soon began to see the benefits of a Scottish alliance as the likeliest means for Charles to regain both his crowns; although the king would need to take the Covenant, it assumed that this would not bind him for long. Jermyn and Sir John Culpeper sought to persuade Charles to this course of action, stressing that there was no specific divine warrant for the Church of England as it stood. There was no reason to sacrifice the crown for the sake of the episcopate, they felt, assuring Charles that he was not 'obliged to perish in company with Bishops meerly out of pitty'.[23] The staunchest, and most intellectually satisfying, defence of the Erastian position came from Thomas Hobbes, however, when a new edition of his *De Cive* was published in the spring of 1646. Hobbes's own views on a Scottish alliance are unclear, but he enjoyed the patronage of men, including Jermyn and the Marquess of Newcastle, who certainly favoured the use of Scottish troops.[24] In any case, Hobbes had little sympathy for episcopacy, and he added to

---

[22]   Henry Hammond, *A view of some exceptions which have beene made by a Romanist to the Lord Viscount Falkland's discourse Of the infallibilitie of the Church of Rome* (London, 1646), sig. A2r. The quotation forms part of the preface added by Hammond.

[23]   *State Papers Collected by Edward, Earl of Clarendon*, ed. Richard Scrope and Thomas Monkhouse (Oxford, 1767–86), ii, 261.

[24]   W. Cavendish to J. Pell, 27th November, 1646, in Noel Malcolm and Jacqueline Stedall, *John Pell (1611–1685) and his correspondence with Sir Charles Cavendish: the mental world of an early modern mathematician* (Oxford: Oxford University Press,

his text some sharp words against the authority of bishops. His distaste for clerics who claimed independent power was crystal clear.[25]

Exile had deepened the Erastian sentiments of these men rather than created them, and their thoughts seem to have resonated with royalists both abroad and at home. Although Jermyn and Culpeper were unusual in their disillusionment with the Church of England, they were entirely conventional in claiming that the Church should be ordered along lines most conducive to peace and settlement. Indeed, many royalists, as well as parliamentarians, saw a magisterial religion in a markedly positive light. For the Church of England had been, as all agreed, established by law, and most Englishmen saw her, at least in some sense, as subject to the magistrate and to the natural laws which governed all social and civil life. While there had been instances of strong claims to *jure divino* episcopal authority in the Laudian church, even Laud himself had been careful to tie together the power of the bishops and the crown. It was commonly held that the Church could therefore be legally altered if this became necessary, and even such royalists as Falkland and Chillingworth would have agreed.[26] Even those royalists deeply committed to the retention of episcopacy defended the Church, because they saw in it the means to preserve the crown and social order – its value here on earth was the greatest proof that it carried God's seal. Edward Hyde, for example, saw episcopacy as divinely ordained, but he stressed that this should be understood as meaning that it was, like monarchy, the best form of rule on earth. For him, Presbyterianism was to be avoided because disorder would inevitably follow.[27] But the political and social value of episcopacy was no longer quite so obvious to Charles and his supporters in the late 1640s. Charles swallowed his disdain for Scottish Presbyterianism and chose in late 1647 to cast in his lot with his northern suitors. As they demanded, he agreed to take the Covenant and to establish a Presbyterian church, but only for three years.[28]

Gardiner famously claimed that the royalist party was first of all an episcopal party,[29] but by 1647 Charles's supporters – and especially those abroad – were

---

2005), p. 495; Margaret Cavendish, *The life of the thrice noble, high and puissant prince William Cavendishe, Duke, Marquess and Earl of Newcastle* (London, 1667), p. 58.

[25]   Hobbes, *De Cive*, annotation to vol. vii, p. 11 (Hobbes, *On the Citizen*, ed. and trans. by Richard Tuck and Michael Silverthorne (Cambridge: Cambridge University Press, 1998), p. 81.

[26]   Lucius Cary, Lord Falkland, *A speech made to the House of Commons concerning episcopacy* (London, 1641), pp. 14–15; William Chillingworth, *The apostolical institution of episcopacy demonstrated* (London, 1644) also argued for the 'conveniency' rather than the necessity of episcopacy.

[27]   Brian Wormald, *Clarendon: politics, history and religion* (Cambridge: Cambridge University Press, 1951), pp. 289–91.

[28]   David Scott, 'Rethinking Royalist Politics: Faction and Ideology 1642–49', in *The English Civil War: Conflict and Contexts, 1649–49*, ed. John Adamson (Basingstoke: Palgrave Macmillan, 2009), pp. 36–60; *Constitutional Documents*, ed. Gardiner, pp. 347–8.

[29]   S.R. Gardiner, *History of England, from the Accession of James I to the Outbreak of the Civil War, 1603–1642*, 10 vols (London: Longman Green & Co., 1883–84), ix, 281.

no longer so sure of their ecclesiological preferences. If the Church of England were to weather this storm, it would need solid intellectual support, proof against the attacks upon it from home and abroad. Ministers would need to show why the church was worth defending, as an institution distinct both from the civil magistrate and from the Roman see. John Spurr and Jeffrey Collins have suggested that strong claims for episcopal authority were forged in the 1650s,[30] and in the remainder of this essay I shall argue that these claims can be fruitfully examined as a response to the problems of exile.

Masterminding the process of reconstruction was Henry Hammond, a divine who had left the relative obscurity of his living at Penshurst to serve Charles I in the 1640s, first as a polemicist and then as a royal chaplain. At Charles's court in Oxford, however, he found familiar company, for he, like so many of those who rallied round the king, had spent time in the 1630s at Great Tew. His priority in the late 1640s, however, was not so much the cause of Charles himself but the Church of England. He realized that it must be able to compete with both the Gallican and Erastian alternatives, if men were to remain loyal through the dark years to come. Against the former challenge, he needed to show that the English Church offered the advantages of such patriotic Catholicism. It would have to include reverence for tradition and for the ancient doctrines of the Church, including the Trinity, combined with the direct authority from Christ and his apostles claimed by the Catholics for their church alone. For Hammond, the English Church had just the right approach to antiquity and the record of history. It offered a balance between the uncritical reliance upon tradition by the Catholics and an 'excessively unreasonable' rejection of it which he associated with the Socinians.[31] It simply was not necessary to look to the Catholic Church as the vehicle for Christian history and tradition, for the Church of England herself carried the ancient doctrines in her veins.

If Hammond's project were to succeed, it would be crucial to nuance the claims for 'the Bible only' as the grounds of the faith of the Church of England. In theological terms he would need to show the centrality of Church history and of the creeds. In that way, he could protect the doctrine of the Trinity and provide some grounds for resolving controversies beyond pure scriptural exegesis. Yet Hammond did not want to abandon the principles of reason and critical judgement which he associated with Great Tew and with the conversations he had shared there, especially since several of his friends had died in the service of the royalist cause. He began, therefore, to shape the legacy of Tew in a manner more suitable for the present times. Falkland had left an unpublished critique of papal infallibility which had circulated among his friends and among some Catholic discussants; in 1646 it was printed with a preface and an answer to some manuscript objections

---

[30]   John Spurr, *The Restoration Church of England, 1646–1689* (New Haven and London: Yale University Press, 1991), pp. 138–43; Jeffrey R. Collins, 'The Restoration Bishops and the Royal Supremacy', *Church History*, 68 (1999), 549–80.

[31]   Henry Hammond, *A Letter of Resolution to six quaeres of present use in the Church of England* (London, 1653), p. 32.

by the Catholic, Guy Holland. Both of these additions were written by Hammond, and they shifted the emphasis of Falkland's work in a particular direction. Whereas Falkland had emphasized the contradictions within ecclesiastical tradition in order to shift the focus to the words of scripture, Hammond wanted to show that the critical judgement which Falkland had defended could be used to draw truth from that tradition. Falkland's 'reasonings about *tradition & authority of fathers*' had been designed, he claimed, not to 'make them vile or meane to any, but only to reduce them *in ordinem*, to prove them not infallible'.[32]

The Church Fathers and ancient authorities were important, because they provided the lens through which the scriptural text was to be read. Hammond saw that if scripture were divorced from tradition, then it would be nigh on impossible to hold the line against the European anti-Trinitarians or the English sectarians. In this context he began to place great emphasis upon the creeds, for they had been accepted by the Church of England and by all other western churches. Hammond argued that the creeds provided credible and authentic statements of Christian belief, which could be accepted by all Christians. In the Nicene and Athanasian creeds, full and explicit affirmations of the doctrine of the Trinity could be found. By suggesting that these documents provided evidence of the consensus prevailing in the early Church, Hammond sought to sidestep the knotty problem of providing scriptural support for the Trinity. At least, this seems to have been Hammond's plan when in 1648 he drew up a proposal for religious settlement for Charles. In it, he wanted to ensure that 'the three creeds [i.e. the Apostles', Nicene and Athanasian Creeds] may not be exposed to public contradiction'. His settlement would not have required the 'explicit beliefe of every one of them [i.e. the articles of the creeds]' by all communicants, however, and he felt that there was space inside this framework for individual interpretation.[33]

Even creeds could not be definitive, and Hammond saw it as the duty of the bishops to preserve harmony by upholding these foundational statements of doctrine and controlling their public interpretation.[34] This leads us to the second plank of Hammond's argument: the importance of episcopacy. For Hammond, it was necessary to show that all bishops, and not merely the Bishop of Rome, could claim authority from Christ himself. The unity of the Church of England could only be maintained by and through the episcopal hierarchy. And the English episcopate was, he insisted, every bit as valid as the Roman – there was no need to resort to Catholicism, as Cressy had done, to find a true church.

Defending the independent authority of the English bishops, both against Catholic claims and against the Presbyterian agendas of the Scots and parliamentarians, became one of Hammond's key priorities in the late 1640s and 1650s. He did this by insisting that the government of the Church was no less important than the doctrines which it taught, for both rested upon apostolic

---

[32] Hammond, *A view of some exceptions*, pp. 93–4.

[33] Bodleian Library, Tanner MS 57, fols 399–400.

[34] Henry Hammond, *A Letter of resolution*, pp. 365–6.

authority.[35] The model for church government which had received the endorsement of the apostles was as binding as the precepts of Christ which they had set down. For Hammond, this meant that the justification for episcopacy was not its 'conveniency', found out by experience, but its introduction as part of the new covenant revealed by Christ. Like the doctrines of Christianity, it could neither be known nor defended by natural law arguments, but must be accepted on the strength of the historical record. Rather than base episcopacy upon the positive commands of English law, therefore, he utilized instead the positive commands of Christ. The need to show that episcopacy was based on more than simply English statute seemed particularly acute in 1647, when Charles looked set to agree to parliamentary abolition of bishops as a distinct order. By August 1647 Hammond could write of church government as among the 'matters of Christs institution, which have no foundation in the Law of Nature', and he could use these ideas to answer the Erastian claims of royalist exiles, including Hobbes. Christ had left bishops to rule the primitive church, and present-day ecclesiology must be determined by the record left of Christ's original commands.[36]

Hammond's claim for the scriptural basis of episcopacy was neither new nor particularly secure. The ecclesiology of the New Testament had long been disputed, and the heated discussions of the Westminster Assembly had done little to resolve the problem.[37] The historical record of the early Church provided much more promising grounds on which to construct a solid defence of episcopacy, and Hammond was much encouraged by the direction of contemporary scholarship. Once more, Europe led the way, but here the English exposure to continental currents of opinion could have a positive bearing on the Church of England. The European debate over episcopacy centred upon the letters of Ignatius, which seemed to prove that bishops had existed as a separate order as early as the first century AD. The authenticity of several of these letters had been called into question, most recently by Claude Salmasius and David Blondel, who were (in the 1640s) both supportive of the Presbyterian agenda in Scotland and England. But the tide was turning in favour of the letters – in the mid-1640s James Ussher, Archbishop of Ulster, and Isaac Voss found some more early manuscripts which seemed to confirm the disputed sections. Less scholarly reasons also played a part: Salmasius seemed to forget his earlier Presbyterian stance when he took up his pen against the English Republic. The time had never been better to show the world that episcopal authority was anchored in early Church history and had no need of the Pope to lean on.[38]

---

[35] Hammond, *Considerations of present use concerning the danger resulting from the change of our church government* (London, 1645), pp. 6–7

[36] Hammond, *Of the power of the keyes, or Of binding and loosing* (London, 1647), p.1; for his critique of Hobbes, see pp. 81–4.

[37] As is shown clearly in Robert S. Paul, *The assembly of the Lord: politics and religion in the Westminster Assembly and the 'grand debate'* (Edinburgh: T & T Clark, 1985).

[38] H. de Quehen 'Politics and scholarship in the Ignation controversy', *Seventeenth Century*, 13 (1998), 69–84; Alan Ford, *James Ussher: Theology, History, and Politics in*

Hammond had used the writing of Ussher and Voss in 1647, during those critical months of negotiation over the future of episcopacy. But that had been in his tract *Of the power of the keyes*, written for Anglophone readers.[39] In the 1650s he wanted to reach a European audience, to prevent and to answer the attacks made upon English episcopacy by foreign Catholics as well as Presbyterians. The result was his *Dissertationes Quatuor* (1651), subtitled 'in which the rights of bishops are founded upon scripture and primitive antiquity, against the opinion of Blondel and others'.[40] In a slightly later tract, *Of Schisme* (1654), he also sought to locate the establishment of episcopacy in England before the time of Augustine. In that way, he could show that it was independent, both of Rome and of any English monarchy. To leave such a church was, he argued, nothing less than the heinous sin of schism.[41]

Having shown that the English episcopate was not only necessary, but also equal in status to other, foreign bishops, Hammond could press home his claims for the Church of England. Hammond wanted to show that his conception of episcopal authority provided a space for the Church to exercise the spiritual powers which Christ had granted to his apostles, although the magistrate had responsibility for the outward morality and cohesion of society. These spiritual powers could only be exercised by the clergy, for they, where they were trusted and duly ordained, had influence upon the wills of men. Faith, as distinct from compliance with a moral code, could not be coerced, but once reasonable men had chosen to embrace Christianity they would see the benefits of adhering to the advice of the clergy.[42] A Church based upon scripture and reason but governed by an apostolic episcopate could, Hammond felt, withstand the political upheavals of the English Revolution. Furthermore, it could hold its own intellectually against the Catholic claims for certainty or sectarian claims for revelation. For the rest of his life, until his death on the eve of the Restoration, he would pour his efforts into strengthening and promoting this vision.

III

The experience of exile, desertion and disillusionment prompted sustained reflection, and the ideas developed during these years were not without their effect.

Early-Modern Ireland and England (Oxford: Oxford University Press, 2007), pp. 237–9; Salmasius later defended episcopacy in his *Defensio regia pro Carolo I*.

[39]   Hammond, *Of the power of the keyes*, pp. 20–21.

[40]   *Idem., Dissertationes Quatuor, quibus Episcopatus Jura ex S. Scripturis et Primaeva Antiquitate adstruuntur, contra Sententiam D. Blondelli et Aliorum* (London, 1651).

[41]   *Idem., Of Schisme* (London, 1654). See also John Packer, *The Transformation of Anglicanism 1643–1660: With Special Reference to Henry Hammond* (Manchester: Manchester University Press, 1969), pp. 80–83, 104–12.

[42]   See, especially, his tract *Of the Power of the Keyes*, where the preface discusses his preferred system of church government, and *Of the Reasonableness of the Christian Religion* (London, 1650).

Throughout the Interregnum the importance of the episcopate, the sole and authoritative source of spiritual jurisdiction and legitimate ordination, would be emphasized by the circle of divines around Hammond, a circle which included the future bishops Gilbert Sheldon and Peter Gunning. Hammond, in particular, wanted to attach these spiritual powers to the bishops without calling into question either the powers of the magistrate, based as they were on natural law, or the role of conscience, which would always remain free. The Church of England, founded upon bishops who held their office from the Apostles, could stand on her own, able to mediate in unique fashion between the claims of the state and of the individual. The 1640s and 1650s, then, was a period of rapid education for the Church and her divines. She may not have come of age by the Restoration, yet she was at least a headstrong adolescent, capable of asserting her institutional independence against the crown and her own divine status against the papacy.

Chapter 6
Exile in Europe during the English Revolution and its Literary Impact

Nigel Smith

I

The account we give of exiles abroad is impoverished, or at least incomplete, if we let it stop at the people who became exiles and look only at what happened to them. Exiles did not just languish in foreign courts, houses or caves, hoping to receive correspondence from home, and writing the odd angry justification of themselves. They interacted with the natives of their new places of residence, and these people took note of them. Native people looked carefully at the exiles and in some cases made something of them and their experiences in their own writing. It is a circumstance that has been explored in intellectual and science history, but is far less acknowledged, if it is, in religion, politics and literature.[1] This, then, is an account of one aspect of the impact of the exiles on seventeenth-century Europe and, in particular, on European literature.

This chapter consists of readings of two pieces of literature, a poem and a play, that put English and Scottish seventeenth-century royalism in two international contexts (in Holland and parts of Germany). Accompanying this is a very brief look at a comparable Italian literary scene. My intention is to explore the cultural impact of the civil wars on continental literary culture, and thereby to show in a provisional way how very different cavalier royalism becomes when placed in the context of continental literatures. Comparative historical studies of the early modern world have largely been dormant for at least 40 years: since the discussion surrounding the 'general crisis' of the period died out. Yet there are no less than 669 works concerned with the English Revolution published between 1640 and 1669 in German, and to take a smaller perspective, of the 157 Dutch works catalogued by W.P.C. Knuttel for 1651, 26 are concerned with matters English.[2]

Exiles were but one part of the traffic of peoples around early modern Europe, certainly central and western Europe, as opposed to the more isolated British

---

[1]   See Noel Malcolm, *De Dominis (1560–1624): Venetian, Anglican, Ecumenist and Relapsed Heretic* (London: Strickland & Scott, 1984); Malcolm, *Aspects of Hobbes* (Oxford: Oxford University Press, 2002).

[2]   W.P.C. Knuttel, *Catalogus van de Pamfletten-Verzameling Berustende in de Koninklijke Bibliotheek*, 9 vols in 10 (The Hague, 1889–1920; Utrecht: HES, 1978), vols 1.2, 2.1.

Isles. Exile and banishment were part of the scenery of political life as much as was imprisonment. Throughout early modern Europe various kinds of people regularly circulated, such as military, diplomatic and artistic personnel. Within the German-speaking world, specialists were regularly recruited across and between principalities. Grand Tours featuring a privileged nobleman and his tutor began from various parts of Europe and proceeded to the famous centres in France, the Netherlands, Italy, Spain and elsewhere. For many, education was the strongest force for travel and long-term residence abroad.[3] Thus, the Italian and the Dutch universities were at different times major centres of international learning, and hence the gathering of many different peoples from other lands. It is within this context of travel and transitory residence that mid-seventeenth-century English exiles must be understood, a context that in fact guaranteed a far greater range of the impact of those exiles, as residents in western Europe took their experience of the English royalists or republicans further east. Nonetheless, the English exiles were noticeable, for they came in numbers to Holland, the Spanish Netherlands and France in particular, and they immediately began to play a prominent role in the political lives of their new homes. We might say that they transformed their destinations, and helped to start the great obsession with English culture and letters that is such a mark of eighteenth-century Europe.

The impact of English events and travelers on Italian letters was rapidly felt. New work by Stefano Villani shows that in Italy, and in particular in Venice, in the circles surrounding the Academy of the Incogniti, many travelers from England, including true royalist exiles during the later 1640s and 1650s, were consulted for the purposes of ambitious newsbook chronicles.[4] According to Villani, Gualdo Priorato followed English political events and wrote widely about them in his works. He knew the bookseller James Allestry, who visited Italy c.1650 in order to find manuscripts of classical authors to be published in England, and to acquire books to be re-sold on the English market. In September 1650 Priorato consulted Englishmen in order to gain as detailed as possible a picture of the trial, judgment and execution of Charles I. The royalist Robert Bargrave met Gualdo Priorato at Venice in the 1650s, near the bookseller and publisher Paul Baglioni, and conversed with him about politics. In these Italian histories, there is a uniformly 'pro-royalist' attitude, despite admiration for Cromwell's military prowess.

Villani finds the historian Gregorio Leti working in an opposite way to Vittorio Siri and the other historians already mentioned. They thought that they had to adhere

---

³   The English aspects of this story have been told by John Stoye, *English Travellers Abroad, 1604–1667: Their Influence in English Society and Politics*, rev. edn (New Haven and London: Yale University Press, 1989); Edward Chaney, *The Grand Tour and the Great Rebellion: Richard Lassels and 'The Voyage of Italy' in the Seventeenth Century* (Geneva: Slatkine, 1985). See, too, the references made to Grand Tourists in Timothy Raylor's Chapter 1, this volume.

⁴   The following four paragraphs are entirely indebted to Stefano Villani's essay 'English Radicalism and 17th Century Italian Movements', delivered at the 'Rediscovering Radicalism' conference, Goldsmiths College, University of London, 21–23 June 2006.

closely to the documentary evidence and considered other sources of information to be merely accessory. Leti, on the other hand, privileged gossip, hearsay and other unreliable sources, emphasizing the more curious, odd and interesting aspects of a story. For Leti, the documents serve, for the best hypotheses, to integrate the narrative, but they are not its fundamental and constituent components. Leti fused together and re-elaborated these peculiar anecdotes and pieces of gossip into a more or less coherent narrative. From this point of view Leti's works are in many respects symptomatic of a violent reaction to, in Villani's formulation, the kind of 'sclerotic' historiography which, in slavish fidelity to documents, mislaid the actual meaning of the events being narrated. Leti's works seem to foreshadow a new way of writing history, and they are certainly related to the fashioning of historical narrative from newsbook sources that we find among English writers such as Marchamont Nedham.[5]

There is further evidence of the fusion of history and romance in the tragedy *Cromuele* (1673), by Girolamo Graziani, which comprises a series of incestuous treasons, misunderstandings, disguises, love affairs and extreme passions, in which exile, flight and disguise are significant features. For Graziani, the English ordeals had an exemplary and paradigmatic value.

Besides the diplomatic channel, English political writings published in Latin and French were of great importance for the Italians, whether they were produced by royalists, parliamentarians, republicans or Cromwellians. These works circulated widely in Italy. The republican government in 1650 started a newspaper – the *Nouvelles Ordinaires de Londres* – published in the French language and specifically aimed at the continental audience, which also continued to be published after the death of Cromwell and through the Restoration until January 1661.

II

A closer look at other literary examples shows how closely they participate in the politics of the three kingdoms as well as that of continental Europe, or states and regions therein. To this extent, a Dutch poem of late 1650, *Schotse Nederlage Door den Generael Olifier Cromwel*, is a true example of the dual perspective introduced by exilic status. It is, as it were (but not strictly so), an 'Horatian Ode' in Dutch on Cromwell's return from Scotland, precisely the campaign for which Marvell's *An Horatian Ode upon Cromwell's Return from Ireland* summons 'forward youths' in the summer of 1650 for action in Scotland, after the brutal successes of the Irish campaign. It seems to have been written after the defeats of Musselburgh and Dunbar (3 September 1650), and before the death from smallpox of the Stadholder Willem II on 6 November. All that was to come during the next year, including the Battle of Worcester in September 1651, which gave final security to the English free state, is not foreseen. The conjunction of the battlefield with the uncertain flow of information begins the poem, and in this respect it is

---

[5]   Joad Raymond, *The Invention of the Newspaper: English Newsbooks 1641–1649* (Oxford: Oxford University Press, 1996).

typical of civil war literature: the poet had heard a false rumour that Cromwell had been captured. The poem is decidedly monarchist and therefore almost certainly Orangist, but its perspective displays none of the sense of a defeated culture of the English royalists, none of their sense of the martyred glory of Charles I, or indeed anything of the sense of living within the English print culture of the 1640s, shared by much English verse on both sides of the main divide. Rather, it reverses English millenarian polarities, in keeping with the Dutch engraving showing Cromwell as the Whore of Babylon, complete with dress, ringlets of hair and ribbons.[6] Despite the devastatingly effective victories achieved by Cromwell in Ireland and Scotland, and clean contrary to the sense of Cromwell as divine instrument in much English writing, including Marvell's poem, Providence is merely waiting to lay low General Cromwell and the Parliament:

> Recht en goet sijn Gods oordeelen,
> Hy laet elck zijn Rolle speelen
>   Is het quaet of is het goet:
> Yder moet met my gelooven,
> Of hy most Gods eer verdooven.
>   Dat het so geshieden moet,
> Sint men CARELS Hals gingh breecken,
>   Kon men met het selfd geweer
> Al die Parlementsche koppen,
> Nu eens met een slagh af kloppen.
>   Dat riep vreek, was leer om leer.

[God's judgments are right and good, he allows each one to play their role, be it bad or good; Everyone must believe this with me, or make themselves deaf to the praise/honour of God, that things have come to pass in this way. Because if men broke Charles's neck, men can with the same weapon knock all the Parliamentarians' heads. That declares itself as tit for tat.][7]

More than merely Orangist, there is also a distinctively international perspective in this poem, perhaps understandable in the context of the Peace of Westphalia of 1648 that ended the Thirty Years War, yet also registering the horror and incomprehension that the civil wars in the three kingdoms caused on the continent:

> K' Wens dat Godt u wil verwekken,
> Dat het tot sijn eer mach strekken,

---

[6]   Jan van den Bosch, *Kort Beworp vande dry Teghenwoordighe aenmerckens-weerdighe Wonderheden des Wereldts* (Cologne, 1656). See Laura Knoppers, '"The Antichrist, the Babilon, The Great Dragon": Oliver Cromwell, Andrew Marvell, and the Apocalyptic Monstrous', in *Monstrous Bodies? Political Monstrosities in Early Modern Europe*, ed. Laura Lunger Knoppers and Joan B. Landes (Ithaca: Cornell University Press, 2004), pp. 93–123.

[7]   For help with translations I am most grateful to Peter Davidson, Jane Griffiths and Andrew Fleck.

    Al het geen wat ghy begint.
En dat eens u Oreloogen,
Die ons liken doen de ogen.
    Geen meer Broeders en verslint.

[I wish that God will wake you up, and that he might turn to his end all the things you have begun. And that all your civil wars that offend our eyes may devour no more of your brothers.]

Supporters of the English Parliament and the new commonwealth are regarded as subject to a collective illusion, from which they will probably wake when it is too late to save each other. This may carry an allusion not merely to parliamentarian apology but also to outright republican ideology, a feature that had already struck several observers. The poem acknowledges the military and literary appropriateness of republican panegyric for the 'Parliamentary gentlemen': precisely such a poem as Marvell's 'An Horatian Ode'.

The poem invokes a Catholic-Protestant alliance of neighbouring monarchs – Portugal, Spain, Denmark and France – who are summoned to invade England and expel Cromwell. William of Orange, however, is to remain at home: the poem is probably sensitive to the struggle within the United Provinces in 1650 between Willem and the Province of Holland over the size of the army. William had imprisoned eight members of the provincial assembly and had dispatched an army to occupy Amsterdam. It was an extremely tense situation; William's death towards the end of the year ushered in the 22-year-long period of republican pre-eminence within the Dutch state.

Like an English royalist poem, however, it responds to the circumstances of defeat by acknowledging internal division: in its view caused by the treachery of the Scots. So, if God's Providence is at work, Cromwell is punishing the Scots on God's behalf for their initial rebellion against the king in 1639, and their subsequent siding with the English Parliament: 'Old heroes, scum of the Scots,/I'll hold back from mocking.' The poem alludes to the published English reasons for the invasion of Scotland and apparently accepts them. The 'hero' invoked at l. 67, near the top of the second column, could be General David Leslie, the defeated Scottish commander, who had previously commanded the Scottish Covenanting army that had crucially reinforced the English Parliamentary forces; it does not appear to be the Scottish royalist commander Montrose, who had been executed by the Covenanters earlier in 1650, or Prince Charles, who had been proclaimed king by the Scottish Parliament on 5 February 1649, but who at this point was moving between different Scottish actions before his ill-fated invasion of England in 1651. More surprisingly, the Irish, who have certainly suffered severely, have also received just punishment on account of earlier perfidies. The poem offers a greater consolation than is usually present at this point in time in English royalist poems, since it imagines a circle of divinely directed violence that is perfectly legitimate in Cromwell's current victories, and which will land next on the head of the Parliament (the brief history of the republic and the Protectorate is of course yet to come). It will do so especially if men – especially foreign monarchs – rise to intervene.

The poem appears to be rendered mostly in the voice of 'Truth', unnamed as such, but outraged by the lies in circulation. Now it is time for some truths, says the poem, and these are delivered in a series of proverbial figures. The poet exploits the pun (already evident in the work of Cromwellian panegyrists and satirists in England) on 'door' ('by' or 'through' in Dutch but sounding exactly like English 'door', connoting 'pathway to' or 'means to'). Thus, the poem and the acts the poem describes are one, so that Cromwell's military prowess is a kind of (dastardly) poetry. This may be an attempt to show that Providence finally masters all actions: 'God makes of their actions his own.' (l. 31). In one of a number of similarities with Marvell, there is a sense of a new age of heroism arriving: 'old heroes' will do no longer (some of the republicans, like John Hall, thought they were returning to an age of old heroism). The poet also realizes that in praising Providence he risks praising Cromwell: he explicitly distances himself from this charge ('I wish that God will put you to flight, that he, to his glory, might strike you to the nothingness from which you came'), and yet acknowledges that the New Model Army is better disciplined and even more humane than the Scots army (the treatment of Scottish prisoners after Dunbar was hardly charitable), and that Cromwell does not deserve to be defeated by anyone except Prince Charles. Perhaps, says the poet, he might be allowed to slip away, as the Stuart who is not mentioned directly by name, Prince Charles, emerges as the rightful conqueror at the end of the poem.

At any rate the poem is more proof of the interaction of Dutch and English politics, even inside the Dutch republic, and of English, Dutch and Scottish politics.[8] As we have seen, the resolution of the Thirty Years War in 1648 had nearly resulted in a Dutch civil war, with the Orangists invoking the aid of the English royalists, and Amsterdam calling on the New Model Army. The playwright Joost van den Vondel had described William II as Rehoboam, also a figure that Milton had identified with Charles I in *The Tenure of Kings and Magistrates* (1649). Milton noted the willfulness of William II in *Pro Populo Defensio Anglicano* (1651). William's sudden death from smallpox in late 1650 was seen as an act of Providence: God was removing him from the scene just when he was becoming most dangerous. Later on in Vondel's view William was Phaeton, cast down from audaciousness.[9]

Is the poor or at least very odd Dutch of the poem an indication of the fact that it may well have been written by an English exile in the Hague, even one of the factions attached to the House of Orange, and taking sides in a very English way within the royalist phalanx on the matter of the future of the royals? Certainly the Dutch in the poem is markedly 'unliterary' and even incomprehensible in places.

---

[8]   This triangulation is a key aspect of the argument in John Kerrigan, *Archipelagic English: Literature, History, and Politics, 1603–1707* (Oxford: Oxford University Press, 2008).

[9]   Joost Van den Vondel, *Faeton of Reuckeloze Stoutheit (Phaeton, or Reckless Audacity)*, (Amsterdam, 1663).

These matters, along with the poem's precise genre and prosodic and stylistic features, will have to wait for another occasion.

III

A second example offers a less immediately contingent perspective, since it is a play by a playwright with a distinctive vision of the role of tragedy and its connection with kingship: Andreas Gryphius's *Ermordete Majestät oder Carolus Stuardus* (1657, rev. 1663). Gryphius is today considered one of the foremost figures of the German literary baroque; he was a Silesian lawyer who travelled extensively in Europe and resided in several cities, including Leiden, Paris, Venice and Stettin as well as his native Glogau. In Gdansk he may well have begun his long interest in English politics in 1634, through meeting Charles I's ambassador there, the Scot, Francis Gordon. His last two years as a student in Leiden coincided with the first two of the English Civil War. Here he met Salmasius, the future confuter of Milton in respect of the regicide, but also some longstanding exiles from an earlier confrontation: the Winter Queen, Elizabeth of Bohemia (daughter of James VI and I), and her daughter Elizabeth, the *Pfalzgräfin* (who was taught by Descartes; the two maintained contact for the rest of his life). In the summer of 1644 Gryphius embarked on a Grand Tour as a tutor to the young Pomeranian nobleman Wilhelm Schlegel, beginning at The Hague on 4 June 1644, but soon departing for Paris. That Gryphius was able to visit Richelieu's library is evidence of access to high places, and it is hard to see how he can have avoided the many English exiles in the French capital, especially given his contacts. He saw Henrietta Maria arrive at Angers on 14 August 1644, and, very moved, wrote a sonnet for her. Schlegel and Gryphius then traveled to Venice, and possibly carried a message from the English Queen to the Senate in Venice, begging support for Charles's cause. In 1649 he accepted the post of Syndic to the principality of Glogau, having turned down an offer from Great Elector (*Großer Kurfürst*) Friedrich Wilhelm of the Chair of Mathematics at Frankfurt an der Oder. In Glogau at this time was a Scottish immigrant, the naturalist John Johnstone, with whom Gryphius became associated. Gryphius's knowledge of English history and the civil war was intensive. His play is indebted to *Eikon Basilike*, Thomas Edwards, Salmasius, George Horn, du Moulin, Heylyn, Philipp von Zesen and other publications, and the notes that came with the second edition cited further historical and political works by Camden, Polydor Vergil, de Thou, Reggius and Buchanan.[10]

While much of this material is continental in source, some of it was English, and clearly Gryphius was able to obtain both kinds of books even in the relative eastern remoteness of Glogau. Libraries were being constructed in the German

---

[10]   See Janifer Gerl Stackhouse, *The Constructive Art of Gryphius' Historical Tragedies* (Bern: Lang, 1986); Günther Berghaus, *Die Quellen zu Andreas Gryphius' Trauerspiel 'Carolus Stuardus'. Studien zur Entstehung eines Historisch-Politischen Märtyrerdramas der Barockzeit* (Türbingen: Niemeyer, 1984).

principalities, with western European books being acquired by agents in places like Paris, Brussels and Amsterdam. The most famous case here is that of August, Duke of Braunschweig's library at Wolfenbüttel. It was also the case that Gryphius was in correspondence with some exiles, and book gifts from his correspondents were almost certainly another means for obtaining information.

His interpretation of events in *Carolus Stuardus* is that the trial and execution of the king is an example of worldly injustice, as instanced in the engraved frontispiece to both editions. In this respect the play might be seen as hyper-Stuart, a dramatic extension of *Eikon Basilike*. There is no criticism of Caroline policy, no position of critique from within the royalist spectrum, and in this regard Gryphius's contribution to absolutist and divine right thought is well-attested.[11] Instead, Gryphius underlined in his notes to the play his belief that Charles's policy in respect of Scotland in 1638–39 was thoroughly well grounded in law. Gryphius's metaphysical interest in time is evident enough, but it is harder in this work, as has been alleged, to see links to Silesian mystics like Abraham von Franckenburg, or his sharing with the advanced tolerationist thinker of the sixteenth century, Dirk-Volkertzoon Coornhert, the idea of a central religious truth that rises above religious confessions yet is not incompatible with them: a Nicodemist and Familist perspective.

Another Dutch connection is with the plays of Joost van den Vondel, who converted to Catholicism in 1640–41.[12] *Mary Stuart or Tortured Majesty* (1646) presents Mary Queen of Scots as the victim of a Machiavellian Elizabeth I and international intrigue.[13] The parallels with the plight of Charles I at this time are obvious: there is open castigation of puritanism, and in presenting Mary as a latter-day Christ, Vondel was affirming his now strong belief in divine right monarchy. James VI of Scotland and future James I of England, Mary's son, is warned to keep them in check, and it was known by 1646 that his son, Charles I, had consummately failed to do this (l. 1128). The First Anglo-Dutch war was five years in the future and Vondel was speaking against the official views of the republic: he seemed to delight in finding these positions. Vondel is, however, not uncritical of Mary, and clearly sides with a rational analysis of her predicament and with the free will that we see her exercise, as opposed to the blind partisanship and bigoted intolerance of her chaplain. Here, Stoicism becomes a position shared by two playwrights despite different faiths and politics: Vondel was born into an Anabaptist family, but became a Roman Catholic, whereas Gryphius was a Lutheran; Vondel was an anti-Organist

---

[11]   See Dirk Lentfer, *Die Glogauer Landesprivilegen des Andreas Gryphius von 1653* (Frankfurt: P. Lang, 1996).

[12]   The connection between the two plays is discussed at greater length in James A. Parente, *Religious Drama and the Humanist Tradition: Christian Theater in Germany and in the Netherlands, 1500–1680* (Leiden: Brill, 1987).

[13]   For a translation, see Joost van den Vondel, *Mary Stuart or Tortured Majesty*, trans. with Introduction and Notes by Kristiann P. Aercke (Ottawa: Dovehouse Editions, 1996).

republican, whereas Gryphius perforce is sympathetic to the plight of all monarchical and princely dynasties, and knew several members of the Orange family.

The play moves between highly authentic material – letters and speeches from Strafford and Laud, and other materials derived from *England's Memorials* (and where it has been suggested that Gryphius may have been inspired by the visual material and circulated miniature paintings that came with this kind of book) – to spectacular prophetic sections with various prophets and ghosts that appear to be Gryphius's own inventions, but whose form derives from Jesuit drama and the *Kunstdrama* of the German courts. In this respect Gryphius was working with a reduced two-part stage, whereas the Jesuit plays often exploited the martyrological theatre of a three-part stage, left to right, each with a curtain, thereby enabling the progressive display of acted emblems. 'I am convinced that this bloody tragedy cannot be portrayed more movingly than if this deposed prince is presented to the audience and the reader as he himself painted himself with his own colors in the face of death', and, significantly, he goes on: 'when all decorative and metaphoric language comes to an end and disappears as mist.'[14] And yet his own reworking of these speeches is heightened poetically: *schwulst* is the German stylistic term. To this extent his plays belong with some of the pamphlet drama of 1648–50, although with far greater compositional complexity, and notably unlike the heroic tragedies of the Restoration, where the anxiety of the king's head can only be indirectly remembered.[15] Belonging to a different tradition in a different language, Gryphius's drama is able to confront and expatiate on the matter of the regicide far more openly than any English example. It is notable that the execution of the king actually takes place on the stage and is witnessed and commented upon by six girls looking down, as it were, from windows above the scene of execution, quite unlike any other dramatic representation of the regicide and the classical tradition where the death of a hero takes place off stage.

From Salmasius, Gryphius developed a defence of the utter righteousness of absolute monarchy. He therefore accepts Salmasius's explanation of the events of the 1640s as a religious war in which the Presbyterians set up a crisis of authority, which was then exploited by the Independents, who actually put the king to death. But in Gryphius's second version of the play Fairfax is a hero, since it is he who is responsible for the failed plot to rescue the king from Hampton Court; Lady Fairfax is the real force behind this enterprise, and a failure of communication, partly caused by Lady Fairfax's compromised conviction, that leads to its failure. The source for this view and the dialogue form itself was in Maiolino Bisaccioni's *Historia della Guerre Civili de questi ultimi Tempi* (Venice, 1655), one of the earliest attempts to explain the general crisis of the seventeenth century. From Galeazzo Guaido Priorato's *Historia delle Revolutioni di Francia, Libro Secondo* (Venice, 1655) came the depiction of the assassination of Isaac Dorislaus in May,

---

[14]   Gryphius, V, 285, Werke, IV, 158; trans., Stackhouse, p. 90.

[15]   Nancy Klein Maguire, *Regicide and Restoration: English Tragicomedy, 1660–1671* (Cambridge: Cambridge University Press, 1992).

1649 in the United Provinces, and the sense that assassination was a justified demonstration of God's higher justice at work. From *The Indictment, Araignment, Tryal and Judgement* of the regicides came ample source material to make a wicked character out of Hugh Peter, one responsible in large part for the regicide, rather than an abettor: the terms on which the real Peter was tried. Nonetheless, extracts of Peter's sermons appear in the text. Version B seems more concerned to explore the religious factionalism of the 1640s than version A. A true exile text that seems to have found its way into Gryphius's hands was a sermon by Henry Leslie delivered in the 1650s to the exiled Charles II at Breda.[16]

Each Act is punctuated with a chorus; in Act I, a chorus of murdered English Kings, speaking pseudo-pindaric odes, denouncing the illegality of Charles I's trial, confidently announces that divine vengeance is at hand, the force of their conviction backed by our knowledge that they too are victims. It is notable that the chorus is an integral part of the work: this again relates in part to Jesuit dramatic influence. No Protestant could easily accept the presence, as another denunciatory ghost, of Mary Stuart. *Carolus Stuardus* has been compared to Shakespeare's *Richard II*, but in this context, and that of the wavering Lady Fairfax, the play with which it more readily fits is *Macbeth*, and this makes Milton's interest in Shakespeare's Scottish play, his possible attempt at rewriting it in late 1648 and 1649, and his own association of Presbyterian lack of conviction or duplicity with the play's female characters, more palpable.[17] The Chorus of Sirens, rendered in highly elevated language, reflects the apocalypticism felt by Gryphius at the challenge to monarchy in several parts of mid-seventeenth-century Europe. This role is taken up later by the Chorus of Women, but is their fainting a reflection of the literal imagery of the depiction of the regicide, reflecting a painting of the regicide with a continental source?[18] The Chorus of Religion is designed to show the betrayal of piety by political ambition. This is amplified by the introduction in the second edition of Poleh, the remorseful visionary character with a remarkable soliloquy, based, it is most persuasively argued, on Alderman Thomas Hoyle of York, who committed suicide exactly one year after the regicide, and who was widely but wrongly believed to have been one of the king's judges.[19] Poleh's guilt trauma is revealed through deluded dreams and real visions, rendered theatrically, of the future justice that will fall on the regicides.

---

[16]   Karl-Heinz Habersetzer, *Politische Typologie und Dramatisches Exemplum* (Stuttgart: Metzler, 1985), pp. 24–31.

[17]   For the career of Macbeth and its performance in the context of seventeenth-century Anglo-Scottish relations, see Kerrigan, *Archipelagic English*, pp. 91–114.

[18]   John Weesop, Eyewitness Representation of Execution of Charles I, Private Collection; Bridgeman Art Library.

[19]   R.J. Alexander, 'A Possible Historical Source for the Figure of Poleh in Andreas Gryphius' *Carolus Stuardus*', *Daphnis*, 3.2 (1974), 203–7. Hoyle appears misspelt as 'Hople' in Johann Georg Schleder's *Theatrum Europaeum* (Frankfurt am Main, 1663), 1124, thereby supplying Gryphius with the beginnings of an anagram.

The play has been criticized for having no motivation through the development of cause and effect. Charles does not change, and remains full of fortitude against his enemies throughout, whatever his imagined fate. This is part of the play's Stoicism. Cromwell and Fairfax have been regarded as uninteresting characters, but their stichomythic exchanges do have interest for anyone who knows about the civil war, and Gryphius's informed interest in their motivation is evident (even if Fairfax is misrepresented as a guilty parliamentarian). There was also an editorial change: in the second edition, the lines of Fairfax and Cromwell were simply swapped round, changing Cromwell from relatively indecisive to fountain of rebellion:

Crom.	The great day breaks, on which we will be free.
Fairf.	The time of all times that will be praised or condemned.
C.	At the outset only an eternally blooming praise is seen.
F.	Neither you nor I can know that.
C.	It stands to me and you to act rightfully.
F.	Still more for God and fortune to enforce what we arbitrate.
C.	Have not God and fortune crowned the weapons up till now?
F.	Often, the final retreat ridicules the first victory.
C.	It cannot go awry. We stand for Church and home.
F.	That goes for Stewart as well, whom we now condemn.
C.	We condemn him who raved against us.
F.	Whom all of Europe and all of Albion loved.
C.	We have come too far to turn back.
F.	Only hope his decline does not crush us too.
C.	He oppresses! Let my mortal enemy fall with me then.[20]

The degree to which Peter in particular is spiritedly represented has led to the suggestion that from this understanding of Independent ideology comes Gryphius's way of expressing his Protestant opposition to Viennese Habsburg military interference in Silesia:[21]

Hugo Peter. […] I feel your omnipotence / Lord! Use it for our salvation /
And arm punishment and vengeance with the just axe.
You give the holy crowd the power to bind kings;
And wind chains and manacles on the nobles.
Who ever imagined it? Light aims for the day /
Indeed, it shows clearly / how, like when the last blow
will lay horror upon the world in an instant,
We will pass judgment over nation and king /
And carry out the judgment that God planned against you
When your throne was chosen for God's earthly seat.
They hurry! I must go! Lest I compromise a thousand lives.

---

[20]   All Gryphius translations included herein are part of an ongoing (and therefore as yet unpaginated) translation project commissioned by myself and Angiras Arya.

[21]   Elida Maria Szarota, *Geschichte, Politik und Gesellschaft im Drama des 17. Jahrhunderts* (Bern: Francke, 1976), p. 139.

Let me go now to witness the miracle,
The miracle, seeing which, I will need to see nothing else.
What does the world have to show after showing this?

The debate on the legitimacy of Charles I's kingship, on whether he has renounced it and become a tyrant, is as vital as the interest in blood-guilt and sacrifice:

    F.   One dares something often that is not always possible.
    C.   Who is it that's pushing us toward the Bishop?
    F.   They whom the Church authorities call the eldest. [?]
    C.   And don't you see, that they are trying to burn white [?]
    F.   I am not the one who can see into the hearts of the people.
    C.   It sickens you that our group of Independents thrives.
    F.   They who took part in robbing the bishop.
    C.   It only hurts those who approved of his greed.
    F.   British law does not agree with us.
    C.   British law may be a law bad for Britons.
    F.   The people's law forbids regicide.
    C.   One cannot hear the law over the sound of drums and trumpets.
    F.   Trumpets and drums owe fealty to the King.
    C.   Back when there was a king. Charles is no king.
    F.   We are sworn to protect the King's head.
    C.   The King's death erases our oaths.
    F.   And so England loses its crowned head.
    C.   Along with everyone who believed in such a head.
    F.   Calidon, defied, will search for its King again. [*Calidon: Scottland*]
    C.   If it searches in weapons / it will be struck down armed.
    F.   It has more claim to Charles' head than we.
    C.   What Calidon has to sell is of no interest to me.
    F.   It is concerned for its King's life.
    C.   It gave up the King to us Britons.

In Gryphius's view the high point of Cromwellian rebellion is a threatened overcoming of God's will:

    A.   What if your own house burns in the future?
    C.   We will find future solutions for the flames.
          Time is passing! I seek not to do
          what is beyond my power. The request is pointless.
          As incapable as you are of splitting the foundation of the earth:
          you are just as incapable today of stopping the blade of justice.
          Because nothing more can save him / nothing, I say to you / believe me:
          Even if God himself stood here in this very moment.

One is reminded of Moloch's threat to overwhelm the throne of God in Milton's *Paradise Lost* (II. 60–70): as it were, threatening to destroy God. Finally, the encounter of the allegorical figures of Religion and Heresy makes for a psychological study of the will to truth in a crisis; an explanation of how something like regicide comes about. Far from placid, it is utterly vital, at once horrifying and sobering.

The clue for discovering the context of *Carolus Stuardus* lies in the dedication of the play to Princess Elizabeth of the Palatinate (1618–1680), daughter of Frederick and Elizabeth of Bohemia, niece of Charles I, sister of Prince Rupert, and cousin of Friedrich Wilhelm (1620–1688), Elector of Brandenburg, the notoriously fierce ruler of Berlin, who successively frustrated the burgers of that city, yet encouraged commerce and religious toleration (although Protestant sectaries, Catholics and Jews were not officially permitted to worship, they were in fact tolerated if they kept a low profile), established colonies along Africa's Gold Coast, and played a major role in building what would become the Kingdom of Prussia.[22] An intervention in the English Civil War by Brandenburg had been discussed in 1646, although Friedrich Wilhelm would soon find himself in the aftermath of the Peace of Westphalia, torn between Swedish, Polish and Imperial allegiances and tensions. It has been suggested that the first edition of 1657 may have been a rallying cry for a joint Brandenburg-Stuart-Orange invasion of England against Cromwell.[23] There is no doubt from this viewpoint that the play is full of political intent as well as religious vision.

The play may also have been performed at Heidelberg, where the Elector Karl-Ludwig was a nephew of Charles I. It has also been suggested that it was possibly adapted in the Rhine valley to be more like the plays of the wandering (English) players by Cologne journalists such as Christoph Kormart. A Cologne troop may have produced the play in 1657, probably abandoning verse for prose and concentrating on ghost and torture scenes. There was a further possible performance of the play at a school in Thorn in 1650, and then a certain performance at Zittau in 1665. A play about the execution of Charles I was performed at Altenburg in 1671; again perhaps this was *Carolus Stuardus*. Before these later dates, it is believed to have circulated in manuscript among Gryphius's friends without his knowledge.

IV

This argument does not claim that the continental response to English parliamentarianism and radicalism was wholly hostile: we still have to explain, for instance, the two Leveller petitions published in Holland and in Dutch in 1652, one addressed to the States General at the start of the First Anglo-Dutch War, and there is the broader and deeper impact of Quakerism and other forms of enthusiasm in northern Europe. However, while the history of English civil war royalism in terms of its continental dimensions, and in respect both of exile and diplomacy, has been written, the literary impact is very largely a blank page.

---

[22]   See Derek McKay, *The Great Elector: Frederick William of Brandenburg-Prussia* (Harlow: Longman, 2001).

[23]   Habersetzer, *Politische*, p. 54.

It is important literature too, having a defining impact in some cases on the continental scene from which it emerged. To what extent English writers paid attention to the continental response is a question that remains to be answered. There is a great deal still to do in this area: in this respect it might even be possible to rewrite the significance of the English Revolution itself as we discover the full dimension of the exile canon.

Chapter 7
Abraham Cowley and the Ends of Poetry

Christopher D'Addario

I

In the waning years of the seventeenth century, in his *Dedication to the Aeneis*, John Dryden looked back at one of the damaged lives of the century's civil wars as he discussed the failed potential of the royalist poet Abraham Cowley, 'the darling of his youth':

> For through the Iniquity of his times, he was forc'd to Travel, at an Age, when, instead of Learning Foreign Languages, he should have studied the Beauties of his Mother Tongue [...]. Thus by gaining abroad he lost at home: Like the Painter in the *Arcadia*, who going to see a Skirmish, had his Arms lop'd off: and return'd, says Sir *Philip Sidney*, well instructed how to draw a Battel, but without a Hand to perform his Work.[1]

The harsh finality of Dryden's evocation of the maimed painter of the *Arcadia* underlines the extent to which Dryden saw only the deleterious effects of geographic exile on Cowley's writing; and the fictionality of the analogy, coming from an author who had made a rather different choice after political defeat and disappointment, tends to belie a surprising, if perhaps self-justifying, callousness to the loss itself, a callousness already hinted at in the balanced poise of his closing judgment of Cowley's writing life: 'thus by gaining abroad, he lost at home'. According to Dryden, Cowley's flight to the continent in the 1640s and 1650s, while providing him with the knowledge and first-hand experience of the heroism and tragedy of which literature speaks, deprived him of the leisure and immediate circumstances with which he could perfect the elegance of expression necessary for the heights of Parnassus. Apparently, at least for the learned, elite Dryden, aesthetic distance and close study of one's native language are necessary for the creation of literature. Dryden may even be remembering Cowley's own famous admission in the *Preface* to his 1656 *Poems* that his damaged fortunes and psyche had stifled his artistic genius: 'how can [wit] choose but wither in a long and sharp winter? A warlike, various and a tragical age is best to write of, but worst to

---

[1]   *The Works of John Dryden*, ed. Niles Hooker and H.T. Swendenberg, Jr., 20 vols (Berkeley: University of California Press, 1956–2006), v, 331–2.

write in'.[2] These statements of Cowley and Dryden reveal particular assumptions concerning the relationship between the artist and history, one where the artist belongs on the sidelines, observing and reacting in peace and at a remove, rather than participating or being swept up in the harsh realities of war and exile.[3]

But of course both Cowley and Dryden, and numerous other exiles in the seventeenth century, continued to write through political hardship and war, despite their laments. The portrait of the artist removed from the mire of politics persisted well into the last century, and has perpetuated the unfortunate and misleading professional division of seventeenth-century literature into the imagined categories of Renaissance (largely ending in 1640) and Restoration (beginning with the return of Charles II and, one assumes, the return of literature to England). Recent scholars, however, have thankfully ignored these boundaries and fruitfully explored the impact of the civil war and political conflict more generally on literature and culture in the period.[4] Attendant with this examination of the artist-at-war, so to speak, is a growing interest in the cultural and artistic effects of and reactions to the experience of exile.[5] In this essay, I outline more specifically some of these effects and reactions through a study of Abraham Cowley, a poet who felt the artistic difficulties of exile keenly, and explored them at length, most substantially in his *Pindariques*. Throughout these poems, as his lament in the *Preface* attests, Cowley seems insistently aware of his disrupted poetic life and, connectedly, of the semantic effects of his removal from the living stream of the English language. The results are both a sustained questioning of the entire poetic endeavor and the unique construction of a poetics of exile that investigates the pervasive polyvalence of language itself.

---

[2]   Abraham Cowley, *Poems* (London, 1656, n.p.). All further citations to Cowley's poems will be from this edition and cited in-text.

[3]   Both Cowley and Dryden may more specifically have been thinking of Ovid's laments over his banishment in the *Tristia*, 1.39–44. It should be noted that the necessity of leisure and peacefulness to the literary imagination, and its attendant picture of the poet-artist removed from the fray of politics and polemic, was certainly not unanimously agreed upon in the seventeenth century.

[4]   For a recent critique of seventeenth-century periodization, see Steven Zwicker, 'Is There Such a Thing as Restoration Literature?', *Huntington Library Quarterly*, 69 (2006), 425–50.

[5]   Edward Corp has edited two substantial collections of essays on the Jacobite court in exile: *A Court in Exile: The Stuarts in France, 1689–1718* (Cambridge: Cambridge University Press, 2004), and *The Stuart Court in Rome: The Legacy of Exile* (Ashgate: London, 2003). See also Geoffrey Smith, *Cavaliers in Exile* (Basingstoke and New York: Palgrave, 2003); Jason Peacey, 'Order and Disorder in Europe: Parliamentary Agents and Royalist Thugs, 1649–1650', *Historical Journal*, 40 (1997), 953–76; Marika Keblusek, 'The Exile Experience: Royalist and Anglican Book Culture in the Low Countries, 1640–1660', in *The Bookshop of the World: The Role of the Low Countries in the Book Trade, 1473–1941*, ed. Lotte Hellinga et al. (Houten: HES & De Graaf, 2001), pp. 151–8. Two recent conferences have brought together a substantial number of scholars to discuss the royalists in exile: 'Englishmen Adrift', in Ghent, in April 2006; and 'Exile in the English Revolution and its Aftermath', in London, in July 2006.

In the above passage from *The Dedication to the Aeneis*, Dryden focuses on the detriment of Cowley's exile to his poetry because, in his predecessor's poems, Dryden sees an inexactness of expression that reveals a loose grasp of the semantic nuances of his native language. However, despite Dryden's critique (and Samuel Johnson's more famous dismissal of Cowley's metaphysical style), recent critical consensus has taken a far more positive view of Cowley's poetics. Since Robert Hinman's *Abraham Cowley's World of Order*, many readers of Cowley's mid-career poems, particularly the Pindaric odes, have largely emphasized the rational empiricism that underlies his poetic style and philosophical stances.[6] The dominant picture we have now of Cowley is of a poet intensely concerned with the empiricism of Francis Bacon's new philosophy and with creating a poetry that focused on natural phenomena and the representation of distinct moments of experience.[7] In these recent studies, Cowley has usefully been placed not at the end of a line of poets beginning with Donne, but rather amidst the continental philosophical and intellectual milieu of the royalist exiles in France, particularly William and Margaret Cavendish, William Davenant, Edmund Waller, Kenelm Digby and Thomas Hobbes.[8] Spurred by interactions with Marin Mersenne, Pierre Gassendi and other French intellectuals, these exiles became deeply interested in the material world, in understanding human actions as a consequence of natural, sensual causes and in the correct expression and representation of these phenomena.

As they attempted to resituate themselves, with varying degrees of success, in the often unfamiliar environment of Paris, royalist exiles felt the attraction of a poetry and philosophy that grasped on to the substance of daily life in order to remake it into coherent imaginative creations. Central to the apprehension of and investigation into immediate reality for exiles such as Hobbes, Davenant and Cowley was the development of a reformed English language that had its basis in experience rather than eloquence or a received academic lexicon. Drawing on Bacon's critique of traditional academic disputation and philosophy, Hobbes had even in 1640 attacked the arbitrary names and reasoning of scholarly learning.

---

[6]   Robert Hinman, *Abraham Cowley's World of Order* (Cambridge: Harvard University Press, 1960), esp. pp. 92–134. For later developments of Hinman's thesis and the influence of Bacon and Hobbes on Cowley, see David Trotter, *The Poetry of Abraham Cowley* (Totowa, N.J.: Rowman and Littlefield, 1979), pp. 109–38; Charles K. Smith, 'French Philosophy and English Politics in Interregnum Poetry', in *The Stuart Court and Europe: Essays in Politics and Political Culture*, ed. R. Malcolm Smuts (Cambridge: Cambridge University Press, 1996), pp. 177–209; Achsah Guibbory, 'Imitation and Originality: Cowley and Bacon's Vision of Progress', *Studies in English Literature*, 29 (1989), 99–120; Mary Elizabeth Green, 'The Poet in Solomon's House: Abraham Cowley as Baconian Apostle', *Restoration*, 2 (1986), 68–75.

[7]   See, especially, the summaries of Hinman, *Abraham Cowley's World of Order*, p. 134, and Green, 'The Poet in Solomon's House', 73–4.

[8]   For which, see Smith, 'French Philosophy', pp. 188–200; James R. Jacob and Timothy Raylor, 'Opera and Obedience: Thomas Hobbes and *A Proposition for Advancement of Moralitie*, by Sir William Davenant', *Seventeenth Century*, 6 (1991), 205–50.

He would impart his version of rationalism to his fellow exiles while in Paris, as the Cavendish circle sought after a language both empirically grounded and politically useful.[9] Cowley notably takes up Hobbes's attack on the current state of learning in his Pindaric to his mentor, lamenting the debasement of philosophy, and specifically philosophical discourse, since Aristotle's 'reign':

> So did this noble *Empire* wast,
>   Sunk by degrees from glories past,
> And in the *School-mens* hands it perisht quite at last.
>   Then nought but *Words* it grew,
>   And those all *Barb'arous* too.
>   It *perisht*, and it *vanisht* there,
> The *Life* and *Soul* breath'd out, became but empty Air.
>   ('To Mr. Hobbes', 27–33)

The movement towards degeneration and dissolution consistently reappears in other contexts in Cowley's *Pindariques*, and should be seen as a central concern in these poems. What should be emphasized is the nature of this intellectual decay, a decay predicated upon a failure of philosophical language to hold its substance until it becomes 'empty Air'. With their metaphoric gesture toward political dissolution, the lines also resonate for the royalist exiles who had witnessed the collapse of the Stuart regime. Later in the poem, Hobbes appears hopefully as a conquering hero who returns the empire of philosophy, and its debased language, to its former glory (an appropriate association when one considers Hobbes's political programme in *Leviathan*). Cowley's political metaphor implicitly reproduces Hobbes's emphasis in *Leviathan* upon the connection between the reformation of language and the creation of a well-ordered state.

Elsewhere, Cowley would also envision the true poet as attempting to reground language in objective experience. So, in 'To Sir William Davenant, Upon His First Two Books of *Gondibert* ...', Cowley, echoing Hobbes's judgment of Davenant's *Gondibert* in the 'Answer' to Davenant's theoretical preface, would praise the former Poet Laureate's romantic epic for representing actual experience instead of the fantasies that had populated heroic poetry up to this point: 'Thou like some worthy knight with sacred arms/Dost drive the monsters thence and end the charms' (ll. 5–6). Cowley goes on to expand his critique of supernatural poetry, a critique that most likely derives from Davenant's own theories in his Preface to *Gondibert*, to include Protestant representations of a frightful Italian past:

> By fatal hands whilst *present Empires* fall,
> Thine from the Grave *past Monarchies* recal.
> So much more thanks from humane kind does merit
> The *Poets Fury*, then the *Zelots Spirit*.
> And from the *Grave* thou mak'est this *Empire* rise,

---

[9]   On the Cavendish's circle's interest in political obedience and the reformation of language, see Jacob and Raylor, 'Opera and Obedience', 215–31.

Not like some dreadful *Ghost* t'affright our Eyes,
But with more Luster and triumphant state
Then when it *crown'd* at proud *Verona* sate.
(ll. 11–18)

The poem takes a distinctly contemporary turn here as Cowley takes a political jab at the more radical, anti-Catholic puritans back in England who have created imaginary ghosts and demons to populate the Italian past. Instead, Davenant's natural and positive representation of the kingdom of Lombardy avoids zealous superstition even in the face of a supposedly widespread anti-monarchism. The emphasis on a mimetic and realistic poetry for Cowley thus takes on political importance, as he concludes his commentary: 'So *God-like Poets* do past things reherse,/Not *change*, but *Heighten* Nature by their Verse' (ll. 21–2). Significantly, the removal of the fantastic and the supernatural that Cowley praises here also underlies Hobbes's attempt, in *Leviathan*, to justify an authoritarian sovereign by denying the spiritual as a legitimate motivation for political action. In its evocation of the contemporary political crisis in England, Cowley's panegyric also identifies the supernatural as politically subversive and argues that the poet should rather restrict his or her language to the bounds of known or accepted experience, striving to mould his words to represent this reality accurately, pleasantly, and in an elevated manner.[10]

That Cowley's positive judgments of Davenant's attempt at a 'naturalistic' poetics, and of Hobbes's reformation of philosophy, should turn its eyes towards the political situation back in the homeland is worth elaborating on here. In both poems, Cowley distinguishes his fellow exiles' empirical reformation of words from the misuses and abuses of the language occurring in England under parliament. For Cowley, and indeed for many other royalist exiles, Hobbes and Davenant's English adheres more closely to reality than the English spoken and written by those at home. Cowley's praise of Hobbes and Davenant thus attempts to confer a semantic legitimacy upon the exiles' writing when these writings, and the exiles, sorely needed it. As they fled to the continent and from power, the royalist exiles were forced to recognize that they also had given up authority over key terms such as 'loyalty', 'obedience' and 'just'. Cowley himself recognized the centrality of language to the political struggle in his Preface to the 1656 *Poems*, where he ostensibly decided to leave off writing for party and give up contesting controversial words: 'The Names of *Party*, and *Titles* of *Division*, which are sometimes in effect the whole quarrel, should be extinguished and forbidden in peace under the notions of *Acts* of *Hostility*'. The desire for linguistic oblivion in this sentence signals an insightful recognition of the power of language and a deep anger over its malleability during times of political crisis. Fleeing royalists such as Cowley were forced to admit the duplicity of the English language as it turned

---

[10]   Hobbes also makes this point in his 'Answer to Davenant's *Preface to Gondibert*', in *Critical Essays of the Seventeenth Century*, ed. Joel E. Spingarn, 3 vols (Bloomington: Indiana University Press, 1957), ii, 61–2.

at the moment of their defeat and exile. The royalists' interest in re-grounding the language in empirically based reasoning should thus be seen as a reaction to the unmooring of meaning that political revolution and the experience of exile entails. The writings and debates undertaken by the Cavendish circle in the 1640s and 1650s, and specifically this circle's interest in an obedience engendered largely through language, sought to counteract or overcome this semantic instability. Yet, as much as Hobbes, for example, seeks a normative semantics that will instill political obedience in *Leviathan*, he remains persistently nervous over the fixity of language, over its ability to represent accurately. After all, it is precisely because of his relativist epistemology that Hobbes asserts the need for sovereign control of how words mean.

Not surprisingly, then, there is a certain self-consciousness to much that is written in the royalist exile; authors seem sharply aware of the provisionality of what they have created. Because exile is profoundly disruptive and disorienting, and because language seems unmoored from its original fixedness, exiles tend to evince a heightened consciousness over the willfulness of the act which makes language mean what they want it to mean. This anxiety, further, tends to shade over into a more general questioning of the value of such assertions even within the texts themselves. Indeed, exilic writings, in many ways, can often be read as sustained reflections on (and provisional answers to) the purpose and efficacy of imaginative creation. Does poetry, and writing generally, as W.H. Auden has asserted, really make 'nothing happen'?[11]

II

It is a question that plagued Abraham Cowley as he continued his poetic efforts while searching for a stable existence on the continent in the 1650s, and later as he prepared his 1656 *Poems* for publication. Cowley's Preface has caused sustained controversy over the extent of its amelioration and retreat from the poet's royalist political beliefs, but I would like to leave aside these questions to consider the Preface as a retreat of a different sort, a retreat from a faith in the importance of poetry.[12] Nowhere is this more evident than when Cowley turns to discuss the reasons for his 'retirement' from the artistic life. According to the Preface, he has

---

[11] 'In Memory of W.B. Yeats', in *Collected Poems*, ed. Edward Mendelson (New York: Random House, 1976), p. 197.

[12] The commentary on these sentences is extensive and began soon after their publication. Thomas Sprat excised these lines in the posthumous Restoration edition of Cowley's poems (London, 1668) to remove any taint of political amelioration. See also, Annabel Patterson, *Censorship and Interpretation: The Conditions of Writing and Reading in Early Modern England* (Madison: University of Wisconsin Press, 1984), pp. 150–52; Thomas N. Corns, *Uncloistered Virtue: English Political Literature, 1640–1660* (Oxford: Clarendon Press, 1992), pp. 256–9; and Stella Revard, 'Cowley's "Pindarique Odes" and the Politics of the Inter-regnum', *Criticism*, 35 (1993), 393–410.

refrained from writing poetry due to his melancholic state: 'Neither is the present constitution of my *Mind* more proper then that of the *Times* for this exercise'; and here he interestingly corrects himself quickly, 'or rather divertisement'. With this correction, Cowley noticeably and self-consciously devalues poetry to something to pass the time, as he makes clearer a few sentences later: 'The *Soul* must be filled with bright and delightful *Idea's*, when it undertakes to communicate delight to others; which is the main end of *Poesie*'. We should not miss Cowley's deliberate refutation here of the Renaissance Horatian commonplace that poetry should both delight and instruct. The claim seems strange considering the moral and philosophical seriousness of the debates over the uses of poetry that Cowley, Davenant, Hobbes and others had held in the 1650s. Indeed, this seriousness is clearly evidenced in the later poems of Cowley's 1656 volume, the *Pindariques* and the *Davideis*, as well as in the subsequent claims in the Preface itself concerning the nobility and utility of poetry and the wholesomeness of its nourishment. However, Cowley did abandon his Biblical epic, and the sentiments earlier in the Preface seem to follow through on this abandonment by questioning the value of such poetic effort, at least coming from the author himself.

The inconsistency in Cowley's attitude towards the ends of poetry that we can see in the Preface signals a poet ruminating on the purposes of the writing life as he looks back upon his experience during the civil war. Despite his attempts to devalue poetry, Cowley still defended his poetic efforts as original and groundbreaking in the Preface, and even if he eventually abandoned such grand attempts as the *Davideis*, he did in fact maintain these ambitions through much of the 1640s and 1650s. Thus, we should not see his disappointment as all-consuming and permanent (he did, after all, return to writing), but rather as one side of a struggle to comprehend what writing and language can do in the face of exile and defeat. Indeed, throughout the 1656 *Poems*, and particularly in the ruminative *Pindariques*, Cowley seems centrally and intensely concerned with understanding what, if anything, poetry can 'make happen'. Even though the answers that Cowley provides in the *Pindariques* are far from unequivocal, it is this very inconsistency that illustrates the extent to which he is obsessed with gaining some finality concerning the efficacy of poetic action as he repeatedly returns to this question, seemingly never satisfied with the conclusion that he reaches.

From the start of the sequence of original poems in the *Pindariques* it is clear that, for Cowley, poetic creation is complexly engaged with the passage of time, the yearning for eternity and the inevitability of death. These concerns are by no means unique to Cowley in the seventeenth century, although we should certainly see the upheavals of defeat and exile as sharpening Cowley's awareness of the transitory nature of human life and its achievements. 'The Resurrection', the first of Cowley's original Pindarics, begins with the assertion that poetry is necessary to the memorialization of virtue and introduces the desire for verse to transform mortal existence into immortal material. In this opening stanza, he describes verse as a 'midwife' to virtue, and when virtue dies, verse:

with comely pride
Embalms it, and erects a *Pyramide*
That never will decay
Till *Heaven* it self shall melt away,
And nought behind it stay.
(ll. 8–12)

The erection or creation of imaginative structures impervious to the exigencies
of time is a recurring desire in many of the *Pindariques*. So, in 'The Muse', poetry
not only crystallizes the present moment with accurate, empirical reflection, but
also, through this creative ordering, extends the moment for all futurity: 'Nay thy
Immortal Rhyme/Makes this one short Point of Time,/To fill up half the *Orb* of
Round Eternity'. In the very next poem, 'To Mr. Hobs', Cowley closes by confidently
affirming the immortal qualities of Hobbesian philosophical reasoning:

And if we weigh, like *Thee*,
Nature, and *Causes*, we shall see
That thus it *needs must be*,
To things *Immortal Time* can do no wrong,
And that which never is *to Dye*, for ever must be *Young*.
(ll. 90–94)

In these lines, as in 'The Muse', Cowley asserts the permanence of an imaginative,
yet substantive creation, a materialism largely of the mind that has its analogue
in the imagined pyramid that stands in memoriam to virtue in the lines from 'The
Resurrection' above. The purely fictive nature of Cowley's materialist imaginings here
and elsewhere indicates a subjectivism enforced by the physical disruptions of exile,
a necessary retreat into the mind, despite Cowley's empirical claims to the contrary.
Nonetheless, the three-poem sequence at the beginning of the *Pindariques* shows a
poet searching for a theory of imaginative creation that establishes its utility in the
midst of war, exile, and more immediately, loss of life. The poems each emphasize the
ability of poetry to counter these realities, to surmount or even halt the decay of the
world that the royalists must have felt in evidence everywhere in the 1640s and 1650s.
Artistic creation becomes a form of willful resistance, a compensatory creative force
that can generate imaginative objects that are immune to the seemingly inevitable
fragility and loss – particularly for the royalist exiles – that living entails.

However, unlike Hobbes, whose mind seems entirely at home in its own
authoritarian creations, in the *Pindariques* Cowley becomes more preoccupied
with, or perhaps less able to deny, the persistent threat of dissolution to which
the exiles' recent defeats and haphazard existence on the continent gave specific
point. Indeed, at this moment in Cowley's imagination, as much as poetry stood
as a potential shelter from decay, it also brought him to contemplate the reasons
for the need for this shelter: the brevity and vanity of all human existence.[13]

---

[13]   Other critics have noted the inability of Cowley to maintain a consistent faith in the
power of philosophic inquiry or artistic creation. See, most explicitly, Trotter, *The Poetry*

In 'The Resurrection', even as Cowley imagines his verse 'embalming' virtue, he swiftly associates this verse also with the steady march of years and the final days of the world. When he comes to dwell on the second coming in this poem, attendant with this event is a rather dark vision of the scattered atoms of creation coming home, 'where th'*attending Soul* naked, and shivering stands' (ll. 44–5). The resurrection seems as much about the termination of things as about their new beginnings. The shadow that briefly clouds Cowley's inspiration here darkens the mood of the latter poems in the sequence much more extensively. With the exception of 'The Extasie', which envisions an imaginative escape from mortality similar to the earlier odes, the closing six poems seem to turn almost automatically to contemplation of the inevitability of death and the failure of futurity. The opening stanza to 'Life and Fame' is representative of the emptiness that Cowley sees in all human effort as the appositives for 'life' build to an exasperated crescendo:

> *Dream* of a *Shadow*! A *Reflection* made
> From the false glories of the gay *reflected Bow*,
>   Is a more *solid* thing then *Thou*.
> Vain weak-built *Isthmus*, which dost proudly rise
>   Up betwixt to *Eternities*;
>   Yet canst nor *Wave* nor *Wind* sustain,
> But *broken* and *orewhelm'd*, the endless *Oceans* meet again.
>   (ll. 7–13)

The ethereality of the opening two images provides a significant counterpoint to the hopefully materialist imaginings of the earlier poems in the sequence, the fleetingness of an insubstantial life replacing the stability of a creativity based on everyday objects. In the final appositive, Cowley juxtaposes the fragility that he sees accompanying all existence to the inexorable forces of nature that engulf and erase all record of life. The representation of the past and future as indistinguishable, implacable eternities here sharply contrasts with the confidence with which Cowley envisions, in 'The Muse', the poet easily ranging over and ordering the past, and witnessing the birth of future years which 'take their everlasting *Flight*' (l. 55). Yet, it is in the context of the hopelessness of these lines from 'Life and Fame' that we can better understand the yearning for such control over temporality elsewhere in Cowley's poems.

Nonetheless, as much as this darker vision of human achievement drives the search for a poetic escape from its implications, at the same time it argues for the impossibility of such an escape, emphasizing the vanity of these efforts, the extent to which we are deceived by our own impossible dreams. If the experience of exile forces the individual habitually to look back for explanation and to look forward in hope, Cowley increasingly seems to have recognized the futility of such endeavors.[14]

---

of Abraham Cowley, pp. 133–4, as well as Guibbory, 'Imitation and Originality', 110, and Hinman, *Abraham Cowley's World of Order*, p. 58.

[14]   For such imaginings in other, more recent exiles, see Svetlana Boym, *The Future of Nostalgia* (New York: Basic Books, 2001).

Thus, it is notable that even in his panegyric upon the supposedly miraculous abilities of his close friend, the doctor Charles Scarborough, Cowley closes the poem by lamenting the ultimate uselessness of Scarborough's efforts:

> Ah, learned *friend*, it grieves me, when I think
> > That *Thou* with all thy *Art* must dy
> > > As certainly as *I*.
> And all thy noble *Reparations* sink
> Into the sure-wrought *Mine* of treacherous *Mortality*.
> > > (ll. 94–8)

Just as Dr. Scarborough's medicinal 'art' proves ineffectual, in other Pindarics it becomes clear that poetry also fails in its struggle against mortality. In fact, Cowley specifically chides poets for the pride with which they toil away at their 'monuments' and laments, half ironically, the particular misfortunes that seem to attend the writing life. While 'The Muse' offers one response to Auden's assertion concerning poetry, the closing to 'Life and Fame' ruefully gives the lie to such ambitions: 'We *Poets* madder yet then all,/With a refin'ed *Phantastick Vanitie*,/ Think we not onely *Have*, but *Give Eternitie*' (ll. 41–3).

Cowley holds poetry up for special scrutiny here because he finds in all earthly language an emptiness of meaning that frustrates the poet's artistic aims. More specifically, in Cowley's mind the inevitability of death is directly connected to our inability to name things accurately and, more generally, to the corruption of all human language. 'Life' is the last of the original *Pindariques* and perhaps his most pessimistic commentary on writing, language and the human condition. The opening stanza elaborates on the disjunction between word and thing that is caused by our mortality:

> We're ill by these *Grammarians* us'd;
> We are abus'd by *Words*, grosly abus'd;
> > From the *Maternal Tomb*,
> > To the *Graves* fruitful *Womb*,
> We call here *Life*; but *Life*'s a *name*
> That nothing here can truly claime.
> > > (ll. 1–6)

The broken metre of the opening line to the poem signals a more substantial and permanent disruption to poetic creativity evinced by the theme of the following lines. The ironic critique of the emptiness and vanity of life that appears consistently in the *Pindariques* here shades over into an admission that the 'nonsense of our language' merely represents shadows, 'the empty dreams which in Death's sleep we make'. As the inversion of the conventional Renaissance rhyme of 'tomb/womb' suggests, the immediate yet fleeting realities of life on earth prevent humans from comprehending the emptiness of these realities and, more importantly for the poet, the wrongness of the words that we use to describe them. In an intriguing note that accompanies these opening lines, Cowley denies true 'being' for all humans since 'that which has more degrees of *Privation*, or *Not-being* then of *Being* (which is the case of all *Creatures*) is not properly said to *Be*; and again, That which is in a perpetual *Fieri* or *Making*, never is quite *Made*; and therefore never properly *Is*'. The note serves as a significant philosophical repudiation of the materialist poetics that Cowley had outlined in 'The Muse'. Indeed, in this poem, at this moment, Cowley denies a material existence to all earthly things, and, as result, denies the possibility of an empirical language based on objective experience. Instead, his exile has here forced him to recognize the futility of attempting to grasp on to a reality that is merely transitory and entirely fleeting.

We can thus see in Cowley's more pessimistic moments a turn toward linguistic relativism that is occasioned by the sudden throes of fate attendant upon the experience of exile and political defeat. The connections between his acceptance of the fleeting realities of human existence and language and the royalists' political misfortunes become clearer in 'Destinie', a poem that reflects specifically yet cryptically on the events of the civil war. While the opening stanza has occasioned much debate over its political sympathies, I would like to focus rather on the second stanza and its attempted erasure of any partisan politics in the poem. This stanza, generally, reveals the complete inability of the political figures from the opening stanza to control their own actions, a revelation that forces the speaker to reflect further upon the emptiness of appearances and, more generally, of political judgments:

> And some are *Great*, and some are *Small*,
> Some climb to *good*, some from *good Fortune* fall,
> Some *Wiseman*, and some *Fools* we call,
> *Figures*, alas, of *Speech*, for *Destiny plays us all*.
> (ll. 29–32)

Cowley, in the half distantly ironic, half despondently serious pose that seems endemic to much of the series, reveals a sense of helplessness here in the face of the implacable movement of history. This helplessness, further, leads Cowley to sound a note familiar from other poems in the *Pindariques*, an admission of the inability of language to name things permanently and directly. The appearance of this familiar complaint in this specifically political lament suggests the impact of the experience of defeat and exile on Cowley's vision of the poetic endeavour. Immediately after the second stanza, in a seemingly unexpected digression that is typical of the odes, Cowley imagines a covenant to which his 'Queen', the poetic muse, forced him to agree:

> *Hate* and *renounce* (said she)
> *Wealth, Honor, Pleasures*, all the *World* for *Me*.
> [...]
> Content thy self with the small *Barren Praise*,
>   That neglected *Verse* does raise.
> (ll. 38–9, 42–3)

In the preceding lines that deny the efficacy of language, we might see the traces of the associative path that led to this wistful contract with the muse. The turn toward linguistic relativism in the second stanza seems immediately to have brought to mind for Cowley the visible failures of his poetic life, the failures of poetry to make something happen.

III

Cowley never fully submitted to these more despondent thoughts, however, and elsewhere in the *Pindariques*, and particularly in the Brutus ode, we can see him struggling to achieve a poetry that admitted the malleability of all language without descending into defeatist silence. 'Brutus' is one of only two Pindarics that Cowley published without any editorial notes, yet it seems clear even from the opening lines that the ode forces the contemporary reader to consider the author's presence and intentions. The poem begins, 'Excellent *Brutus*, of all humane race,/ The best till *Nature* was improv'ed by *Grace*' (ll. 1–2), a strongly unexpected characterization of the republican hero from a former royalist exile, especially considering the frequent parallels drawn between Brutus and Oliver Cromwell in revolutionary pamphlets of the period.[15] From the start, the reader is asked to rectify the poem's sentiments with his or her knowledge of the author's apparent royalist sympathies, and either must read these lines ironically (certainly still a possibility) or else reconsider what Cowley in particular meant by the words 'Excellent', 'Brutus' and 'best' – is this poem a conciliatory panegyric to Cromwell, or does it ask us to reorient our understanding of the basis for such praise and concomitantly the meanings of these signs?[16] By stopping the reader before he or she starts, so to speak, Cowley draws attention to the interpretive possibilities, the semantic instability, of the very language with which he has begun his poem.

The questions that arise from the opening lines of the ode are, in fact, intrinsic to the allegorical mode that Cowley chooses here to investigate political action and choice in a time of upheaval. As theorists of allegory have argued extensively, this form, because of its complex interpretive processes and its violation of grammatical categories, engages in persistent self-referentiality and thus emphasizes the capacity of language to mean multiple things simultaneously.[17] As allegory

---

[15]   T.R. Langley, 'Abraham Cowley's "Brutus": Royalist or Republican?', *Yearbook of English Studies*, 6 (1976), 41–52.

[16]   The political questions have continued to intrigue modern critics. Recent and extensive commentaries include: Ruth Nevo, *The Dial of Virtue* (Princeton: Princeton University Press, 1963), pp. 119–27; Langley, 'Abraham Cowley's "Brutus"', 41–52; Patterson, *Censorship and Interpretation*, pp. 154–7; Corns, *Uncloistered Virtue*, pp. 263–5; Revard, 'Cowley's "Pindarique Odes"', 395–6.

[17]   See Angus Fletcher, *Allegory: The Theory of a Symbolic Mode* (Ithaca: Cornell University Press, 1964), pp. 228–61, and his investigation into the polysemous ambivalence of the late Renaissance form; Maureen Quilligan, *The Language of Allegory: defining the genre* (Ithaca: Cornell University Press, 1979), esp. pp. 26–68. Gordon Teskey has emphasized the productive rift in meaning at the center of all allegory, in *Allegory and*

strives towards linguistic fullness, it also becomes an inquiry into the otherness of meaning so expected of poetic language, an inquiry into the truth inherent in individual words and ultimately this truth's variability. Such a mode would surely have appealed to Cowley at a time when the very processes through and authorities from which words obtained meaning seemed to be disintegrating before them. If allegory forces a self-consciousness concerning interpretive practices in the writer and reader, then Cowley, already keenly aware of the volatility of the English language, seems to have turned to this mode to contemplate and comment upon the linguistic shifts engendered by the revolutions of government.

In the Brutus ode, Cowley seems intent upon evaluating the nature of political virtue, the meaning of the word 'virtue', through the classical type Brutus. Does Brutus's faithfulness to the republic, his refusal to serve Caesar, constitute true virtue (a question certainly that resonates in the context of the civil war, execution of Charles and rise of Cromwell)? The exact parallels between Brutus, Caesar and contemporary figures seem secondary at times to the answers to this question, although they do add a rich layer of contemporary urgency to the entire poem. Instead, Cowley's allegory fluctuates between the normative and the ironic in its evaluation of Brutus, not necessarily or solely to obfuscate Cowley's political meaning, but rather to highlight the difficulties of locating such meaning at a time when the English language kept shifting suddenly.[18] The opening of the second stanza seems particularly subtle:

> From thy strict rule some think thou didst swerve
> (*Mistaken Honest men*) in *Caesars* blood;
> What *Mercy* could the *Tyrants life* deserve,
> From him who kill'd *Himself* rather than *serve*?
> (ll. 15–18)

The mention of the 'mistaken honest men' who see in Brutus's killing of Caesar a departure from virtue reminds the reader that all did and do not see Brutus's actions as consistent or virtuous; and the final line – 'From him who kill'd Himself rather than serve' – seems to hover between praise and approbation, inviting the reader to read ironically, if he or she is apt to hear any positive connotation in the word 'serve'. The possibility of ironic praise in a contemporary, Cromwellian context is heightened in the next stanza's closing lines: 'There's none but *Brutus* could

---

Violence (Ithaca: Cornell University Press, 1996), pp. 3–31. In *The Ruins of Allegory: 'Paradise Lost' and the metamorphosis of epic convention* (Durham: Duke University Press, 2001), Catherine Gimelli Martin argues that with the advent of scientific realism, late Renaissance allegories tended to embrace 'linguistic modulation' and investigate the ways words mean in the face of the decline of the certainties of the divine wholeness of sacred language.

[18] In my emphasis on Cowley's interest in investigating the shifting grounds for linguistic authority, I differ from recent interpretations of Cowley's *Pindariques* as coded allegories that are cautiously directed to Interregnum readers. See, especially, Patterson's emphasis on functional ambiguity in *Censorship and Interpretation*, pp. 146–57, and Revard's more 'royalist' reading of Cowley's poems in 'Cowley's "Pindarique Odes"'.

deserve/That all men else should *wish* to *serve*./And Caesar's usurpt place to him should proffer;/None can deserv't but he who would *refuse* the *offer*' (ll. 43–6). The difficulty of reading these lines as solely serious or ironic demonstrates that Cowley is more concerned at these moments with opening interpretive possibilities, with illustrating the polyvalence of the poem's political vocabulary.

Indeed, the rest of the second stanza does not continue to praise Brutus but rather laments the natural tendency of humans to misperceive the truth amidst the babble of competing definitions spurred by the corrupting influence of personal prejudice and custom. The poem's observations, as well as the reading experience it creates, compel the reader to contemplate the variability of political language. It is not surprising, then, that the poem's final stanza does not elaborate on Brutus's virtues, but rather on the emptiness of the word 'virtue' itself, at least in an earthly context. In Brutus's destruction, we are meant to see the frailty of virtue in the face of the 'odde events,/*Ill men*, and wretched *Accidents*' (ll. 65–6) that inevitably destroy its embodiments. Fate exposes human, political virtue as 'An idol onely, and a *Name*' (75). In relation to Christ's divine intervention upon which the poem closes, this virtue remains provisional, and thus prideful. The poem illustrates the inevitable reliance of the definition of human virtue, and by extension the entire range of the poem's language, upon the vagaries of fate and accident.

Such vagaries were often the focus of royalist lament during the 1650s, and we have already seen in the *Pindariques* Cowley's own complaints over the haphazardness of existence and its deleterious effects on the creation of meaning. Yet, Cowley's political allegory seems also an attempt to record and admit the polyvalence of political language during a 'warlike and tragical age'. Rather than emphasizing the futility of language, in its opening stanzas the Brutus ode explores the ways in which political conflict can be semantically generative, the ways in which uncertainty and change can transform language and produce oscillations in meanings, however momentary. We might consider Cowley's poem alongside not the coded allegories of royalist romance but, instead, Marvell's 'An Horatian Ode', another piece that seeks to record political ambivalence during this time of historic change. Like Marvell's ode to Cromwell, 'Brutus' emphasizes the possibility of seeing in the presentation of these figures, in each word, both praise and irony. And like Marvell, who seemed to have believed that it was poetry's special place to display such complexity in the midst of revolution, Cowley also finds a temporary and partial answer to his questioning of the efficacy of poetry in the generative ambiguities of the Brutus ode. I would suggest, finally, that for Cowley, this ode, with its fluctuations between the normative and the ironic, demonstrated poetry's, and specifically allegory's, special ability to recognize and display the instability of language. But this is a truth, of course, that also contains the seeds of the same form's futility.

Chapter 8
'Not Sure of Safety': Hobbes and Exile

James Loxley

No paradox of contemporary politics is filled with a more poignant irony than the discrepancy between the efforts of those well-meaning idealists who stubbornly insist on regarding as 'inalienable' those human rights, which are enjoyed only by citizens of the most prosperous and civilized countries, and the situation of the rightless themselves.[1]

I

'The Decline of the Nation-State and the End of the Rights of Man', a central chapter in Hannah Arendt's *Origins of Totalitarianism*, sets out one of the book's continuing provocations. Meditating on the fate the shifting and various mass of exiles generated in mid-twentieth-century Europe, Arendt discerns perplexities. The exile, stripped of his or her civil rights, should have stood revealed as an individual endowed with inalienable human rights, and therefore capable of making a legitimate claim for recognition on the modern European polity which proclaims its fidelity to such notions. But this had not happened. Instead, 'those whom the persecutor had singled out as scum of the earth – Jews, Trotskyites, etc. – actually were received as scum of the earth everywhere; those whom persecution had called undesirable became the *indésirables* of Europe.'[2] Far from being embraced as fellows by the peoples to whom they looked for refuge, exiles carried their stigma with them. They found themselves as estranged from the rights of man as they were from those of the citizen when they were stopped at borders or interned in camps. So for Arendt, the stateless refugee 'has been forced outside the pale of the law', and in that movement shows up an anomaly or awkwardness in our sense that human and civil rights are necessarily complementary or mutually reinforcing.[3] Inalienable, natural rights have turned out to be unenforceable 'whenever people appeared who were no longer the citizens of any sovereign state'.[4] To be expelled

---

[1]   Hannah Arendt, *The Origins of Totalitarianism*, 2nd edn (London: Allen and Unwin, 1958), p. 279.

[2]   *Ibid.*, p. 269.

[3]   *Ibid.*, p. 286.

[4]   *Ibid.*, p. 293.

from a polity, to be forced to fall back on one's humanity, is in fact to be expelled from a humanity that turns out to be co-extensive with citizenship, and at the same time to be reduced to a humanity which is both the ground of right and a mark of its withdrawal. As Arendt puts it, 'a man who is nothing but a man has lost the very qualities which make it possible for other people to treat him as a fellow-man'.[5] The exile's condition is thus one of 'abstract nakedness', or 'mere existence', a life lived as a body or a natural datum; but it is also a condition in which this givenness is juridically visible, since rights are supposed to inhere in us on account of our irreducible, universal, natural humanity. This is the source of the perplexity.

Arendt's formulation of this perplexity has been taken up by a number of thinkers intent on the somewhat suspicious examination of the rhetoric of human rights.[6] But perhaps the most influential recent work to follow explicitly from Arendt's discussion has been that of the Italian philosopher Giorgio Agamben. For Agamben, the perplexing condition of the stateless exile is just one example of a more generally queasy modern politics of the natural, a politics that produces the figure of 'bare life' as the disruption and displacement – but also disavowed condition – of modern citizenship.[7] Agamben therefore extends Arendt's analysis, locating the problem not just in the challenge posed to the Western conjunction of man and citizen by the streams of refugees created in twentieth-century Europe, but more fundamentally in Western discourses of sovereignty and the state. In this, for Agamben, Thomas Hobbes is implicated, despite the radical differences between Hobbesian and Arendtian conceptions of law and right. This is partly because Agamben's analysis of sovereignty engages with the theoretical account offered by the reactionary German jurist Carl Schmitt, who saw himself as developing Hobbesian ideas.[8] But it is also because Agamben follows theorists such as Leo Strauss and Norberto Bobbio in seeing Hobbes's political philosophy as centrally concerned to articulate the relation between the *status civilis* and the *status naturalis*, as therefore thinking civility through its limits, and seeking to test the relationship between different kinds or moments of nature and right.[9] Clearly, it

---

    [5]   *Ibid.*, p. 300.

    [6]   For a representative selection of recent views, see the essays gathered in 'And Justice For All? The Claims of Human Rights', ed. Ian Balfour and Eduardo Cadava, *South Atlantic Quarterly*, 103, 2/3 (2004), 277–96.

    [7]   Agamben, *Means Without Ends: Notes on Politics* (Minneapolis: University of Minnesota Press, 2000); Agamben, *Homo Sacer: Sovereign Power and Bare Life* (Stanford: Stanford University Press, 1998).

    [8]   Agamben, *Homo Sacer*, pp. 8–19, 26–42; Carl Schmitt, *Political Theology: Four Chapters on the Concept of Sovereignty* (Chicago: University of Chicago Press, 2005), esp. pp. 16–52, and *The Concept of the Political* (Chicago: University of Chicago Press, 1996).

    [9]   See Leo Strauss, 'Notes on Carl Schmitt, The Concept of the Political', in Schmitt, *The Concept of the Political*, pp. 81–108, *The Political Philosophy of Hobbes* (Chicago: University of Chicago Press, 1952), and *Natural Right and History* (Chicago: University of Chicago Press, 1953), esp. pp. 166–202; Norberto Bobbio, *Thomas Hobbes and the Natural Law Tradition* (Chicago: University of Chicago Press, 1993), esp. pp. 114–71.

makes sense to suggest that in Hobbes the political significance of the relationship between nature and civility is very much to the point, and therefore the whole political constitution of the human is at issue; yet identifying this significance is not always the easiest or most uncontroversial move. Hobbes stresses both the continuities and the disjunctions between natural and civil right and law: the weighty transition – and also caesura – between Chapters 13 and 14 of *Leviathan* can serve as an exemplary instance of this. Agamben suggests that Hobbes's thinking of right, and of the political human, is not so much an articulation of the civil and the natural as the awkward and mutual implication of the one within the other. For Hobbes, he suggests, sovereign power:

> presents itself as an incorporation of the state of nature in society, or, if one prefers, as a state of indistinction between nature and culture, between violence and law [...]. Exteriority – the law of nature and the principle of the preservation of one's own life – is truly the innermost centre of the political system, and the political system lives off it.[10]

While there may be a bit too much of Schmittian decisionism in his account of sovereignty, even without this influence Hobbes's thought is marked for Agamben by the kind of conceptual awkwardness – paradox, almost – that Arendt locates in the modern thinking and practice of rights.

Despite the fact that his own work on bare life is indebted to the Foucauldian conception of biopolitics, Agamben here displays the distance between his own account and that of his predecessor. Foucault, following Hobbes's own comment on his project, sees him as one of the Capitolian geese 'that with their noyse defended those within it, not because they were they, but because they were there'.[11] For Foucault, Hobbes is accounted 'the father of political philosophy' because he is the staunch defender of 'philosophico-juridical discourse', a paradigmatic instance of the desire to maintain the language of right as the explanatory matrix for all human, social relations. For Agamben, though, as for Arendt, it is precisely the desire to articulate right beyond the bounds of the polis that produces, despite itself, only paradoxically juridical figures, and indeed also summons up that political other of a philosophy of right which Foucault sees Hobbes as aiming to suppress. Both Arendt and Agamben see the exile as one of the figures for this predicament, and the latter also relates this figure, briefly, to the Hobbesian account of sovereignty.[12] Following such hints in the context of more mainstream readings of Hobbes, this essay explores the nature and extent of any perplexity manifested in the solitary, poor, insecure exile.

---

[10] Agamben, *Homo Sacer*, p. 36.

[11] Hobbes, *Leviathan*, ed. Richard Tuck (Cambridge: Cambridge University Press, 1991), 'Dedicatory Epistle', p. 3; Michel Foucault, *Society Must be Defended*, ed. Mauro Bertani and Alessandro Fontana (London: Penguin, 2004), p. 99.

[12] Agamben, *Homo Sacer*, pp. 105–11.

II

The significance of exile for Hobbes is as much personal as it is philosophical. Hobbes's sojourn in France between 1640 and 1651 certainly looks like an exile, and is described as such by a recent biographer.[13] The account Hobbes gave others supports the suggestion that this was not an unforced relocation. Aubrey notes that 'he told me that Bishop Manwaring (of St David's) preach't *his doctrine*; for which, among others, he was sent prisoner to the Tower. Then thought Mr Hobbes, 'tis time now for me to shift for my selfe, and so withdrew into France'.[14] The same suggestion is made in Hobbes's own prose autobiography: having realized that civil war was approaching in late 1640, concerned for his safety, he returned to his friends in France.[15] His fears were not groundless: Hobbes's name, says Noel Malcolm, 'was [...] in circulation as a hardline theorist of royal absolutism'.[16] Roger Maynwaring was among the most notorious of such theorists, and during the Short Parliament moves were made to reopen a parliamentary case against him that the king had managed to head off 12 years earlier; the fear that the treatment Maynwaring had endured in 1628 for promulgating his views was about to be dished out not only to him but also to those with similarly elevated views of royal power, and that the king would not be able to protect his apologists as he had in prior troubles, is what brought him to Hobbes's mind now.[17] The prospect of aggressive moves against those who preached 'for absolute monarchy that the king may do as he list', raised again when the Long Parliament convened in November 1640, appears to have finally decided Hobbes.[18] Yet a stay in France was probably already planned, and was in large part a welcome resumption of a treasured friendship with Marin Mersenne at a point when Hobbes's main English

---

[13] A.P. Martinich, *Hobbes: a Biography* (Cambridge: Cambridge University Press, 1999). See Chapters 6 and 7, 'A Decade of Exile'.

[14] John Aubrey, *Brief Lives*, ed. Oliver Lawson Dick (London: Secker and Warburg, 1949), p. 51. On Maynwaring's fate, see Harry F. Snapp, 'The Impeachment of Roger Maynwaring', *Huntington Library Quarterly*, 30 (1967), 217–32, and Vivienne Larminie, 'Maynwaring, Roger (1589/90?–1653)', *ODNB*, online edn, Jan 2008 [http://www.oxforddnb.com/view/article/18011, accessed 1 Feb 2008].

[15] Hobbes, 'The Prose Life', in Thomas Hobbes, *Human Nature and De Corpore Politico*, ed. J.C.A. Gaskin (Oxford: Oxford University Press, 1994), p. 247; 'T. Hobbes malmesburiensis vita carmina expressa', in *Thomas Hobbes malmesburiensis opera philosophica quae latine scripsit omnia*, ed. William Molesworth, 5 vols (London: John Bohn, 1839), i, p. xv.

[16] Noel Malcolm, 'Hobbes, Thomas (1588–1679)', *ODNB*, online edn, Jan 2008 [http://www.oxforddnb.com/view/article/13400, accessed 15 Feb 2008].

[17] See Quentin Skinner, *Hobbes and Republican Liberty* (Cambridge: Cambridge University Press, 2008), pp. 86–8. I am particularly grateful to Professor Skinner for allowing me to read this book prior to its publication.

[18] Noel Malcolm, *Aspects of Hobbes* (Oxford: Oxford University Press, 2002), p. 16.

patron, the Earl of Newcastle, was preoccupied with affairs of state.[19] As Malcolm suggests, 'with Newcastle distracted by politics, the prospects of a period of quiet study in Newcastle's household had receded; Mersenne's Paris thus became the most natural and alluring alternative'.[20] Hobbes in 1640 is perhaps not best classed as a refugee.

Yet the situation, according to Hobbes at least, was worse 11 years later. In his Latin autobiographies he suggests that his departure from France in 1652 did not constitute the end of exile but was actually the response to a banishment that made him a stateless refugee. Criticized at the exiled Stuart court for maintaining positions in *Leviathan* that were allegedly contrary to royal interests, he found himself 'banished [prohibitus] from the King's household':

> Stripped of the King's protection [protectione regia destitutus], and fearing malicious attacks by Roman clerics whose teachings he had successfully attacked, he had little option other than to take refuge [coactus sit refugere] in England.[21]

Or, as he put it in his verse autobiography (in the English of the anonymous 1680 translation):

> When that Book [i.e., *Leviathan*] was perus'd by knowing Men,
> The Gates of *Janus* Temple opened then;
> And they accus'd me to the King, that I
> Seem'd to approve *Cromwel's* Impiety,
> And countenance the worst of Wickedness:
> This was believ'd, and I appear'd no less
> Than a Grand Enemy [adversis in partibus], so that I was for't
> Banish'd both the King's Presence and his Court
> [Perpetuo jubeor Regis abesse domo].
> Then I began on this to Ruminate
> On *Dorislaus*, and on *Ascham's* Fate,
> And stood amazed, like a poor Exile
> [Tanquam proscripto terror ubique aderat],
> Encompassed with Terrour all the while ...
> Then home I came, not sure of safety there,
> Though I cou'd not be safer any where.[22]

---

[19]   *Ibid.*, p. 16.

[20]   Malcolm, 'Hobbes, Thomas (1588–1679)'.

[21]   'The Prose Life', 249, 'T. Hobbes malmesburiensis vita', p. xvii.

[22]   Hobbes, 'The Verse Life', in *Human Nature*, ed. Gaskin, p. 260, and 'T. Hobbes malmesburiensis', p. xciii. See Gaskin, pp. xlix–l, for details of the translation. Faithful enough to Hobbes's Latin, there are nonetheless some important qualifications to be noted. The Latin translated as 'Grand Enemy' is 'adversis in partibus', and is rendered by Quentin Skinner as 'a member of the adverse party' (see his *Visions of Politics*, 3 vols [Cambridge: Cambridge University Press, 2002], iii, 22), which lacks the explicitly juridical connotations of the English. The English 'Banish'd' condenses a Latin phrase which translates more

Where Maynwaring's example had been the worrying precedent in 1640, now the fate of two representatives of the new Commonwealth, murdered abroad by royalist assassins, looms threateningly large. Here, Hobbes describes himself as akin to an exile not because he shifts abroad, but because he has been deprived of protection and rendered newly and starkly vulnerable. The Stuart court-in-exile is itself a little commonwealth, and once ordered to leave Hobbes has no choice but to seek safety wherever he could reasonably hope to find it.

Of course, this version of his return to England was written some years after the fact, and there is evidence to suggest that it is intended to excuse its author from the persistent accusation that he willingly abandoned the Stuart cause in the early 1650s. Edward Hyde, Earl of Clarendon, claimed not only that Hobbes wrote *Leviathan* to appease the English Republican authorities and thus facilitate his return, but that he confessed as much at the time.[23] Malcolm points to indications that, like the flight to France in 1640, this journey too was substantially premeditated and not a response to a sudden crisis.[24] Nevertheless, this identification of his own plight with that of the exile, and the indication that this might have an exculpatory function, points to the connection that could be drawn between Hobbes's personal circumstances or interests and his political theory. When Hobbes is seeking to justify his own conduct, we might reasonably expect him to do so in a manner that is consistent with the normative framework of his own thought. In which case, Hobbes's claim to have suffered the condition of the exile can only be made fully comprehensible in relation to the place of that condition in his civil science.

Exile is mentioned in each of the major works of political theory that Hobbes produced, and its handling is consistent across them. In *The Elements of Law*, the topic first arises at the end of Chapter XXI, at the point when Hobbes is completing his discussion of the kinds of commonwealth by institution, polities produced by a group of people through the consensual creation of a new civil state. Having considered 'how particular men enter into subjection', Hobbes says, 'it followeth to consider how such subjection may be discharged'.[25] One of the ways in which subjection as such may be dissolved is 'exile perpetual, [...] forasmuch as being out of the protection of the sovereignty that expelled him, [the exile] hath no means of subsisting but from himself' (*EL* XXI, 14, 125). Interestingly, this brief definition of exile is paired with another instance of dissolved subjection:

---

literally as 'ordered to depart forever from the King's household', which again perhaps lacks the judicial connotations of the 1680 version. And 'proscripto', here given as 'Exile', is more commonly translated as 'outlaw'. The English of the 1680 translation is not simply erroneous or misleading, however: there are perfectly good Hobbesian reasons for using such pregnant terms as 'enemy', 'banish'd' and 'exile', as this essay seeks to demonstrate.

[23]   Edward Hyde, Earl of Clarendon, *A Brief View and Survey of the Dangerous and Pernicious Errors to Church and State, In Mr. Hobbes's Book, Entitled Leviathan* (Oxford, 1676), p. 8.

[24]   Malcolm, *Aspects*, pp. 19–20.

[25]   Hobbes, *Human Nature*, ed. Gaskin, XXI, 14, 125. Hereafter *EL*; parenthetical references to chapter, paragraph and page number are included in the text.

'Likewise, a man is released of his subjection by conquest' (*EL* XXI, 14, 125). The situation of the exile and that of the conquered man are similar for Hobbes, but he says little here about the reasons for aligning them in this fashion. The issue arises again a few paragraphs later, though, in the following chapter's handling of 'dominion, or a body politic by acquisition' (*EL* XXII, 1, 126). Once again, exile is treated in conjunction with a handling of conquest. Hobbes here seeks to define the condition of the discharged servant, claiming specifically that 'servants [...] are discharged of their servitude or subjection in the same manner that subjects are released of their allegiance in a commonwealth institutive' (*EL* XXII, 7, 128). Unsurprisingly, exile is the same kind of forced release from subjection in this context as in its earlier appearance: 'no more but manumission given to a servant, not in the way of benefit, but punishment' (*EL* XXII, 7, 128). But again, some of the conditions that Hobbes then chooses to align with exile are noteworthy. He claims that 'new captivity' is equally a necessary end of prior bonds, before going on to argue that a servant who 'is no longer trusted, but committed to his chains and custody, is thereby discharged of the obligation *in foro interno*, and therefore if he can get loose, may lawfully go his way' (*EL* XXII, 7, 128–9).

In *The Elements of Law*, then, exile features as one of a number of related conditions in which the fundamental civil bond of subjection is cancelled: exiles are likened to those conquered by enemies and prisoners, all equally exposed and vulnerable to physical force, stripped of civil personality and the security it brings. In *De Cive*, a translation and development of part of *The Elements*, the mention of exile occurs again at the end of Hobbes's definition of the three kinds of commonwealth by institution and immediately prior to his account of 'dominion'. But now the implications of this account of discharged subjection are spelled out in greater detail, in tune with *De Cive*'s development of the important topic of liberty, and one significant modification is made.[26] Hobbes defines what happens when a commonwealth by institution is dissolved or conquered, and its civil bonds cancelled, before speaking of a different but relevant instance of such cancellation:

> All the citizens together retreat from civil subjection into the liberty of all men to all things, i.e. into natural liberty, which is the liberty of the beasts. (For the state of nature has the same relation to the civil state, i.e. liberty has the same relation to subjection, as desire has to reason or a beast to a Man.) But in addition, individual citizens may rightly be released from subjection by the will of him who holds sovereign power; namely if they go to live abroad. This can happen in two ways: either by permission, as when one gets leave and voluntarily departs to live elsewhere, or by command, as an *Exile*.[27]

---

[26]   Skinner, *Hobbes and Republican Liberty*, pp. 89–123.

[27]   Hobbes, *On the Citizen*, ed. and trans. by Richard Tuck and Michael Silverthorne (Cambridge: Cambridge University Press, 1998), VII, 18, 101. Hereafter *DC*; parenthetical references to chapter, paragraph and page number are included in the text.

So exile is associated here with those occasions on which natural liberty, the desiring, animal condition opposed to 'the civil state', reasserts itself. And while the name of exile applies only to those who have been banished, it is also related to the condition of someone who voluntarily seeks to live beyond the boundaries of the state in which s/he is a subject. In both cases this subjection comes undone, even if the mantle is immediately reassumed in the polity to which the exile goes.

In *Leviathan*, the picture is complicated a little further. Exile appears twice, first – tellingly – in Chapter XXI, 'Of the Liberty of Subjects', and then in more detail during the discussion of punishment in Chapter XXVIII. In the first case it once again features on a list of the ways in which subjection can be dissolved. Captivity in war, or conquest by an enemy, strips a person of their subjection, as does a sovereign's abdication. Hobbes then states that 'If the Soveraign Banish his Subject; during the Banishment, he is not Subject', here differentiating the exile from someone who 'is sent on a message, or hath leave to travel'.[28] These latter voyagers retain their subjection through a kind of exchange agreement between sovereigns; the former, entering 'anothers dominion', is immediately liable to subjection to the place's master. Then, in his discussion of punishment, Hobbes spells out the thinking condensed in his basic definitions of exile in *The Elements*, *De Cive*, and earlier in *Leviathan*:

> *Exile*, (Banishment) is when a man is for a crime, condemned to depart out of the dominion of the Common-wealth, or out of a certaine part thereof; and during a prefixed time, or for ever, not to return into it: and seemeth not in its own nature, without other circumstances, to be a Punishment; but rather an escape, or a publique commandement to avoid Punishment by flight. And *Cicero* sayes, there was never any such Punishment ordained in the City of *Rome*; but cals it a refuge of men in danger. For if a man banished, be neverthelesse permitted to enjoy his Goods, and the Revenue of his Lands, the meer change of ayr is no Punishment; nor does it tend to that benefit of the Common-wealth, for which all Punishments are ordained, (that is to say, to the forming of mens wils to the observation of the Law;) but many times to the dammage of the Common-wealth. For a Banished man, is a lawfull enemy of the Common-wealth that banished him; as being no more a member of the same. But if he be withal deprived of his Lands, or Goods, then the Punishment lyeth not in the Exile, but is to be reckoned amongst Punishments pecuniary. (*L*, XXVIII, 218)

Here, then, the implications of living beyond the dissolution of one's subjection are clarified. Hobbes aligns himself with one side of a long debate in asserting that exile itself is not a punishment, because punishment happens to those subject to the civil law, whereas exiles exist beyond that law. With Cicero, Hobbes avers that exile may also be an escape from punishment, or a refuge from danger.[29] Crucially,

---

[28] Hobbes, *Leviathan*, ed. Richard Tuck (Cambridge: Cambridge University Press, 1991), p. 154. Hereafter *L*; chapter and page references are given parenthetically in the text.

[29] See Agamben, *Homo Sacer*, p. 110.

too, exile makes an enemy of someone who had been a subject, and is therefore contrary to the aim of punishment.

Given this, it is perhaps unsurprising that Hobbes then goes on to describe in detail the condition of enmity itself, in which violence may legitimately be done to someone without recourse to the processes of positive law. Against its enemies, the state may act with apparently vindictive savagery, and in doing so acts entirely in accord with natural law. Such enemies include 'Subjects, who deliberatly deny the Authority of the Common-wealth established', or rebels:

> the nature of this offence, consisteth in the renouncing of subjection; which is a relapse into the condition of warre, commonly called Rebellion; and they that so offend, suffer not as Subjects, but as Enemies. For *Rebellion*, is but warre renewed. (*L*, XXVIII, 219)

As a result of the subject's or the sovereign's actions, then, an instance of the war of all against all appears as a localized enmity. The state may kill rebels or traitors without reference to law, as the enemy is legally visible only as someone beyond its pale; consequently, the apparently juridical status of the exile and the traitor, and the apparently juridical violence to which they are exposed, are in fact not properly juridical at all. As Hobbes says, 'Harme inflicted upon one that is a declared enemy, fals not under the name of Punishment':

> If a subject shall by fact, or word, wittingly, and deliberately deny the authority of the Representative of the Common-wealth, (whatsoever penalty hath been formerly ordained for Treason,) he may lawfully be made to suffer whatsoever the Representative will: For in denying subjection, he denies such Punishment as by the Law hath been ordained; and therefore suffers as an enemy of the Commonwealth; that is, according to the will of the Representative. For the Punishments set down in the Law, are to Subjects, not to Enemies; such as are they, that having been by their own act Subjects, deliberately revolting, deny the Soveraign Power. (*L*, XXVIII, 216)

This is a modification of the position that Hobbes sets out in different terms in Chapter XIV of *De Cive*, where the crime of *lèse-majesté* is defined as a transgression of natural rather than civil law, but '*rebels*, *traitors* and others convicted of *treason*' are nonetheless said to be 'punished not by *civil right*, but by *natural right*, i.e. not as *bad citizens* but as *enemies of the commonwealth*, and not by the *right of government* or dominion, but by the *right of war*' (*DC*, XIV, 165–6). Here, punishment is still the appropriate name for this violence. And in Chapter XXVII of *Leviathan*, the same crime is said to be against fundamental law, itself earlier defined as a subdivision of civil rather than natural law; presumably then, on this basis, the violence inflicted would be a kind of punishment (*L*, XXVI, 199–200, XXVII, 212). Later, in *A Dialogue between a Philosopher and a Student, of the Common Laws of England*, Hobbes argues forcefully against the opinion expressed by Edward Coke in his *Institutes* that the traitor and the enemy are fundamentally distinct. Coke deduced a fundamental difference in legal status for foreign and domestic enemies from the difference in treatment that would be meted out to them if they were captured together. Foreign enemies cannot be proceeded against as traitors; conversely, a domestic enemy in league with a foreign army would not be ransomed.[30] Hobbes, though, complaining that 'Sir *Edw*. Coke does seldom well distinguish when there are two divers Names for one and the same thing', reiterates his account of treason as a form of enmity.[31] He insists that a king may 'Lawfully […] kill a Man, by what Death soever without an Indictment, when it is manifestly proved he was his open Enemy'.[32] The 'law' with which this course of action is compatible is therefore specifically not a civil law. As Hobbes argues:

> For the Nature of Treason by Rebellion; is it not a return to Hostility? What else does Rebellion signifie? *William* the Conqueror Subdued this Kingdom; some he Killed; some upon promise of future obedience he took to Mercy, and they became his Subjects, and swore Allegiance to him; if therefore they renew the War against him, are they not again open Enemies; or if any of them lurking under his Laws, seek occasion thereby to kill him, secretly, and come to be known, may he not be proceeded against as an enemy, who though he had not Committed what he Design'd, yet had certainly a Hostile Design.[33]

The differences between these accounts of the precise juridical status of the traitor perhaps derive from the fact that treason is a specific kind of enmity, based on the renunciation of the basic political relation, the contract on which the state and its juridical capacity was founded. A subject cannot renounce subjection and remain liable to treatment according to judicial proceedings, but this path to enmity does make treason a distinctive hostility. The traitor is marked by the after-image of subjection, and thus hovers on the borders of the law as an ex-subject, his deprivation a chief element in his visibility. And the exile, as someone literally removed from the compass of the law, shares in this peculiar post-civil status. When Hobbes describes himself in his verse autobiography as appearing to be an adversary, 'adversis in partibus', to Charles II in 1651, he might be suggesting that he was merely perceived as an opponent in an informal sense. The more resonant words of his translator, which describe how he was perceived as 'no less/Than a Grand Enemy', are more accurately reflective of the categories of political status set out in his philosophy. The banishment he then suffers confirms, as much as it responds to, this apparent enmity: the exile and the traitor are both names for those who have outlived their subjection.

---

[30]   Edward Coke, *The Third Part of the Institutes of the Laws of England* (London, 1644), p. 11.

[31]   Hobbes, *A Dialogue Between a Philosopher and a Student, of the Common Laws of England*, in *Writings on Common Law and Hereditary Right*, ed. Alan Cromartie and Quentin Skinner (Oxford: Clarendon Press, 2005), p. 73.

[32]   Hobbes, *A Dialogue*, p. 72.

[33]   *Ibid.*, p. 73.

At the same time, it is worth pausing to note the nature of the example for which Hobbes reaches when looking to illustrate the basis for his understanding of treason in *A Dialogue*. The primal scene to which treason reverts here is not the state of nature as such, or a war of all against all; it is instead a scene of conquest. In fact, the Hobbesian account of exile and enmity often presupposes the balance – or rather, imbalance – of forces that such a scene implies. Within such circumstances, the enemy in question is defeated and captive; the outsider or exile is confronted not with a wilderness but a powerful potential sovereign. Persistently seeing these figures in this context not only shapes Hobbes's sense of their status; it also witnesses to the kinds of exigency that made their status more than a theoretical matter for him.

III

At the time of *Leviathan*'s completion and publication, the kind of dubious or shadowy quasi-subject represented by the vulnerable exile or defeated enemy was a particularly urgent locus of political concern. As a number of historians of political thought and writing have argued in the last four decades, Hobbes's third version of his civil science can be read illuminatingly in the context of the Commonwealth's demand that its citizens take an oath promising to obey England's republican regime.[34] That demand made a pressing issue of both the nature of political obligation and the ways in which a change of obligation might be justified, and it has been convincingly suggested that Hobbesian texts and arguments were influential in, and influenced by, the political controversy that followed. Hobbes's potentially dry discussion of the basis and limits of subjection becomes, in this context, of immediate relevance to those disputing whether or not the subjects of the executed king can rightly transfer their allegiance to the regime that has succeeded him. Not, of course, that all those ex-subjects are exiles, exactly, but insofar as their subjection is now in question they are in an analogous position: their sovereign has lost his power to protect them, and some have been vanquished in war. In which case, Hobbes famously says, they may be absolved of

---

[34]   While much has been written in support of this claim, it has not gone unchallenged. For the flavour of all sides to the issue see John Wallace, *Destiny His Choice: The Loyalism of Andrew Marvell* (Cambridge: Cambridge University Press, 1968); Quentin Skinner, 'The Context of Hobbes's Theory of Political Obligation', and 'Conquest and Consent: Hobbes and the Engagement Controversy', in *Visions of Politics*, iii, 264–86, 287–307; Glenn Burgess, 'Usurpation, Obligation and Obedience in the Thought of the Engagement Controversy', *Historical Journal*, 29 (1986), 515–36; Burgess, 'Contexts for the Writing and Publication of Hobbes's *Leviathan*', *History of Political Thought*, 11 (1990), 675–702; Martinich, *Hobbes*, pp. 216–53; Conal Condren, *Argument and Authority in Early Modern England: The Presupposition of Oaths and Offices* (Cambridge: Cambridge University Press, 2006), pp. 290–314; and Jeffrey Collins, *The Allegiance of Thomas Hobbes* (Oxford: Oxford University Press, 2005), pp. 1–10, 115–59.

their allegiance, and therefore of the obligation to obey that constitutes it, because 'the Obligation of Subjects to the Soveraign, is understood to last as long, and no longer, than the power lasteth, by which he is able to protect them' (*L*, XXI, 153). Sovereignty is intended to be immortal, but for Hobbes it is always a matter of capacity or power as well as title, in which case, 'in its own nature [it is] not only subject to violent death, by forreign war; but also through the ignorance, and passions of men, it hath in it, from the very institution, many seeds of a naturall mortality, by Intestine Discord' (*L*, XXI, 153). So if sovereignty is mortal, and dies with its power to protect those who established it, then subjection too dissolves at the point when subjects find themselves without recourse to the protective power of their state.

The question animating the Engagement debate then arises: what ought those who have lost their sovereign to do? In his accounts of dominion and a commonwealth by acquisition Hobbes offers a picture that is particularly pertinent to the early 1650s; indeed, its pertinence is highlighted in the 'Review and Conclusion' appended to *Leviathan*, and this applicability seems particularly to have riled his royalist enemies: Clarendon described it as 'a sly address to *Cromwell*', and suggested that Hobbes was thereby seeking to 'secure the People of the Kingdom [...] to acquiesce and submit to his Brutal Power'.[35] The essentials of Hobbes's view, though, are there in the *Elements of Law* – indeed, it was this text that Marchamont Nedham directly cited in *Mercurius Politicus* and in the second edition of his *Case of the Commonwealth of England, Stated*, to reinforce his arguments in favour of obedience to the republic.[36] In Chapter XXII, Hobbes argues that 'a servant taken in the wars' and kept in chains owes nothing to his new master: he is a slave, owned by 'right of conquest', but in no way obliged to obey his conqueror (*EL*, XXII, 3, 127; 9, 129). However, servants who are permitted to move around are tied to their new masters by 'no other bond but a supposed covenant' (*EL*, XXII, 3, 127). They are therefore parties to an engagement of sorts, and while they continue to be their master's property, they are nevertheless more than slaves.

This distinction between those servants who are merely physically bound and those who are subjects through a covenant of sorts carries through to *De Cive*. Hobbes expands on its implications in a parallel chapter of his Latin treatise where the process of constituting a commonwealth by acquisition is properly delineated. A person enters into this version of the political relation 'if, on being captured or defeated in war or losing hope in one's own strength, one makes (to avoid death) a promise to the victor or the stronger party, to *serve* him, i.e. to do all that he shall command' (*DC*, VIII, 1, 102–3). But some of the defeated fare differently. Not all captives are trusted to be set free from their bonds and make a promise, and if not they do not become obliged to obey their master: 'for an obligation arises

---

[35]   Clarendon, *Brief View*, p. 317.

[36]   Marchamont Nedham, *The Case of the Commonwealth of England, Stated*, ed. Philip Knachel (Charlottesville: University Press of Virginia, 1969); Skinner, *Visions of Politics*, iii, 279–81.

from an agreement, and there is no agreement without trust' (*DC*, VIII, 3, 103). In *Leviathan*, this point is even more sharply stressed. Now, the emphasis is less on trust and much more firmly on the covenant. Hobbes distinguishes between the vanquished and the conquered: the former are merely defeated in war, and therefore in another's power, whereas the latter are those among the defeated who have consented to obey their vanquisher in return for life and protection:

> It is not therefore the Victory, that giveth the right of Dominion over the Vanquished, but his own Covenant. Nor is he obliged because he is conquered; that is to say, beaten, and taken, or put to flight; but because he commeth in, and Submitteth to the Victor. (*L*, XX, 141)

Here, emphatically, Hobbes argues that the consent of an agreement or covenant underpins subjection.

In all these accounts of the commonwealth by acquisition, then, Hobbes places an emphasis on a fundamental political relation – juridical, in Foucault's extended sense – that is an alternative to the sheer power that a victor possesses over those he has beaten. This is not, of course, the social contract of the commonwealth by institution, because it is a covenant between the sovereign and his subjects; nonetheless, it is enough to establish the conquered as subjects, with a subject's liability to all the obligations and sanctions that come with participation in the polity. In setting consent at the heart of the process he is also bringing his account of dominion into line with contract theory. This emphasis on the covenant within dominion is also relevant to the Engagement debate, where what was being demanded was precisely an explicit promise of obedience to a new sovereign power. Interestingly, though, Hobbes's account of how consent is given is developed in the 'Review and Conclusion' in a direction that clearly undermines the significance of a specific verbal promise or act of agreement. There he argues that consent can be tacit, and might therefore be signalled merely by living openly under the protection of a power (*L*, 'Review and Conclusion', 485).

In fact, the centrality of consent to the process of becoming a subject is compromised more profoundly. From the evidence adduced above, those who live on beyond the dissolution of their polity, or beyond the meaningful continuance of their own bonds to a sovereign, are thereby absolved of their status as subjects. Seemingly, therefore, they are completely without any of the marks of civil subjection until such time as they contract, tacitly or expressly, with the dominating power. They are returned to the state of nature, and are presumably open to the obligations of the laws of nature that Hobbes sets out in describing the transition to the commonwealth by institution, obligations that are themselves other than the duties or responsibilities of a subject and are binding only *in foro interno*, 'to a desire they should take place' (*L*, XV, 110). But this sense of the circumstances faced by the vanquished, or those deprived of their sovereign in war, neglects their specificity. This is not a general return to the state of nature: it is, of course, the experience of a vulnerability to an existing power, and any account of the duties incumbent on the vulnerable here should take its bearings from Hobbes's views on the nature of dominion.[37] The consent of agreement or covenant, as we have seen, would seem to be vital, and Hobbes's distinction in *Leviathan* between the vanquished and the conquered would make no sense if it were not; but as Kinch Hoekstra has demonstrated, Hobbes also appears to override this requirement elsewhere in his account of dominion, leading his contemporaries to argue that he derived an obligation for people to obey a power, to become its subjects, merely from the fact of their cringing before its might. Hoekstra suggests that, 'in passage after passage' from *The Elements of Law*, *De Cive* and *Leviathan*, 'Hobbes subscribes to some version of the thesis that sufficient power by itself confers the right to rule'.[38] The implication of this, given Hobbes's consistent claim that the rights of the sovereign and the duties of subjects are reciprocal, is that a power can make its objects subjects against their will, or rather, without their consent. This would suggest that the distinction between the vanquished and the conquered, slaves and servants, those held in chains and those trusted, is in danger of collapsing. Certainly, when Hobbes says in *The Elements* and *De Cive* that a master has 'right' and 'dominion' over both his prisoners and his servants we might wonder what these terms mean, since they apply to possession regardless of the existence of any covenant (*EL*, XXII, 4, 127; *DC*, VIII, 5, 104). This might be thought to make Hobbes at this point a remorselessly *de facto* thinker, grounding right in power, and completely contradicting his emphasis on the fundamental constitutive role of agreement or covenant.

According to Hoekstra, resolving this problem requires attention to two features of Hobbes's thinking. First, there is a crucial distinction between the way in which 'right' applies in the absence of a commonwealth and its functioning within one. Only in the latter case does right entail obligation; in the former, everyone has a right over everyone else, and if one person is able to get another into his power he has merely managed to actualize a right that already existed.[39] The victor's right over the vanquished, therefore, is only the making concrete of an entitlement that everyone in a condition of hostility has over potential opponents. The slave thus kept in chains is an unwilling party to this actualization, and in no sense the subject of a corresponding obligation to obey his 'rightful' master. Yet Hobbes does also seem to suggest that rights entailing obligations can arise from power, and not only where the power in question is divine. This is more than a right of nature, since it involves an obligation to obey on the part of the powerless. How, then, is this reconciled with the requirement for consent?

Hoekstra's answer sees Hobbes building on the notion of a consent given tacitly, a conception that already ensures that 'consent is sometimes stretched vanishingly thin'. Beyond this, Hoekstra argues, we find an argument that 'the covenant of

---

[37]   See Kinch Hoekstra, 'The *de facto* Turn in Hobbes's Political Philosophy', in *Leviathan After 350 Years*, ed. Tom Sorell and Luc Foisneau (Oxford: Oxford University Press, 2004), pp. 33–73, esp. p. 46.

[38]   Hoekstra, 'The *de facto* Turn', p. 62.

[39]   *Ibid.*, pp. 64–5.

obedience [...] can instead be *attributed* when a given will or intention can be understood or assumed'.[40] Assuming that humans will do what is in their own best interests, we can further assume that they will consent to obey an overwhelming power rather than risk their lives in contesting it. The laws of nature would suggest that they ought to consent to do so; according to Hoekstra, Hobbes ends up arguing that 'one *has* consented when one *ought* to have consented', and thus a normative requirement becomes an assumed social fact.[41] Such an intervention into the debate around the Engagement oath would not necessarily persuade anyone of an obligation to take it; rather, it would circumvent debate in pointing out the superfluity of any such explicit consent-giving. And such a doctrine would also emphasize the nature and extent of the exile's quasi-subjecthood: to be free of one power, and to encounter another, would not leave exiles suspended in a state of natural right before their consent is signalled in words or deeds. Instead, their subjection – their constitution as participants in a juridical network of reciprocal obligations and entitlements – would always be immanent in any situation in which they confronted a power capable of killing them that nonetheless offers them an alternative. The limit cases of the exile and the conquered make it abundantly clear that the subjection that appeared to depend on the exercised will of a rational agent, consciously choosing to step into the civility announced by agreement or contract, arises more basically from the physical vulnerability of the living – mortal – human. If the ex-subject appears primarily as the absence of civil status, then the subject is itself stalked by the bare humanity that generates civil status.

So it is perhaps not surprising to find Hoekstra setting out the ultimate implication of Hobbes's line of argument in the claim that 'all of the living have consented to the power over them, if there is one'.[42] The individual without proximity to a superior power is not, though, the exception to this rule that Hoekstra has in mind: 'the only people free of obligation to the present power are the dead (and slaves in shackles)'.[43] These parenthetical latter have not consented, and cannot be assumed to have consented, because they have not been offered life and protection by the victorious foe. No possible agreement has been put to them. They are instead frozen or suspended in the exilic vulnerability on which the possibility of politics depends, but out of which it spins the very different condition of civility. Confined captives are to be grouped with the dead, free of obligation only and exactly to the extent that their natural powers are blocked, condemned to live a life-beyond-life, as those who are always about to die. Exiles are haunted both by their lost subjection and, as Arendt remarked, by the possibility – however momentary – that they will not find a new commonwealth in which they can become subjects once again.

---

[40] *Ibid.*, p. 67.
[41] *Ibid.*, p. 69.
[42] *Ibid.*, p. 68.
[43] *Ibid.*, p. 68.

IV

The language of obligation, though, is not the only lens through which Hobbes perceives the predicament of the exile, and it is not the only way in which this figure presents a potentially difficult image of political and natural life. Elsewhere in his work, instead of speaking of an obligation to obey – assumed or otherwise, normative or contractual – Hobbes describes the situation of the vulnerable in the following terms:

> If a Subject be taken prisoner in war; or his person, or his means of life be within the Guards of the enemy, and hath his life and corporall Libertie given him, on condition to be Subject to the Victor, he hath Libertie to accept the condition; and having accepted it, is the subject of him that took him. (*L*, XXI, 154)

In the 'Review and Conclusion', as part of his effort to clarify 'in what point of time it is, that a Subject becomes obliged to the Conqueror', he refers back to this element in his argument and resorts to the same terms:

> Therefore for farther satisfaction of men therein, I say, the point of time, wherein a man becomes subject to the Conqueror, is that point, wherein having liberty to submit to him, he consenteth, either by expresse words, or by other sufficient sign, to be his Subject. When it is that a man hath the liberty to submit, I have shewed before in the end of the 21. Chapter. (*L*, 'Review and Conclusion', 484)

For the Hobbes of *Leviathan*, then, the ex-subject is at *liberty* to consent to the rule of the power confronting him, and this emphasis makes a vigorously renewed appearance in later, more autobiographical writings. Responding to John Wallis, in a 'letter' published in 1662, Hobbes sought to refute accusations that he betrayed his king in returning from France to England and submitting to the post-regicide regime.[44] His defence invoked the account of political obligation and its limits that he had crafted in his treatises, with a particular focus on *Leviathan* since that was the text his critics suggested had been written primarily to justify his coat-turning. Hobbes counter-attacks by arguing that his political theory actually condemns those such as Wallis who had abandoned their obligation to obey Charles I, even when the king still had the capacity to protect them. Speaking of his own situation, he repeatedly insists that he was free of any obligation to the Stuarts when he returned to England. He suggests, tellingly, that having 'gone over' into French exile, he had then 'been driven back again'.[45] He also implicitly aligns his own case with that of the king's loyal servants, who, 'having done their utmost endeavour to defend His Majesties Right and Person against the Rebels', were subsequently 'forced to compound with your Masters, and to promise Obedience for the saving of their Lives and Fortunes'.[46]

---

[44]   Thomas Hobbes, *Mr Hobbes Considered in his Loyalty, Religion, Reputation, and Manners, by Way of Letter to Dr Wallis* (London, 1662).

[45]   *Ibid.*, p. 12.

[46]   *Ibid.*, pp. 19–20.

The nature of the force here is unclear; Hobbes, though, follows this with a categorical statement in their (and his) defence:

> They that had done their utmost endeavour to perform their obligation to the King, had done all that they could be obliged unto; and were consequently at liberty to seek the safety of their Lives and Livelihood wheresoever, and without Treachery.[47]

Citing his own words from the 'Review and Conclusion' to *Leviathan*, Hobbes repeatedly insists on this 'liberty' – seven times in five pages.[48]

What, then, is this liberty of the ex-subject or exile? Liberty, as a significant body of recent research has shown, is an important and heavily freighted term for Hobbes, yet views on its meaning and place in his thinking remain various.[49] For Philip Pettit, the Hobbesian vision of liberty is bipartite, divided between 'non-obligation' on the one hand, and 'non-obstruction' on the other. Liberty in the former sense characterizes the condition of those who are not bound by agreements to perform or refrain from certain actions, and Pettit suggests, following Annabel Brett, that here Hobbes's usage converges on the late-Scholastic and post-Scholastic definition of 'natural liberty'.[50] Natural liberty, in this account, is the freedom we possess when we are not yet bound by the kind of covenant that establishes society: in the state of nature, therefore, we are not yet obliged to anyone, and fully in possession of our liberty. Pettit claims that this kind of liberty is described by Hobbes in *Leviathan* as natural right. It therefore denotes both a fundamental entitlement and, negatively, an absence of obligations as social facts, rather than as normative, *in foro interno* requirements.[51] Liberty as non-obstruction, by contrast, is a freedom from external impediments to the full exercise of our corporeal will and capacities. Whether or not we possess this kind of liberty is apparently a matter of natural or physical fact: a river constrained by banks or channels is denied the liberty to go where its powers would take it, and the liberty possessed by humans is fundamentally of the same kind (*L*, XXI, 145–6). For the Hobbes of *Leviathan* this kind of liberty is identified as 'Liberty in the proper sense', or 'the proper signification of the word' (*L*, XXI, 147; XIV, 91).

In his account of the development of Hobbes's thinking on freedom, Quentin Skinner has disputed the claim that natural liberty for Hobbes is fundamentally

---

[47]   *Ibid.*, p. 20.

[48]   *Ibid.*, pp. 20–24.

[49]   Quentin Skinner, 'Hobbes on the Proper Signification of Liberty', in *Visions of Politics*, iii, 209–37; Skinner, *Hobbes and Republican Liberty*; M.M. Goldsmith, 'Hobbes on Liberty', *Hobbes Studies*, 2 (1989), 23–39; Annabel Brett, *Liberty, Right and Nature: Individual Rights in Later Scholastic Thought* (Cambridge: Cambridge University Press, 1997); David van Mill, *Liberty, Rationality and Agency in Hobbes's* Leviathan (Albany: State University of New York Press, 2001); Philip Pettit, 'Liberty and Leviathan', *Politics, Philosophy and Economics*, 4 (2005), 131–51.

[50]   Pettit, 'Liberty and Leviathan', 137.

[51]   *Ibid.*, 137, 141.

a concept of non-obligation.[52] He suggests instead that Hobbes's view of natural right, and indeed of liberty more generally, is multifaceted, encompassing the juridical language of entitlements, the negative theory of freedom from obligations, and a sensitivity to the extent of and impediments to an agent's powers to act. The primary significance of Hobbes's accounts of liberty lies in their attempts to resignify the term in the face of his opponents' political rhetoric. Such attempts reach a climax in Chapter XXI of *Leviathan*, where Hobbes takes it upon himself to recast the potent republican or neo-Roman notion of the 'free-man' in his own terms. In asserting that the subjects of the Leviathan are as free as the citizens of a republic, Hobbes draws on all aspects of his definition of liberty to make his case. He insists that '*A* FREE-MAN, *is he, that in those things, which by his strength and wit he is able to do, is not hindred to doe what he has a will to*' (*L*, XXI, 146). In demonstrating that this is true of the Hobbesian subject and the republican citizen alike, he invokes his account of liberty in its 'proper sense', as 'corporall Liberty; that is to say, freedome from chains, and prison', as well as the suggestion that the subject has authorized the laws to which he is subject, and is therefore to an important degree his own governor (*L*, XXI, 147–8). He also defines the liberties of the subject in what Skinner calls the 'purely juridical terms' of inalienable rights and limits to obligation: since people contracted with each other or the commonwealth in order to protect themselves, and they are obliged to it only for as long as it can fulfil this end, they remain in full possession of their natural rights or 'true Liberty' to refuse a command wherever obedience would contradict it (*L*, XXI, 150).[53]

The disagreement between Skinner's and Pettit's views on liberty in Hobbes is perhaps best explained as that between a primarily expository and a primarily analytical account. Seeking to separate out the main strands making up Hobbes's usage of the term, however, Pettit draws on an analytical distinction of Skinner's own making: 'obstruction represents loss of liberty in "the sphere of nature"; obligation the loss of liberty in "the sphere of artifice"'.[54] The sphere of nature would appear from this to be the physical realm of bodies in motion, while that of artifice would seem to be the world of rights, agreements and obligations. If this is the case, though, the liberty of the subject in the sphere of artifice is primarily a matter of natural fact, what Hobbes actually calls in *Leviathan* 'natural liberty' (*L*, XXI, 147), while freedom in the sphere of nature is principally a juridical status, precisely the plenitudinous possession of a 'natural right' that survives residually for every subject after covenants have been made. It is worth noting, in this connection, that the chapter that aims to set out the Hobbesian account of the liberty of the subject is also that in which the fullest account of 'corporall' or physical liberty is to be found. The theory of human liberty in Hobbes would on this evidence appear to be somewhat convoluted: not confused, in the sense of

---

[52] Skinner, *Hobbes and Republican Liberty*, p. 35.

[53] *Ibid.*, p. 166.

[54] Pettit, 'Liberty and Leviathan', 140–41, drawing on Skinner, *Visions of Politics*, iii, 225. Skinner returns to the distinction in *Hobbes and Republican Liberty*, pp. 162–3, 170–71.

logically discontinuous or incoherent, but precisely – as Arendt claimed of the modern conception of human and civil rights – perplexed.

The liberty of the exile or ex-subject of which Hobbes so insistently speaks is itself an instance of this, and it restates the interpenetrations of physical and juridical, natural and civil (these only insecure oppositions, as should be evident by now, are not synonymous) that have been noted in earlier sections of this essay. The passage from Chapter XXI of Leviathan cited above mobilizes the distinction between liberty as non-obligation and as non-obstruction to make its point: if life and 'corporall Libertie' are given to an ex-subject by a power with which he is confronted in return for his subjection to this power, then 'he hath Libertie to accept the condition' (L, XXI, 154). This can best make sense if the latter kind of liberty is not here synonymous with the former, if indeed it is precisely the freedom of those who have been released from their prior obligations to take up new ones and become, in so doing, someone else's subject. By the same token, only if this kind of liberty is at least partly a freedom from obligation can its invocation by Hobbes in his own defence actually serve to refute his accusers. All people free to move around and act according to their wills retain the physical liberty to break the law, as Hobbes suggests (L, XXI, 146), and both Skinner and Pettit have pointed out;[55] yet when he insists against Wallis that he and other royalists were at liberty to submit to their conquerors, he must be making a juridical claim. Anything else would not cut the exculpatory mustard. Stripped of the status of subject, the natural human revealed is only more insistently the focus for a language of liberty-as-right. Yet this liberty is also a mark of their vulnerability, the risk that their freedom to exercise their powers will be abruptly curtailed by confinement or death.

Equally significant, however, is the way in which this liberty is generated through the projection of subjects into a post-civil state. These humans are therefore testament to a temporality of subjection, a difference between before and after, that is itself a transition across the conceptual boundaries between natural and civil, physical and juridical; their identities bear the marks of these differences and of this temporality, allowing Hobbes's readers to see this as a narrative of political metamorphosis in which conceptual oppositions and relations can be explored. And insofar as these oppositions are convoluted, then those identified by them appear to perplex the philosophical project of which they are a part. In this way exiles, like other ex-subjects, are a defining case for the intelligibility and applicability of political and juridical categories, and their value as such a case depends on their being deprived of the less obviously fraught or ambiguous political identity conferred by membership of the commonwealth. Exposed in this way, humanly at risk, the stakes of any commonwealth appear in the starkest possible form. From this perspective the Hobbesian exile animates, however fleetingly, a problem of political definition that can certainly claim affinity with modern and contemporary worries about the relationship between the citizen and the outsider.

---

[55] Skinner, *Hobbes and Republican Liberty*, pp. 158–60, 170–73; Pettit, 'Liberty and Leviathan', 144–5.

Chapter 9
'A poor exile stranger': William Goffe in New England

Philip Major

I

If, as the essays in this volume have argued, the English Revolution had a pronounced and hitherto underappreciated European dimension, its aftermath had equally far-reaching and neglected ramifications in North America. Any genuine reassessment of the Revolution's chronology and geography, any full reconfiguration of the space of political exile in this period, should look to acknowledge them. In this respect, the experiences and writings of William Goffe are of uncommon interest. Goffe, and his father-in-law, Edward Whalley, were Major-Generals during Cromwell's experiment with military rule in the mid-1650s. They were also, more seminally, members of a select group of onetime parliamentarians which was to be conspicuously excluded from the king's mercy in the Bill of Indemnity and Oblivion signed on 29 August 1660: the regicides, signatories to the death warrant of Charles I in January 1649.[1] This chapter turns the microscope of history and literary analysis on Goffe's consequent exile in New England, for which he sailed (with Whalley) from Gravesend on 12 May 1660.

In America, the legacy of the regicide exiles is substantial and secure. Most significantly, their story of resistance to monarchy was latched onto by supporters of American Independence in the 1780s and 1790s; Ezra Stiles, the first president of Yale, used his book *A History of the Three Judges of King Charles I* (1793) as the basis for a partisan and influential defence of nascent American democracy and of tyrannicide. To this day, there is an intersection in New Haven, Connecticut, bearing the names of Goffe and Whalley, along with that of John Dixwell, another regicide fugitive, and the subject of the final essay in this collection, by Jason Peacey. In Britain, sustained examination of the regicide exiles in America has been conspicuous by its absence. Nonetheless, Goffe's life in New England affords us the opportunity, as I have indicated, to see beyond the Revolution's English and continental European theatres; it also assists us in developing still further some of the key exilic themes pervading this book: the choice of the place of refuge; the

---

[1]   12 Car. c.11, *Statutes of the Realm*, 2nd edn, 12 vols (London, 1963), v, 231–2; *JHC*, viii, 85. As well as the regicides already mentioned, three public servants who were excepted from the Bill consequently fled into and died in exile: Andrew Broughton, John Phelps, and Edward Dendy. See *ODNB*.

sustaining role of religion; the impact of exile on the family; the response of the host community; and the attitudes of the exile to the motherland.

The bare facts of this story are explicable enough. Goffe's and Whalley's exiles were long and drawn out: neither man was to see England, or his family, again. Landing more than 10 weeks later at Boston, they first moved on to Cambridge, then, in 1661, to New Haven, Connecticut, at one point reportedly hiding in a cave for a month, or, according to probably more exaggerated accounts, three years. They settled in remote Hadley, Massachusetts, in 1664, where they were housed secretly in the Reverend John Russell's house, Whalley dying there in 1674 and Goffe five years later. For a short time they were joined by Dixwell.

There are, however, more complex issues surrounding their exile which merit and require closer analysis. The first concerns location – the reasons why Goffe and Whalley chose New England as their place of refuge. Security, clearly, was of prime concern: the possibility of detection in the vastness of far-away New England, with its limitless potential for further penetration inland, doubtless appeared considerably more remote than, for instance, in small and nearby Holland. There, the arrest (and subsequent execution in London) in 1662 of three other regicides – John Barkstead, Miles Corbet and John Oakey – was soon to vindicate this line of reasoning.

Security was also a factor, and probably the deciding one, in Goffe's leaving England for Massachusetts without his wife, Frances, and their three children, Anne, Elizabeth and Frances. Travelling, and then living in exile, with just the one other male companion (Whalley) would clearly draw less attention from would-be Crown informers. Again, subsequent events – i.e., the fact that both Goffe and Whalley were able to survive undetected by government officials for nearly two decades – seem to have justified this strategy. Relatedly, that Frances was never to join her husband in New England indicates that up until the 1670s they considered a reconciliation between them to be a seriously compromising undertaking, strongly implying that government spies were still, years into the Restoration, looking to detect and apprehend the regicides in New England.[2] Goffe's and Whalley's eschatological outlook was another, complementary influence here, providing the other-worldly perspective which allowed for a long, perhaps final separation on this earth to be accepted with equanimity. For all his longing to be reunited with his wife, Goffe could reflect earnestly that 'These are dying times, wherein the Lord hath been and is breaking down what he hath built, and plucking up what he hath planted, and therefore it is not a time to be seeking great things for ourselves.'[3]

Intertwined with the immediate question of safety, and the two exiles' millenarian religious outlook, was another important consideration: the reputation New England, and Massachusetts in particular, had firmly established – indeed, its *raison d'etre* – as a haven for those in England seeking religious liberty, a subject which has attracted

---

[2]   As Jason Peacey shows in Chapter 10, this volume, Dixwell remained incognito for even longer, i.e., until 1690.

[3]   *Thomas Hutchinson Papers*, 3 vols (London: Print Society, 1865), iii, 186.

an enormous amount of critical attention.[4] Not all of those in the first great wave of emigrants to the New World in the 1620s and 1630s – for example, those seeking the economic gain offered by The Virginia Company – were nonconformist émigrés.[5] However, the many that *were* in that bracket – and it has been estimated that 21,000 Englishmen and women chose a new life in New England in the 1630s, the majority of them settling in Massachusetts[6] – had attempted to build, in John Winthrop's celebrated phrase, a 'City on a Hill'. For puritans like Goffe and Whalley, looking west from Old England, this community was a saving remnant keeping alive a puritan theocracy that had collapsed on their side of the Atlantic.

Goffe and Whalley would also have appreciated that the religious sympathies of New England had translated into strong and active support for the republican regimes of the civil wars and Interregnum, so that the signal part they had both played in the execution of the king was more likely to win favour from, rather than appal, their prospective hosts. New England ministers like John Cotton and John Wheelwright had been regular and influential friends and correspondents with Cromwell, with whom they shared millenarian views, and who as Protector treated New England with particular sympathy, allowing Massachusetts, for example, to produce its own currency. John Endicott, Governor of Massachusetts, who was to play an important role in securing the exiles' safety, referred tellingly to an annual statement of solidarity with Cromwell, issued by colonial leaders as 'an anniversary acknowledgement of our obligation'.[7]

If exile were to be their only expedient in the unpropitious circumstances of May 1660, the regicides knew they would also enjoy practical as well as ideological support. A fugitive life in New England, that is, also held out the prospect of tapping

---

[4]   Among the most influential contributions to this corpus have been: Perry Miller, *The New England Mind: The Seventeenth Century*, 2nd edn (Boston: Bacon Press, 1965); David Cressy, *Coming Over: Migration and Communication between England and New England in the Seventeenth Century* (Cambridge: Cambridge University Press, 1987); Virginia Anderson, *New England's Generation: The Great Migration and the Formation of Society and Culture in the Seventeenth Century* (Cambridge: Cambridge University Press, 1991); Francis J. Bremer, *Congregational Communion: Clerical Friendship in the Anglo-American Puritan Community* (Boston: Northeastern University Press, 1994). See, also, for more recent perspectives, Joseph A. Conforti, *Explorations of Personal Identity from the Pilgrims to Mid-Twentieth Century* (Chapel Hill and London: University of North Carolina Press, 2001); John McWilliams, *New England's Crisis and Cultural Memory: Literature, Politics, History and Religion, 1620–1860* (Cambridge: Cambridge University Press, 2004); Joseph A. Conforti, *Saints and Strangers: New England in British North America* (Baltimore: John Hopkins University Press, 2006).

[5]   For details of economic development in the first three decades of the seventeenth century associated with The Virginia Company, see Robert Brenner, *Merchants and Revolution: Commercial Change, Political Conflict, and London's Overseas Traders, 1550–1653* (London: Verso, 1993), esp. Chapter 3.

[6]   Bremer, *Congregational Communion*, p. 109.

[7]   *Ibid.*, pp. 178–9.

into the sustaining influence of the transatlantic congregational communion of the godly, with its ethos of collegiality, evidenced by the flow of ministers, pamphlets, letters and prayers across the Atlantic, knitting together the puritan brethren. Indeed, it was with testimonial letters from several English clergy members of this communion that Goffe and Whalley were to arrive in Boston.[8] Both men, moreover, had strong, pre-existing ties with puritan communities in New England. The Reverend John Davenport, who issued a direct invitation to them in 1660 to come to New Haven, the colony he had founded, was a close friend and colleague of William Hooke, Whalley's brother-in-law. In England, Hooke was to harbour Frances Goffe and her three daughters.[9] This neatly illustrates the usefulness and importance for the regicide exiles of the intercontinental network of supporters, which provided both financial and spiritual sustenance during their exile, and its interwoven subset of wider kith and kin.

II

On arriving in Massachusetts, Goffe and Whalley were immediately invited to the home of the colony's Governor, John Endicott. As a hostile source, the deposition of the aptly named loyalist, John Crown, which relayed the warm welcome they received, can be held as reasonably reliable, though with the caveat that his account may have been used in part to explain the failure of the colonial authorities to arrest them. Crown declared it was reported that Governor Endicott:

> Embraced them, bade them welcome to New England, and wished more such good men as they would come over. That they were visited by the principal persons of the town [...]. That they then resided in Cambridge University [...] where it was reported they were held in exceeding great esteem for their piety and parts; that they held meetings, where they preached and prayed and were looked upon as men dropt down from heaven.[10]

In this respect, it was a welcome every bit as effusive as that extended in 1662 to Edmund Ludlow and his fellow regicides by the authorities at Vevey, Switzerland, where, Ludlow reported:

> we were received with the greatest kindness and affection both from the magistrates and people [...] the principal magistrate, accompanied by most of the members of the Council [...] giving us thanks for the honour they said we did the town in coming to reside among them.[11]

---

[8]   *Ibid.*, p.218.

[9]   Mary-Peale Schofield, 'The Three Judges of New Haven', *History Today*, 12 (1962), 346–53 (p. 348).

[10]   *CSPC*, v, 54.

[11]   *The Memoirs of Edmund Ludlow*, ed. Charles Firth, 2 vols (Oxford: Clarendon Press, 1894), ii, 344.

Although it was soon to be complicated by concerted pressure to execute a warrant for their arrest, the palpable sense of civic pride here displayed by the Massachusetts authorities attests to the high standing Goffe and Whalley had attained as military and political figures during the republic. Aside from his role as a Major-General, it should be noted, Goffe had led Cromwell's regiment at Dunbar, and his own regiment at Worcester; he had also been a prominent figure at the Putney Debates of 1647, and an MP in 1654 and 1656, before being appointed to the House of Lords.[12] He was even spoken of as a possible successor to the Lord Protector.[13] Whalley, Cromwell's cousin, fought with distinction at Marston Moor and Maidstone, and took a leading role at the sieges of Banbury, Worcester and Colchester. He, too, had been an MP and a member of the House of Lords. The Nottinghamshire commissioners, like their Massachusetts counterparts, had been impressed with the calibre of Whalley, their newly promoted Major-General, thanking Cromwell for appointing, in January 1656, 'our native countryman, of an ancient and honourable family, and of singular justice, abilitie and piety'.[14] The historian Lemuel Welles claimed that 'No such prominent Englishmen as Whalley and Goffe visited New England during the colonial era, and even the English generals who came during the French and Indian War and during the Revolution were children at warfare compared with Cromwell's old officers.'[15]

Clearly, to be regarded by local dignitaries as 'men dropt down from heaven' presented advantages to the regicide fugitives, both in terms of being accepted within New England communities and, by extension, of avoiding capture. Indeed, the fact that, as Crown reported, they 'held meetings' in Boston signals how freely they were able to conduct themselves, at least initially. At the same time, the esteem in which they were held was a double-edged sword. Notwithstanding the physical safety it helped ensure, and though their letters fail to provide many clues, it is quite feasible that New England provincialism engendered in men of such standing a sense of declension. As Major-Generals a few years earlier, they had full responsibility for implementing important and wide-ranging policies across a number of counties, answerable only to the Protector. They had also, as we have seen, been MPs, and significant landowners for their services to parliament. Divested of public status, their transformation into exiles in the North America of the 1660s can have been no small culture shock to them, not least in the frontier wilds of Hadley, Massachusetts, a town incorporated as recently as 1661, and resided in by a mere 50 families.[16]

---

[12]   Schofield, p. 347.

[13]   E.B. Arnold, 'A Sussex Family during the Commonwealth', *Sussex County Magazine*, x (1936), 740–43 (p. 741).

[14]   Christopher Durston, *Cromwell's Major Generals: Godly Government during the English Revolution* (Manchester: Manchester University Press, 2001), p. 40.

[15]   Lemuel Welles, *The Regicides in Connecticut* (New Haven: Yale University Press, 1935), p. 2.

[16]   On 15 November 1658, Richard Cromwell granted Goffe crown lands in Ireland worth £500 a year, 'calling to mind the great worth and merit of our truly and well-beloved

Allied to this point, one of the key gaps in our knowledge is a clear understanding of what Goffe and Whalley actually *did* during their years in exile. We know from one of his journal entries that Goffe attended lectures in Boston, and from his correspondence from Hadley that he was 'carrying on a little trade here among the Indians'.[17] That the primary sources reveal little more, however, is unwitting evidence that once they had moved inland from Boston, at least, the imperative of evading capture trumped all other considerations. This dictated that the admiration they evidently inspired could not, for safety's sake, be translated into commensurate public, official duties within the host community.[18] The eighteenth-century Governor of Massachusetts, Thomas Hutchinson, who had access to the whole of Goffe's journal, not merely a copy of the fragment which now remains, was in no doubt that there was a keenly felt loss of prestige by both men; that they perceived themselves as big fish in a small pond:

> Their diary for six or seven years contains every little occurrence in the town, church and particular families in the neighbourhood. These were small affairs, and they had [...] for a few years of their lives been among the principal actors in the great affairs of the nation; Goffe, especially, who turned the members of the little parliament out of the house, and who was attached to Oliver and to Richard to the last.[19]

This aspect of their displacement points up one of the key differences between regicides like Goffe and Whalley and earlier, royalist exiles. However welcome they were made, and though did not face the language difficulties often encountered by royalists on the European mainland,[20] the regicides had to lie much lower.[21]

William Lord Goffe'; *TSP*, vii, 504. Goffe is also recorded as having purchased items at the sales of goods belonging to the royal family, 1649–52 (*CSPD* 1670, Addenda, p. 666). For an indication of the regional isolation of Hadley, and a map of Hadley itself in 1661, indicating its small-town, outpost nature, see *Historical Atlas of Massachusetts*, ed. R.W. Wilkie, (Amherst, MA: University of Massachusetts Press, 1991), pp. 17–18.

[17] 'Letters and Papers of the Regicides', *Collections of the Massachusetts Historical Society*, 4th Series, 8 (1868), 122–5 (p. 141). This source hereafter cited as *CMHS*.

[18] A similar picture emerges in the case of John Dixwell. See Jason Peacey's essay, this volume.

[19] Caroline Newton, 'Letters of a New England Exile', *Americana*, 14 (1920), 208–26 (p. 220). Goffe's journal was irrecoverably lost through fire in 1765.

[20] John Glad has argued that 'the loss of language is probably the most decisive factor in determining exile; it is what makes exile so wretched for the writer'. *Literature in Exile*, ed. John Glad (Durham and London: Duke University Press, 1990), p. 41.

[21] Goffe and Whalley lived secretly in the cellar of Rev. John Russells's house in Hadley for years. Cora Lutz remarks how Stiles 'marvelled that this arrangement was kept such a close secret among the members of the family and a very few of friends that the hiding place was never discovered.' See Cora Lutz, 'Ezra Stiles and the Legend of Hadley', *Yale University Library Gazette*, 73, 3–4 (April, 1998), 115–23 (p. 121). For a plan of 'The Judges' Chamber', where the regicides resided in Russell's house, taken from Stiles's

The intelligence network of the English Republic, led by Secretary of State Thurloe, was extensive; it was, however, looking for intelligence on plots rather than, as in the case of Restoration governments, to execute retributive arrest warrants. This is one reason why, as evidenced in their letters, both Goffe and Whalley threw themselves into the intellectual, spiritual and communal consolations of the transatlantic congregational network, in order to recover the day-to-day cachet among their peers which the 'small affairs' of Hadley failed to provide.

This is not the only conclusion we can draw from Hutchinson's words, though. The very fact that Goffe took the trouble to meticulously record, over several years, 'every little occurrence in the town, church and particular families in the neighbourhood' also displays a striking adaptability to his new environment. Notwithstanding the secrecy of their whereabouts, and the perennial danger of exposure, Goffe and his father-in-law, as far as they could, evidently immersed themselves in Hadley's quotidian affairs: those on a corporate, religious and social level. It is important to discern the psychological impulse behind this; the extent to which an enforced isolation impels them to look to the minutiae of their immediate locality as an exilic survival technique, as much as anything to stave off boredom, analogous to an Ovidian study of Tomis. For these deeply pious men, then, preserving oneself for years in exile sometimes appears to have required more – or rather, less – than the sustaining of Revelatory, cosmic belief in the Second Coming, and the attendant regular correspondence with kindred spirits in the congregational network, crucially important as these were. It needed, in addition, a multi-layered engagement, perhaps even bordering on the obsessive, with day-to-day events at the micro level, however comparatively banal. It is this sometimes curious blend of the millenarian and the mundane – a single letter by Goffe to his wife can span a discussion of the Book of Revelations and his need, or otherwise, for a periwig – which provides much of the fascination in Goffe's response to exile in New England.[22] Of course, in the millenarian mindset the cosmic and the local can rarely be neatly segregated. As has been said of the journals of one of Goffe's illustrious puritan correspondents, Increase Mather, who for 11 years relayed letters to the fugitive Goffe via the minister of Hadley, John Russell, 'A diary was but the daily balancing of the writer's success or failure in doing God's will [...]. A Puritan diary read in any other light is unintelligible.'[23]

History, see Sylvester Judd, *History of Hadley* (Springfield, MA: H.R. Hunting and Co., 1905), p. 212.

[22] *CMHS*, 134, 142. For an excellent recent study of the significance of Revelation to New England settlers, see Kevin Sharpe, 'Transplanting Revelation, Transferring Meaning: Reading the Apocalypse in Early Modern England, Scotland and New England', in *Shaping the Stuart World 1603–1714: The Atlantic Connection*, ed. Allan I. Macinnes and Arthur H. Williamson (Leiden, Boston: Brill, 2006), pp. 117–146.

[23] K.B. Murdoch, *Increase Mather: The Foremost American Puritan* (Cambridge: Harvard University Press, 1925), p. 89.

III

Though the supplementary and ancillary sources hitherto examined have their strengths, the key to a deeper understanding of Goffe's exile lies in a close examination of his correspondence. Yet, while most of this was published (by the Massachusetts Historical Society) as long ago as 1868, it has, since then, attracted little critical attention. Excerpts from only a small number of letters have been cited, and these have either been subsumed into works on New England letters generally, or quoted sparingly in biographical sketches. To date, it appears that only one article has been published (in 1920) which offers something approaching a detailed critical analysis of the collection as a whole.[24] Furthermore, the secondary literature on Goffe, in particular, has concentrated disproportionately on the colourful if highly speculative 'Angel of Hadley' story, in which the ageing former Major-General (Goffe) suddenly appears as if from nowhere in 1675 to lead the inhabitants of Hadley in successfully repulsing an Indian attack during King Philip's War.[25] For the purpose of this study, then, these understudied letters provide invaluable source material on the preoccupations, psychology and attitudes of the regicide exiles in North America.

Goffe's correspondence is notably diverse in content; it includes news of family and friends, political developments in Old and New England, and copious exegetical interpretation. Common to almost all of it, however, is the notion that letters act as an emotional safety valve. As a medium for the expression of affection, in particular, it addresses the fundamental question of separation from loved ones, and articulates more of Goffe's own, invariably biblical, justification for the sundering of the family unity. Thus, we find admiration for his wife's constancy expressed in the following lines from a letter of July and August 1672:

> I cannot but be Deeply sensible of your greate and long continued affliction [...]
> what a mercy is it that the Lord is pleased to give you such a hearty Desire, (as
> you expresse in your last) to be contented to want the enjoyment of that which
> God our heavenly father seeth meet to withould from us though otherwise never
> so much desired.[26]

For Goffe to have been so demonstrably anxious about the suffering of his wife in England is brought into sharper focus upon consideration that as one of Cromwell's Major-Generals in 1655–56 he was often preoccupied with the difficulties – in

---

[24]   Newton, *Letters*.

[25]   See for example Lutz, 'Ezra Stiles'. The story has been incorporated into numerous fictional works, including Cooper's *Wept of Wish-ton-Well*, Hawthorne's *The Gray Champion*, and Scott's *Peveril of the Peak*. Sargent comments more generally that 'Few episodes in the history of the British American colonies intrigued nineteenth-century novelists and playwrights more than the flight of the Puritan regicides to New England', in M.L. Sargent, 'Thomas Hutchinson, Ezra Stiles, and the Legend of the Regicides', *William and Mary Quarterly*, 3rd ser., 49, 3 (1992), 431–48 (p. 431).

[26]   *CMHS*, p. 139.

hindsight, the comparatively minor difficulties – his wife experienced in settling into their new home in Winchester. In May 1656, he writes to Thurloe asking to be excused from a forthcoming meeting with Cromwell in London, on the grounds that:

> having brought my wiffe and family to this place, I should have been verie glad to have staied with them till my wiffe were a little better acquainted with this place, which she doth not very much rejoyce in at present; and my leaving her heere alone is the thing att present she greatly dreades'.[27]

We can readily imagine how much his concern in New England for his wife's well-being was magnified by the huge distance now separating them. Goffe's sympathy for his wife's 'greate and long continued affliction' operates on different levels. Chiefly it displays genuine sorrow, but it also subtly, and solipsistically, reinforces his own consolatory perception that she cannot forget him. Furthermore, if unintentionally, it subverts the pervasive millenarianism we witness in his letters, in which time's intensity foreshortens not only the physical distance between England and New England but also the passing of the months and years.

The submission to, and desire to enjoy, divine Providence, as witnessed here, is an exilic survival mechanism employed – and, less cynically, an integral belief held – by many exiles in this period. It is bound up with the comforting belief that if God has 'visited our transgression with a rod & our iniquity with stripes', then this in turn only confirms that he continues to have a loving plan for the exile, that 'His loving kindness he hath not taken from us'. By extension, and in Goffe's case, divine approbation for the Good Old Cause has not been abandoned.[28]

There are other passages in his letters, nonetheless, where the exigencies of exile induce Goffe, the apparently inscrutable and steadfast millenarian, to explicitly reveal the depths of his suffering. In his letter of 1671, for example, he is 'not only a stranger, but a poor exile stranger'; his written words couched meekly as 'these weake Breathings' and 'these poor lines'. In his letter to Frances of 1672 he portrays himself, even more starkly, as 'a poore, broken, useless vessell'; and in a letter to Increase Mather of 1677 he is falteringly 'peeping [...] through the crevises of my close Cell to discern the signes of my Lords coming.'[29] It is with these and other similarly wistful reflections in his correspondence that Goffe's seemingly unceasing faith in the divine plan being worked out for him needs to be contrasted.

Throughout Goffe's letters, it is not always easy to appraise the extent to which the condition of exile itself animates the reactions we witness from him. Clearly, his long-distance and long-lasting physical displacement had a significant impact on him, but it is plausible to argue that on occasion its effect was to exacerbate self-perceived, pre-existing weaknesses in his character, rather than to transform a previously sanguine personality into 'a poore, broken, useless vessell'. It is worth

---

[27]   *TSP*, iv, 765.

[28]   'William Goffe to his Wife', *CMHS*, p. 139.

[29]   *Ibid.*, pp. 128, 129, 140, 159. See, also, Durston, *Cromwell's Major-Generals*, p. 45.

noting, in this respect, that his correspondence with Thurloe during his career as a Major-General in the 1650s, years before he arrived in New England, projects, perhaps counter-intuitively, a sense of fragility, humility and perpetual unworthiness. On one occasion he enquires apologetically of Thurloe:

> If you thinke fitt, I beseech you present my most humble service to his highness, for whom I pray without ceasing and can, I hope cheerefully sacrifice my life in the service, if it need be; but I wish he doe not repent the laying soe great a trust upon soe poor and inconsiderable a creature.[30]

Similarly, another letter to Thurloe betrays a man who, for all his conviction that he is serving God's cause, is already susceptible to feelings of isolation, and whose axiomatically deep faith in a divine plan does not always translate into unshakeable confidence in his own abilities. This provides further insight into the way in which the sometimes delicate nature of Goffe's disposition – he has been described by one commentator as 'a curious mixture of messianic recklessness and temperamental weakness'[31] – may have been preyed upon, rather than necessarily formed, by his new circumstances in exile:

> I tell you by the way of my intended proceedings, that if you like them not, I may be helped by your counsel, for I am here much alone. ... If I be mistaken in this my way of thinking, I hope, I shall be better advised by you. ... You see how fully I deliver my thoughts to you, which I do in hope that the Lord will manifest His presence with me in this difficult affair, to me difficult, because I am weak.[32]

In his letter of July and August 1672, already cited, another key component of Goffe's correspondence can be observed. Here, he is responding to his wife's letter of October 1671, in which her recurrent feelings of dislocation from her husband are laid bare: 'The Lord make us truly thankful, & give us hearts to be wiling to be without what he will not have us to injoy, thou never so much desired by us', Frances writes. The way in which her husband's reply echoes her words, not simply her sentiments, is striking: 'enjoyment' matches 'injoy', and 'though otherwise never so much desired' matches 'thou never so much desiered'.[33] In one respect, this echoing effect is simply an effective means of accurately referring to the letter he is responding to; on the other hand, and more intriguingly, it also represents an attempt, on a literary level, at a form of transatlantic reunion. That is, in replicating his wife's vocabulary almost word for word, Goffe is making a consciously closer

---

[30]   *CSPT*, iv, 190.

[31]   Anthony Fletcher, 'The Religious Motivation of Cromwell's Major-Generals', in *Religious Motivation: Biographical and Sociological Problems for the Church Historian*, ed. Derek Baker (Oxford: Basil Blackwell, 1978), pp. 259–66 (p. 263).

[32]   Newton, *Letters*, 214, *CSPT*, iv, 151.

[33]   *CMHS*, pp. 133, 155.

connection with her; by sending back to her the very words she has written to him, he is demonstrating the encouraging fluidity and potency of their interchange. In this way, the written word not only constitutes a mutually binding exilic discourse, but embodies, as it were, shared objects which freely traverse, back and forth, the distance between correspondents. In the process, it is reassuringly demonstrated that just as the semantic gap between words is bridgeable, so, too, is the physical and emotional divide between those who write them.

Interlinked with this notion is the strategy adopted by Goffe and his wife of recommending to each other a particular passage of scripture. For example, Frances advises him in a letter of 1662:

> We have seen that word in the 5th of Job, in some measure, made good to you. Read the 12th verse; from the 11th to the end of the chapter, there is much comfort to those in our condition; as also 91 Psalm'.[34]

The Bible becomes, as it were, a shared reference point in a complex and confusing exilic terrain. It does so not just because of the mutual perception of its inherently consolatory content, but also because, at a distance of 3,000 miles, it allows, at the level of an individual verse, for the buttressing of an often fragile interconnectedness between separated believers. It provides a sense of certainty over exactly what it is that the absent spouse will be reading. All of this during a period in which, it has recently been argued, the ideal of companionate interpersonal relations 'had long been promoted with particular vigour by puritans, and was especially strong among dissenters, where a stout and reciprocal affection between partners seemed to support them in an age of persecution'.[35]

If letters per se, and exilic coping mechanisms within them like the repetition of words, help to span the various physical, emotional and spiritual distances between Goffe and his wife, what can be inferred from the ubiquitous use of pseudonyms and ciphers in this correspondence? First, it should be noted that assuming another identity was not confined to letter-writing for Goffe; it is known from his journal – itself written in a form of shorthand – that while on board the *Prudent Mary*, the ship on which he sailed for the New World, he and Whalley adopted the names of Edward Richardson and William Stephenson respectively, so as to avoid detection.[36] Yet, while these names were soon discarded when the sympathetic political makeup of the ship's crew and other passengers became clear, these aliases continued to be used in the correspondence. The context within which such tactics were adopted in Goffe's letters is important to grasp. Like other New Englanders, most notably John Winthrop, Goffe knew full well that his correspondence was vulnerable to confiscation or censorship by hostile English authorities, agents eager to know

---

[34] Thomas Hutchinson, *The History of Massachusetts*, 3rd edn, 2 vols (Boston, MA, 1795), i, 532.

[35] Gordon Campbell and Thomas N. Corns, *John Milton: Life, Work, and Thought* (Oxford: Oxford University Press, 2008), p. 339.

[36] Hutchinson, *History of Massachusetts*, i, 28.

where he may be taking refuge and to snuff out any residual republican trouble he may have been minded to foment in England.[37]

Discovery of Goffe's true identity was an ever-present danger. In April 1672, Frances warns him: 'be carefull what you write for all the lettars we receve comes from the post house.'[38] Goffe, in reply, is 'glad you have informed me of it, for I would not make my letters too chary, to you.'[39] Other correspondents exhibit a similar fear of exposure; William Hooke, for instance, writes to Goffe in June 1663: 'You may know mee heereafter by D: G: Letters are soe often broke up that many are loth to write their names.'[40] For these reasons Goffe usually wrote to his wife using the assumed name of Walter Goldsmith, addressing her as his 'mother'. She reciprocated by signing herself Frances Goldsmith. It is not necessarily the most sophisticated of undercover names: as was the case with John Dixwell, who used the assumed name of James Davids, Goffe's alias has the same initials as his real name. Clearly, for Goffe (and Dixwell) the retention of one's own initials was a small but important means of preserving one's identity, bearing out John Glad's argument that the anonymity associated with the loss of one's name is one of the three main causes of despair in the early stages of exile.[41] In another twist to this idea, it is noteworthy that Ludlow and Cawley, regicide exiles in Switzerland, retained in their correspondence their correct first names, preferring instead to change their surnames, to Phillips and Johnson respectively.[42] Augmented by the employment of ciphers, particularly prevalent in his correspondence with the wider transatlantic congregational network, the use of such code names is widespread in Goffe's letters. It contributes to his construction of a rhetoric of exile, helping to construct not only a discreet mode of literary transmission, but also a psychologically empowering language of secrecy and furtiveness.

IV

Though Goffe's letters register the apparent immateriality of space and distance, it would be a mistake to attribute this to a lack of interest on his part in the fate of his native land. On the contrary, his correspondence teems with questions, thoughts, reflections and interpretations on England, both spiritual and political. Indeed, these provide the ingredients for some of the most profound and affecting tensions in Goffe's letters: tensions between the 'peculiar mercy' he perceives God as reserving for the people of New England and God's design for Old England; between reconciliation to his new home and an acute interest in his former; between

---

[37] See Cressy, *Coming Over*, pp. 223–4.

[38] *Hutchinson Papers*, iii, 163.

[39] *CMHS*, p. 136.

[40] *Ibid.*, p. 125.

[41] *Literature In Exile*, p. 118.

[42] See the letters from exile by both men published in *Memoirs of Edmund Ludlow*, ed. Firth, ii, 479–508.

the sinfulness of Old England, which in his eyes vindicated his flight, and his lasting hopes for its salvation. In one sense, Goffe's ruminations on England are entirely consistent with his views on the converse, 'elect' nature of New England. Certainly, when his judgement on England is filtered uncompromisingly through the prism of his millenarianism, what is most noticeable is just how damning it can be. This is nowhere more evident than in his letter to Increase Mather, as late as 1676, with its wonderful double quality of anxiety and celebration, in which Goffe claims to:

> see a greater glory prophesied of in Rev: 14; the 5 first verses, then hath yet app[eard] in any of the protestant nations of Europe, which yet is to be expected before the Destruction of Rome, for which my soul longeth, and I am much persuaded that the Beginning of it will be in Great Br[itain.]. But oh, the terrible things that are to be expected God will do there, in order thereunto, and Blessed are those that shall be found worthy to escape the things that are coming to passe.[43]

For all his own hardships of the past 16 years, Goffe still considers himself one of the 'Blessed' who have escaped the 'terrible things ... that are coming to passe' in punishment for England's manifold iniquities; on this evidence, any kind of benign emotional tie to the homeland, other than with friends and family, seems hard for him to sustain.

In another sense, though, Goffe's attitude towards the England he left behind is imbued with a tangible sense of sadness, sympathy and nostalgia, which nevertheless carries a significance beyond adherence to the simplistic maxim of distance lending enchantment. While in his letters the motherland is often portrayed as subject to God's wrath and judgement, Goffe seldom, if ever, takes a detached or complacent view of developments there. The terminology he employs, as much as anything else, suggests this. Replying to Frances in July 1672, for example, he 'cannot but tremble to think what may become of *poor England*, whose sins are grown to a great Height', echoing the 'pore England' punished by 'the great fier in London' and other subsequent 'Joygments' portentously evoked in his wife's latest letter.[44] In the same reply, Goffe continues:

> Yet the Lord that would have saved Sodom for the sake of 10 Righteous will, I hope, be gracious to *our poor native country*, for the sake of the many thousands (as it may be reasonably hoped) that are therein. There is a great stock of prayers going up for you in this countrey, which I doubt not the Lord will answer.

In the same vein, in a letter to William Hooke of August 1674, Goffe exhorts: 'Oh, that the inhabitants of *poor England* would learn righteousness'. It is a critical yet sympathetic tone towards the home country, consonant with that of other puritan migrants to the New World, many of whom, like one Edward

---

[43] *CMHS*, p. 158.
[44] *Ibid.*, pp. 136, 133.

Johnson, declared that they were 'going from England to pray without ceasing for England'.[45] Goffe's choice of words here can be instructively contrasted with the curiously distant language he sometimes applies to his adopted land. More than a decade after arriving in New England he can refer to it as merely 'this country', such as when remarking to his wife, in 1672, that 'the aire of this countrey in the winter is exceeding pearcing.'[46] The vocabulary Goffe employs here is determined in part by his need to keep his country of refuge secret to any would-be interceptor of his letters. Even so, the unambiguously warm descriptions of his new home noted earlier are significantly qualified by such – at best – neutral terms, resulting in the emergence of a noticeably ambivalent overall tone. Like many exiles, Goffe appears to have seen himself as being caught between worlds, with England always a very present absence.

The aftermath of the English Revolution, then, was played out on more than one continent. The years spent by William Goffe and Edward Whalley in New England open up North America as an important new frontier in the study of exile born of the English Republic. And they bear scrutiny in their own right for the insight they afford into varieties of exilic coping mechanisms and survival strategies. Close reading of Goffe's correspondence, a poignantly emotional lifeline in exile, illustrates the prime influence on and significance to Goffe of his puritan belief system, which, as with so many who ventured to the New World, was only reinforced by the potent symbolism of surviving the hazardous transatlantic voyage. Relegating the importance of physical contact, and emphasizing the transience of temporal affairs, his religious temper coloured his thoughts on enduring permanent separation from the wife and children he perforce left behind. It does not, however, fully dispel the notion of a man of unexpected, self-confessed mental frailty; nor does it preclude a sometimes paradoxical attitude in exile both towards New England and his native country, which he was both relieved to escape from and assiduous in praying for.

---

[45]   Bremer, *Congregational Communion*, p. 107.
[46]   *CMHS*, p. 142.

Chapter 10
'The good old cause for which I suffer': The Life of a Regicide in Exile

Jason Peacey

I

Scarcity of archival evidence has ensured that the lives of the exiled regicides have received little scholarly attention. What is known about this group suggests that, if their lives were not necessarily nasty, brutish, and short, they nevertheless faced constant threats from royalist agents. Some died of old age and in their beds, but at least one was assassinated, and three more were captured and repatriated, before being tried and executed. Only one of those who fled to Europe, Edmund Ludlow, left any appreciable record of the search for friends in an alien environment. Our understanding is dramatically enhanced, however, by neglected evidence relating to the three men who escaped to New England, William Goffe, Edward Whalley, and John Dixwell, the latter of whose papers are particularly revealing. This chapter scrutinizes Dixwell's experience, not merely in order to understand how he survived into old age, but also to examine his attitude to his past, his current circumstances, and his plans for the future. To be an exile was to regard one's reason for absence from England as being political in nature and temporary in duration, and as such it is important to appreciate Dixwell's relationship with the motherland, his perception of his status and identity while abroad, and his views regarding returning home. What factors kept him in New England, and what, if any, pulled him homeward? Did he set down firm roots in the colonies, or did he consider himself to be merely a temporary resident, biding his time until a propitious moment to return?

Such questions can be answered by analyzing an unusual variety of surviving sources: a one-sided and incomplete run of correspondence with his family in England, and with other friends in London and the Low Countries; the papers of clerical and lay settlers in the colonies; the legal papers drawn up by Dixwell in his final years; the testimonies of those who had known him; and oral and eyewitness evidence gathered by Dixwell's first biographer, Ezra Stiles.[1] Such papers constitute a valuable case study with which to supplement the existing

---

[1] Franklin B. Dexter, 'Dixwell papers', *Papers of the New Haven Colony Historical Society*, 6 (1900), 341–4; Ezra Stiles, *A History of Three of the Judges of King Charles I* (Hartford, CT, 1794). For the originals of Dixwell's papers, and Stiles's notes, see Whitney Library, New Haven, MSS 7–8.

composite picture of the mental world of the colonists and their attitudes towards old England.[2] By enabling reconstruction of the political world which Dixwell inhabited, however, such evidence also enhances our appreciation of a vibrant network of religious nonconformists and political radicals, which had its roots in the civil wars, which persisted until the Glorious Revolution, and which spread from England to the Low Countries, and to the New World.

Dixwell's life before 1660 can be quickly summarized. He rose to prominence in Kent after the death of his elder brother in 1644, becoming the trustee of a substantial estate, and guardian of young nieces and nephews.[3] He then became a prominent local parliamentarian, secured election to parliament for Dover in August 1646, and emerged on to the national political stage as an assiduous member of the High Court of Justice, and as a signatory of Charles I's death warrant. Service on the republican Council of State followed, although Dixwell rejected the Protectorate, and made little or no impression upon the three Cromwellian parliaments to which he was returned. A civilian republican in the restored Rump of 1659, he quickly returned to the Council of State, was made lieutenant of Dover Castle, and found little difficulty in taking the required oath abjuring the Stuart dynasty.[4]

Like other regicides, Dixwell faced a stark choice in the spring of 1660: to stay in England and face trial, or to flee.[5] He avoided arrest in May 1660 for long enough to settle his affairs and make his escape, severing the greater part of his financial ties to England by surrendering control of his late brother's estate, and by conveying his own property to a kinsman, Sir Thomas Peyton.[6] Those portions which were not sold were quickly confiscated by the crown.[7] As a single man without dependents or siblings, Dixwell apparently had nothing to keep him in his native country, and he travelled with fellow regicides to Hanau – where he was made a burgess – before seeking sanctuary further afield.[8] By 1665 he was at Hadley in New England, and after a peripatetic existence he finally settled in New Haven, Connecticut, sometime before 1673, under the assumed name of James Davids.[9]

---

[2]   David Cressy, *Coming Over: Migration and Communication between England and New England in the Seventeenth Century* (Cambridge: Cambridge University Press, 1987); Harry Stout, 'The Morphology of Re-migration: New England University Men and their Return to England, 1640–1660', *Journal of American Studies*, 10 (1976), 151–72; William L. Sachse, 'The migration of New Englanders to England, 1640–1660', *American Historical Review*, 55 (1948), 251–78; Andrew Delbanco, 'Looking Homeward, Going Home: The Lure of England for the Founders of New England', *New England Quarterly*, 59 (1986), 358–86.

[3]   'Dixwell papers', pp. 349, 371; BL, Add. MS 20001, fols 48r–v; Add. MS 40717, fols 160, 169–74, 181–99; Centre for Kentish Studies, U270/T267.

[4]   Jason Peacey, 'John Dixwell' (draft biography, History of Parliament Trust).

[5]   *JHL*, xi, 32b, 52b, 101b, 102a.

[6]   BL, Add. MS 40717, fols 175, 177, 181–99; Stiles, *History*, p. 150.

[7]   BL, Add. MS 40717, fols 161–8, 169–74; National Archives, LR 2/266, fol. 1.

[8]   *The Memoirs of Edmund Ludlow*, ed. C.H. Firth, 2 vols (Oxford: Clarendon Press, 1894), ii, 330.

[9]   Stiles, *History*, pp. 125–6.

II

Having explored the circumstances – political danger – in which Dixwell left England, and the degree – apparently total – to which he severed ties with his homeland, it is necessary to examine the conditions in which he lived in exile. This means analyzing his wealth and health, his willingness to settle, and his ability to disguise his true identity and evade capture.

The evidence from Dixwell's correspondence indicates that the ties which he developed to New England were familial rather than financial. In November 1673, he married Joanna, widow of one Mr Ling, although she died almost immediately, and in October 1677 Dixwell entered a second marriage, to Bathsheba How, by whom he had a son, John, and two daughters, Mary and Elizabeth, the latter of whom died in infancy.[10] Aside from his family, Dixwell apparently established only the smallest of networks of friends during more than two decades in the colonies. His relationship with John Davenport, who sought to contact him in the 1660s, is hard to substantiate,[11] and his contact with the other regicides in the region seems to have been negligible.[12] Neither Increase Mather nor the Boston merchant, Humphrey Davie, may have provided anything more that a means of corresponding with England.[13] Although Dixwell naturally received a few visitors, he evidently kept himself to himself. It is only the much later oral testimony of Hezekiah Willis which indicates that he visited Dixwell when a small child in 1682, along with his father, Governor George Willis.[14] Those who clearly did know Dixwell in New Haven, on the other hand, recalled his preoccupation with 'reading and rural walks', his 'reservedness', and his determination to 'lead a retired and obscure life'.[15] The local minister, John Pierpont, later claimed that Dixwell endeavoured 'studiously to avoid public observation and employment'.[16]

Dixwell's only real friends during this period appear to have been three prominent New Haven figures. He certainly befriended the minister Nicholas Street, who named 'James Davids' as an overseer of his will.[17] William Jones, sometime deputy-governor of the colony, later claimed to have had 'personal acquaintance and frequent conversation' with Dixwell.[18] More important was the relationship

---

[10]   *Ibid.*, pp. 128, 156; 'Dixwell papers', pp. 347, 374.

[11]   *The Mather Papers* (Massachussetts Historical Society Collections, 4th series, 8, 1868), p. 127.

[12]   *Ibid.*, p. 154.

[13]   'Dixwell papers', p. 369; *Mather Papers*, pp. 164–5. See: Francis J. Bremer, 'Increase Mather's Friends: the transatlantic congregational network of the seventeenth century', *Proceedings of the American Antiquarian Society*, 94 (1984), 59–96.

[14]   Stiles, *History*, p. 166.

[15]   *Ibid.*, pp. 131, 160.

[16]   BL, Add. Ch. 66210.

[17]   Stiles, *History*, p. 127.

[18]   BL, Add. Ch. 66210.

with Pierpont, who arrived in New Haven in 1674 as Street's successor.[19] Pierpont found Dixwell's conversation 'very valuable', and the two men evidently became close, to the bemusement of their neighbours, and the minister's own wife.[20] It was to Pierpont that Dixwell entrusted sealed private papers in the 1680s, and bequeathed Raleigh's *History of the World*.[21] It was by Pierpont, too, that Dixwell was eventually admitted to the church fellowship at New Haven, in December 1685, in circumstances of failing health and approaching death.[22]

Dixwell's modest and retired lifestyle may have been a matter of necessity as well as choice, and it is likely that he lived in straightened financial circumstances.[23] He pursued no employment or trade, relying instead upon a small estate inherited from his first wife,[24] which was supplemented in December 1680 by a small gift of land by the local authorities.[25] At his death, after nearly 30 years in New England, Dixwell's possessions were valued at only £276, and he could promise his surviving daughter a mere £20.[26] Dixwell's financial and material plight is apparent from his English correspondents. He failed to secure a supply of new books to read, and his friend Francis Prince seems to have failed to locate and transport portions of the library which had been left behind in England,[27] although his niece was able to send 'some of those books you desired' in July 1680, adding that 'if I can meet with a way I have more to send you'.[28] Elizabeth Westrowe also sought to supply more essential items, including a parcel of cloth for a new suit and stockings in August 1678, 'of the colour of the cloth as they wear them here', as well as four shirts, six handkerchiefs, and some cravats.[29] In June 1679, Prince sent a coat and a cloak.[30] That such parcels of supplies did little to alleviate Dixwell's needs is apparent, however, from Elizabeth Westrowe's comment, in March 1683, that 'it grieves me you should suffer any straits', while also apologizing for being unable to send those things that he desired.[31] In addition to sending goods, Dixwell's friends and family felt compelled to send money as well. Prince sent £5 in 1679,

[19] Stiles, *History*, p. 157.

[20] *Ibid.*, pp. 129–30, 157.

[21] *Ibid.*, pp. 136–7, 157; Connecticut State Library, New Haven Probate Records, vol. 2, part 1, pp. 8–9.

[22] Stiles, *History*, p. 128.

[23] *Ibid.*, p. 132.

[24] *Ibid.*, pp. 131–2.

[25] Franklin B. Dexter, *New Haven Town Records II, 1662–1684* (New Haven Historical Society, 1919), p. 406.

[26] Connecticut State Library, New Haven Probate Records, vol. 2, part 1, pp. 8–9; Stiles, *History*, pp. 136–7.

[27] 'Dixwell papers', pp. 366–7, 367–8.

[28] *Ibid.*, pp. 349–50.

[29] *Ibid*, pp. 347–8.

[30] *Ibid.*, pp. 366–7.

[31] *Ibid.*, pp. 353–4, 354–6.

and Elizabeth Westrowe sent £30 in 1685, while on another occasion £11 seems to have been sent to Dixwell through the good offices of Humphrey Davie.[32]

Dixwell's reclusive existence was almost certainly related to the need to evade detection and exposure, and issues of personal safety were another key determinant of the degree to which he was able to settle in New Haven. He must have been keenly aware that there was a price on his head, and that attempts were being made to locate the regicides, and he may have disputed the idea, expressed long after his death, that he was actively protected by Connecticut's governors.[33] Public dealings were consistently undertaken, and private letters written, under the pseudonym of James Davids, and members of his family concealed their true identity, too. The hostile biographer of the regicides, Mark Noble, was probably correct to suggest that the adoption of an alias indicated that Dixwell 'lived in constant fears of being betrayed', even if he had little evidence for his subsequent claim that he privately boasted of his role as a king-killer.[34] Fear of exposure led to caution regarding the reliability of particular merchants and carriers,[35] and to his request that his grave should not be marked with a monument, 'lest his enemies might dishonour his ashes'.[36]

Dixwell's caution clearly paid off. The English government lost track of him after his spell in Hanau,[37] and evidently did not suspect that he had made it to the New World.[38] Charles II and his ministers probably assumed that he had perished in some remote corner of Europe, and in this they knew no more than some of Dixwell's English relatives.[39] Nevertheless, Dixwell's true identity and real whereabouts were not entirely secret. John Davenport evidently knew that Dixwell and the other regicides were at Hadley in 1665, although in mentioning this to one of the town's ruling elders he was cautious enough to refer merely to 'those three worthies', and to put even this phrase into cipher.[40] It can be also

---

[32]   *Ibid.*, pp. 354–6, 366–7, 369.

[33]   *CSPC, 1704–5.*

[34]   Mark Noble, *Lives of the English Regicides*, 2 vols (London: J. Stockdale, 1878), ii, 181–2.

[35]   'Dixwell papers', pp. 350–51.

[36]   Stiles, *History*, p. 135. This explains why Dixwell's grave is marked with a small plain stone marked merely with the letters 'J.D.', the date of his death, and his age.

[37]   Richard Greaves, *Deliver us from Evil* (New York: Oxford University Press, 1986), p. 92; *The Life of Edward, Earl of Clarendon*, 3 vols (Oxford, 1827), iii, 155; Ralph C.H. Catterall, 'Sir George Downing and the Regicides', *American Historical Review*, 17 (1912), 268–89 (pp. 271, 274); *CClSP*, v, 140, 153–6; *Memoirs of Edmund Ludlow*, ii, 330.

[38]   *CSPC, 1661–1688*; J. Hammond Trumbull, *The Public Records of the Colony of Connecticut*, 3 vols (Hartford, CT, 1850–59); Charles J. Hoadly, *Records of the Colony or Jurisdiction of New Haven ... 1653–65* (Hartford: Case, Lockwood & Co., 1858); Dexter, *New Haven Town Records I, 1649–1662* (New Haven Historical Society, 1917). For Goffe and Whalley, see: *CSPC, 1661–8*, pp. 45, 80, 81–2, 87, 96, 160–62, 1103, 1300; *CSPC, 1675–6*, pp. 953, 1067; *CSPC, 1677–80*, pp. 351, 354, 358, 782, 811, 813; *CSPC, 1681–5*, p. 1121.

[39]   Stiles, *History*, p. 160.

[40]   *Mather Papers*, p. 127.

presumed that Dixwell's true identity was known to those colonists by whom he was helped, such as Increase Mather and Humphrey Davie, although even this cannot be stated with certainty, given that all parties consistently corresponded using his adopted name.[41]

Within New Haven, Dixwell's pretence was perhaps harder to maintain. Judging by later testimonies, local residents were clearly suspicious about his true identity, but although speculation was evidently rife that he was not who he claimed to be, he proved difficult to unmask. Writing as an old man in the early eighteenth century, James Heaton recalled that when Dixwell first arrived, 'his clothing, deportment and manifest great education and accomplishments in a little time caused many to conjecture the said gentleman was no ordinary person'. Locals assumed that he 'for some great reasons sought to conceal both his proper name and his character', yet 'people could not be determined in their thoughts'.[42] At much the same time, Dixwell's friend Pierpont claimed that it was immediately apparent that Dixwell was a person of 'manifest great education', and added that he was 'generally supposed to be of another name', given his 'observable wisdom and great knowledge in the English law, state policy, and European affairs'.[43] Pierpont admitted that, as in any small town, there were 'many conjectures' as to the old man's previous life.[44] Writing in 1708 to Dixwell's cousin, Sir Basil Dixwell, 2nd Bt., the current head of the family, Pierpont remembered his first impressions of the regicide's 'accomplishments and accurate gentility', which 'showed him to be no ordinary person'. He added that 'people generally supposed there were great reasons of his reservedness', but added that, while 'they made their guess', they 'could not find him out'.[45] Another of those who gave evidence in the early 1700s, William Jones, claimed that upon his own arrival in New Haven he 'was informed of a gentleman of manifest great education who in other parts of the country endeavoured to lead a retired and obscure life'. Jones went on to claim that, having had 'opportunity of personal acquaintance and frequent conversation with him', he recognized Dixwell from his days at Westminster in the 1640s, although he apparently 'could not recover his true name'.[46] The story, told to Ezra Stiles, that Dixwell's identity had been revealed in 1682 to the young child Hezekiah Willis, has the ring of the apocryphal.[47]

Having successfully covered his tracks for over 20 years, Dixwell was eventually forced to let down his guard. The man who knew him best, Pierpont, finally guessed

---

[41]   *Ibid.*, pp. 164–5; 'Dixwell papers', p. 369.

[42]   Stiles, *History*, pp. 130, 159; BL, Add. Ch. 66210.

[43]   Stiles, *History*, p. 157; BL, Add. Ch. 66210.

[44]   BL, Add. Ch. 66210.

[45]   Stiles, *History*, p. 161. Sir Basil Dixwell (1665–1750) was the grandson of the regicide's elder brother, Mark Dixwell, and the son of the first baronet, to whom the regicide had been guardian after Mark's death.

[46]   *Ibid.*, pp. 155–6, 160; BL, Add. Ch. 66210.

[47]   Stiles, *History*, p. 166.

his true identity, and having confronted Dixwell, was sworn to secrecy.[48] More important was the fact that, as he approached death in his long last illness, Dixwell had to reveal his real name to those who witnessed the legal papers which he prepared, for reasons which will become clear in due course. However, while this ensured that James Heaton was let into the secret of Dixwell's past in 1682, the papers themselves were ordered to remain private until after his death. The reason for such caution was perfectly clear. The recent appointment of the zealous royalist Sir Edmund Andros as governor placed Dixwell's life under renewed threat, and in passing the papers to Pierpont, the regicide explained that 'it was not safe under present changes [that] those writings should be found in his hand'.[49]

III

Dixwell's behaviour in the colonies may be regarded as entirely explicable in the light of fears that his past would catch up with him. Alternatively, the failure to integrate more fully into the New Haven community, in spite of the successful creation of a new identity, and official ignorance regarding his whereabouts, suggests that other factors were at work. This possibility seems to be confirmed by the wording of the deeds and papers which Dixwell passed to Pierpont for safe keeping, in which the regicide invariably referred to himself as John Dixwell of Folkestone Priory. Although there were legal reasons for associating himself with his former status, the omission of any reference to New Haven suggests that Dixwell had never reconciled himself to his New England existence.[50]

Closer inspection of the surviving evidence indicates, moreover, the extent to which Dixwell remained obsessed with English and European affairs, and for reasons more profound than his apparent determination to remain up to date with sartorial fashion.[51] Many of the letters which Dixwell received from England contained pamphlets and newspapers, as in December 1676, when Elizabeth Westrowe sent 'such books of intelligence as I can get'.[52] It was evidently difficult for her to maintain a steady flow of such news while based in the provinces, and in July 1678 she explained that she had withheld a letter 'with expectations of news and more pamphlets, but there is none'.[53] At other times the difficulty lay in the security of the post: in January 1681 she explained that 'I would fain have sent

---

[48]   *Ibid.*, p. 157; BL, Add. Ch. 66210.

[49]   Stiles, *History*, pp. 132, 156, 159; For Andros, see Mary Lou Lustig, *The Imperial Executive in America: Sir Edmund Andros, 1637–1714* (Madison: Fairleigh Dickenson University Press, 2002).

[50]   Stiles, *History*, pp. 143–7.

[51]   See above, p. 170.

[52]   'Dixwell papers', pp. 342–4.

[53]   *Ibid.*, pp. 344–7. Elizabeth Westrowe probably spent much of her time at her second husband's estate in Hertfordshire.

you some pamphlet, but cannot get a passage I can trust'.[54] Dixwell's news also came in the form of detailed political commentary, in letters from friends such as Prince and John Dubois.[55] In June 1679, therefore, Prince wrote from Amsterdam about 'the great fears and troubles that are in England'; outlining news regarding Titus Oates and the Popish Plot, the Exclusion Crisis, and the trial of Stafford, as well as Lauderdale's oppression of the Scots, and the revival of the Covenanting movement north of the border.[56] A letter from Dubois in August 1678 offered an even more detailed account of 'these unhappy times', when men were 'divided into as many factions as sects'. Dubois provided in-depth analysis of European affairs, including the expectation of war with France, before turning his attention to Britain. He wrote of the secret meetings led by Independent ministers such as George Cockayne and Mathew Mead, as well as of the official attempts by the bishops and Lord Chief Justice William Scroggs to silence dissent, and of the flight of some radicals to the continent. Dubois also expressed his own opinions, not least that '[t]he refractory may sometimes be reduced more by lenity than severity', and that 'tis not perhaps a season to persecute the fanatics as they term it, while armies [are] in the field'. Regarding Scotland, meanwhile, he told Dixwell that the nonconformists were 'more heady and more numerous, [and] have been treated more rigorously than those in England'.[57]

IV

Such comments hint at the radical nature of the network with which Dixwell remained associated during his years in New England, in terms of friends as well as family, and this provides a second and more important way of demonstrating the strength of Dixwell's connections with the Old World.

Dixwell's niece, Elizabeth Westrowe, highlights nicely the extent to which networks of political radicals, both inside Kent and beyond, persisted long into the Restoration. In the dying days of the republic she married Thomas Westrowe of Mersham, the son and namesake of one of Dixwell's radical colleagues from Kentish politics in the 1640s and 1650s.[58] In 1676, she negotiated the marriage of her daughter, Eleanor, to John Wildman of Becket in Berkshire, the son of the sometime Leveller leader and plotter against the Protectorate, who had been imprisoned at the Restoration, but who was released in 1667, entered the service

---

54 *Ibid.*, pp. 350–51.

55 For Dubois, see below, p. 176.

56 *Ibid.*, pp. 366–7.

57 *Ibid.*, pp. 358–66.

58 *Canterbury Marriage Licences ... 1619–60*, ed. Joseph M. Cowper (Canterbury: Cross & Jackman, 1894), 1053. See Thomas Westrowe's will, dated 16 September 1653: NA, PROB 11/239, fol. 407v (will of Thomas Westrowe, 1653); PROB 11/432, fol. 341v (Elizabeth Westrowe will). For Thomas Westrowe senior, see Jason Peacey, 'Thomas Westrowe', *History Today* (October 2003), 62.

of the Duke of Buckingham, and drifted towards active plotting against Charles II and James II.[59] Elizabeth's subsequent letters indicate the strength of the political ties which bound the two families, and the extent to which Wildman offered her assistance in hard times, right up to the Glorious Revolution. In December 1676, she told Dixwell that Wildman 'asks most kindly after you', and even after Eleanor's death in 1678, she commented that the Wildmans remained 'my good friends' who 'send you their love and service'.[60] In March 1682 she complained that they were 'the only support I have', and in May 1685 she told Dixwell that they were 'very kind to me and my family and give you their service'.[61] Writing in September 1689, Elizabeth's son explained that their correspondence was now a great deal safer since Wildman had been appointed Postmaster General.[62]

The political and religious radicalism of Dixwell's network extended far beyond his family. The 1673 will of Elizabeth Westrowe's husband revealed his friendship with Dr William Stane, sometime auditor-general and commissary-general in the New Model Army.[63] Although a respectable member of the College of Physicians during the Restoration, and ostensibly politically inactive, Stane evidently remained close to leading Independent ministers such as John Owen.[64] Widow Westrowe also mixed in nonconformist circles, and was friendly with the embattled Independent minister, George Cockayne, in the mid-1670s.[65] Cockayne, of course, had been a close friend of Wildman's since their days plotting against Cromwell in the 1650s, and through him Dixwell's niece may have encountered other radical ministers, such as Henry Jessey, Nathaniel Holmes, and Joseph Caryl.[66]

The Dixwell-Westrowe correspondence also reveals a wealth of other intriguing names. Elizabeth referred, for example, to Major John Bremen, who apparently asked after Dixwell in 1681.[67] A former New Model Army agitator and republican plotter, Bremen spent much of the early 1660s in prison as 'a great fanatic'. He later sat in the Exclusion Parliaments, and was accused of plotting on behalf of Monmouth, before being rewarded with office after the Glorious Revolution.[68]

---

[59]   'Dixwell papers', pp. 341–2. For Wildman, see Maurice Ashley, *John Wildman: Plotter and Postmaster* (London: Jonathan Cape, 1947).

[60]   'Dixwell papers', pp. 342–4, 344–7, 350–51.

[61]   *Ibid.*, pp. 351–2, 354–6. See also Elizabeth Westrowe's will: PROB 11/432, fol. 341v.

[62]   'Dixwell papers', pp. 356–7.

[63]   NA, PROB 11/343, fol. 273v.

[64]   Patrick Little, 'William Stane' (draft biography, History of Parliament Trust); NA, PROB 11/362, fol. 323v.

[65]   'Dixwell papers', pp. 342–4.

[66]   *TSP*, vi, 829–30; *ODNB*; NA, PROB 11/425, fol. 225.

[67]   'Dixwell papers', pp. 350–51.

[68]   *The History of Parliament: The House of Commons, 1660–1690*, ed. Basil D. Henning, 3 vols (London: Secker & Warburg, 1983), i, 709–10; Greaves, *Deliver*, pp. 67, 69, 96, 203; Greaves, *Secrets of the Kingdom* (Stanford: Stanford University Press, 1992), pp. 114, 158, 194, 276, 335, 350.

Another mutual friend was Benjamin Hewling, a London merchant and Baptist, who married the daughter of William Kiffin, and who too was arrested soon after the Restoration. Hewling's sons joined the Monmouth rebellion, while his Baptist daughter, Hannah, married Oliver Cromwell's grandson in 1686.[69] A third friend, John Dubois, was a Kentishman of French Protestant extraction who became a London merchant, common councillor and Whig MP in the Exclusion Parliaments, and who served on the Whig jury which acquitted Shaftesbury of treason.[70]

The importance of such connections lies in locating Dixwell within a network of late seventeenth-century nonconformists and political plotters in exile in the Low Countries. Thomas Westrowe's 1689 letter mentioned friends who were willing to help Dixwell in the Low Countries, including William Histerman and Alexander Henderson, the latter of whom was a prominent Scottish radical.[71] Dubois' son-in-law, Robert Archer of Amsterdam, another of Dixwell's friends, appears to have been involved in surreptitious printing in the Low Countries, to have assisted in preparations for Argyll's expedition to Scotland in 1685, and to have been a close associate of Monmouth, and he too secured office after the Revolution.[72] Francis Prince, yet another of Dixwell's correspondents, was the person to whom Elizabeth Westrowe bound her son as an apprentice, and the person to whom she turned to find a master for another son.[73] A friend of William Kiffin since the mid-1650s, and

---

[69]   Greaves, *Secrets*, pp. 351–2, 354–6, 409; NA, PROB 11/376, fol. 206v; J. Tuchin, *The Bloody Assizes*, ed. Joseph G. Muddiman (Edinburgh: William Hodge, 1929), pp. 55, 75, 94, 105, 117, 127; Gary S. De Krey, *London and the Restoration, 1659–83* (Cambridge: Cambridge University Press, 2005), p. 407; *CCISP*, v, 65; Mark Noble, *Memoirs of the Protectorate House of Cromwell*, 2 vols (Birmingham: Pearson & Rollason, 1784), ii, pp. 443–4; BL, Add. MS 41818, fol. 78.

[70]   *ODNB*; *The House of Commons*, ed. Henning, ii, pp. 237–8; Gary De Krey, 'London radicals and revolutionary politics, 1675–1683', in *The Politics of Religion in Restoration England*, ed. Tim Harris et al. (Oxford: Blackwell, 1990), pp. 144, 149; NA, PROB 11/378, fol. 296v.

[71]   'Dixwell papers', pp. 356–7; Greaves, *Secrets*, pp. 62, 372. See: P.W. Klein, 'Little London: British Merchants in Rotterdam during the Seventeenth and Eighteenth Centuries', in *Enterprise and History: Essays in Honour of Charles Wilson*, ed. D.C. Coleman and Peter Mathias (Cambridge: Cambridge University Press, 1984); A. De Bussey, 'The English Church at Amsterdam', *Baptist Quarterly*, 12 (1948), 423–8; Ginny Gardner, *The Scottish Exile Community in the Netherlands, 1660–1690* (East Linton: Tuckwell, 2004); Alice C. Carter, *The English Reformed Church in Amsterdam* (Amsterdam: Scheltema, & Holkema, 1964); Fred Dentz, *History of the English Church at the Hague, 1586–1929* (Delft: W.D. Meinema, 1929); Charles Grimes, *The Early Story of the English Church at Utrecht* (Chambéry: Imprimeries Réunies, 1930); J. Walker, 'The English Exiles in Holland during the Reigns of Charles II and James II', *Transactions of the Royal Historical Society*, 4th series, 30 (1948), 111–25.

[72]   'Dixwell papers', pp. 358–66; Mark Knights, *Politics and Opinion in Crisis, 1678–81* (Cambridge: Cambridge University Press, 1994), p. 158; NA, PC 2/69, fol. 132; Greaves, *Secrets*, pp. 285, 350; BL, Add. MS 41818, fols 125v, 234v.

[73]   'Dixwell papers', pp. 344–7, 350–51, 351–2, 352–3.

a leading figure in Amsterdam's Congregational community, Prince was one of those merchants to whom Shaftesbury turned for personal protection and financial assistance when he fled into exile in 1682, and who was monitored by Charles II's agents as a result.[74] By the early 1680s, the latter knew that Hewling too was part of the same circle in the Low Countries, and that other associates included yet another of Wildman's friends, the pamphleteer and plotter, Robert Ferguson, sometime Kentish minister and friend of the Independents' patriarch, John Owen.[75] One of the most intriguing members of this group was Prince's close friend Abraham Kick, who had sheltered regicides in the early 1660s, Shaftesbury in 1682, and Slingsby Bethel in 1685.[76] These men were joined by other malcontents in the early 1680s, including another of Cromwell's grandsons, the regicide John Phelps, and the sons of other king-killers such as Thomas Harrison and Daniel Blagrave, as well as a host of 'rebellion-promoting merchants'. The latter were supposed to have been 'the great coffeemen as spread all seditious news', and who were known to have been involved in printing and circulating seditious literature.[77]

Whether or not it is plausible to suggest that Dixwell's behaviour in New Haven was that of someone who was unwilling, rather than merely unable, to settle into colonial life, evidence from his personal papers demonstrates not only that he retained an interest in English and continental affairs, but also that he was a corresponding member of a radical circle of nonconformists and plotters. His links with this group had their roots in Kentish politics and the High Court of Justice, were strengthened by political marriages among his kin, and nurtured in the febrile political atmosphere of the late Stuart crisis.

V

The crucial final stage in this exploration of Dixwell's post-Restoration life concerns his attitude towards the future, and this final section reconsiders what, if anything, might have induced him to leave New England, and what he considered to be the condition of his affairs in Kent, as well as comments made by himself and his correspondents regarding the possibility of his 're-migration'.

Dixwell's papers indicate that the severance of his financial ties with England was not complete after all. He laid claim to some £2,500, apparently owing to him as

---

[74] BL, Add. MS 4157, fol. 106; Greaves, *Deliver*, p. 93; BL, Add. MS 37981, fol. 68; Kenneth Haley, *The First Earl of Shaftesbury* (Oxford: Clarendon Press, 1968), pp. 729–31; William D. Christie, *A Life of Anthony Ashley Cooper, 1st Earl of Shaftesbury*, 2 vols (London: MacMillan & Co., 1871), ii, 458–9.

[75] BL, Add. MS 37981, fols 58, 68.

[76] Richard Ashcraft, *Revolutionary Politics and Locke's Two Treatises of Government* (Princeton: Princeton University Press, 1986), pp. 419–20, 446; BL, Add. MS 41818, fols 107, 206, 274; Add. MS 37981, fols 58, 68.

[77] BL, Add. MS 37981, fols 2v, 4, 68; Add. MS 41818, fols 125v; NA, SP 84, fols 118, 144–v.

trustee of his brother's estate, railed at the treatment he had received from his family, and indicated his willingness to pursue the matter through the English courts, after taking advice from leading London lawyers.[78] Dixwell also laid claim to his own personal estate, and intended to revoke the conveyance made to Sir Thomas Peyton in 1660, despite the fact that the lands had been confiscated, that Peyton had been forced to pay almost £4,000 for their recovery, and that revocation was legally impossible for someone attainted for treason.[79] Nevertheless, it was this attempted revocation which explains the drafting of Dixwell's 1680s deeds written in New Haven.[80] Although such evidence does not necessarily indicate a desire to return to England, other papers make this abundantly clear. First, Dixwell's legal papers demonstrate his ambition that his wife and children, who had never set foot outside of Connecticut, should settle with his family in England in the event of his death.[81] More importantly, his papers also intimate that Dixwell himself sought to return home, and he expressed confidence that 'the Lord will appear for people and the good old cause for which I suffer, and that there will be those in power again that will relieve the injured and oppressed, the lord having given me opportunity to change my condition'.[82]

That Dixwell did not return home reflected the inauspicious political situation in England. This was abundantly clear to him from the letters of Prince and Dubois, which reflected upon 'great discontents', 'great fears and troubles' and 'these unhappy times', and upon the fact that 'God's hand is soar out against us'.[83] It was also evident from the letters of Elizabeth Westrowe. In March 1683, she complained: 'I am still in the wilderness and labouring under many troubles', adding of her family that 'I am a stranger to them all'.[84] In 1678, she wrote of 'my great afflictions' and 'these fiery trials', not least perhaps because her chosen way of worshipping God was commonly considered 'heresy'.[85] Fear regarding the religious and political purity of England – she considered herself to be living in a 'debauched' age – forced her to send her son to Holland for his apprenticeship, and to bemoan the difficulty of finding a match for her daughter who was sufficiently 'honest'.[86]

---

[78]   Stiles, *History*, pp. 138–43, 144–7, 148; 'Dixwell Papers', pp. 371–3, 373–4; *The Oxinden and Peyton Letters 1642–1670*, ed. Dorothy Gardiner (London: Sheldon Press, 1937), p. 110.

[79]   BL, Add. MS 40717, fols 161–8, 169–74, 175, 177, 183–99; Connecticut State Library, New Haven Probate Records, vol. 2, part 1, pp. 8–9; Stiles, *History*, pp. 136–40.

[80]   Stiles, *History*, pp. 139–40.

[81]   *Ibid.*, p. 145; 'Dixwell papers', pp. 373–4. Dixwell's family never made the move to England; Stiles, *History*, pp. 128, 148–50; Z.J. Powers, *New Haven Town Records III, 1684–1769* (New Haven Colony Historical Society, 1962), pp. 101, 136, 209, 238, 298, 319, 334, 431, 441, 482.

[82]   Stiles, *History*, p. 142.

[83]   'Dixwell papers', pp. 358–68.

[84]   *Ibid.*, pp. 353–4. She eventually moved to London: NA, PROB 11/432, fol. 341v.

[85]   'Dixwell papers', pp. 344–8.

[86]   *Ibid.*, pp. 344–7, 352–3.

If such comments help to explain why Dixwell refrained from risking the journey to England, others indicate that such a trip was seriously considered. In August 1678, Elizabeth Westrowe explained: 'I hope for an opportunity to tell you more than this, for if you come into Holland I will come and meet you'. She expressed 'the joy I have in the hopes of seeing you [...] where we shall have more freedom than this opportunity will give me of a discourse'.[87] In July 1680, she wrote that 'we would be glad of an opportunity of seeing one another if it were the will of our good God, but we must wait on the wise disposer of all things, whom doth what pleaseth him with kingdoms and families'.[88] In March 1683, she hoped that 'the lord will give us the comfort of seeing one another in this world; if not, yet in another where all things will be made known and all the works of darkness be brought to light'.[89] In the wake of the Glorious Revolution, however, Thomas Westrowe explained that it was now safe for Dixwell to return. He explained that, 'finding all things going so well and our king is bent to the honest party, I have endeavoured to get your pardon which I doubt not but to obtain and also an act of parliament to back it'. He went on to suggest that Dixwell's family should 'make all the haste you can possible to Amsterdam in Holland where I have friends that will receive you and you may be as safe as where you are'. Westrowe had already made arrangements for friends in Amsterdam to accept bills of exchange, adding that such documents would also find 'due honour' in London. The only reason for advising 'the greatest privacy' was because some of Dixwell's kinsmen 'may else do you a mischief, they having spoken very threatening things of you'. This appears to have been the only reason why 'Wildman thinks it the best way to come first to Amsterdam [...] he knowing it a place that you may be safe in, he having been there three years without danger or fear'.[90] These do not appear to have been the comments of someone who did not already know of Dixwell's desire to return to England, and the only reason for the regicide's failure to act upon such advice seems to have been that death came rather sooner than Westrowe's letter.[91]

VI

There is one curious epilogue to the story of Dixwell's later life which provides the final piece of the puzzle surrounding the surviving documentation and the attempt to reclaim his English estate. In 1710, John Dixwell junior travelled to England in search of his patrimony, armed with a letter from Pierpont to Sir Basil Dixwell, 2nd Bt., a letter of introduction from Cotton Mather (Increase Mather's son), as well as certified copies of New Haven records, and depositions of those who had known

---

87 *Ibid.*, pp. 347–8.
88 *Ibid.*, pp. 349–50.
89 *Ibid.*, pp. 353–4.
90 *Ibid.*, pp. 356–7.
91 *Ibid.*, pp. 356–7, 357–8; Stiles, *History*, p. 135.

his father in New England.[92] The aim was clearly to prove that he was the son of the regicide, and although it was emphasized that he 'comes not over because he is any wants or straits', the trip was clearly made with a view to reclaiming 'their father's estate'.[93] This initiative evidently and rather predictably failed, but the childless Sir Basil eventually changed his mind, and his 1732 will declared that at least part of his estate was to pass to his American cousins, specifically the regicide's grandson, Basil Dixwell, whom he acknowledged as the son of 'my great uncle, Colonel John Dixwell'.[94]

This rather touching story provides a fitting conclusion to an attempt to demonstrate that Dixwell was an exile rather than merely an émigré. The documentation relating to his life after 1660 reveals the nature of his interaction with those among whom he took shelter, a man who adapted to life in an alien environment without ever truly embedding himself within its society, and a political firebrand who appears to have lost none of his earlier zeal. Dixwell the regicide expressed not so much the nostalgia for Old England so familiar among inhabitants of the colonies, as a determination to retain his links with political allies in England and in other places of exile, and to restore the fortunes of his family and his cause. The 'good old cause' was something for which Dixwell was willing to suffer, but it was also something towards which he continued to strive.

---

[92] Stiles, *History*, pp. 160–62; BL, Add. Ch. 66210.

[93] Stiles, *History*, pp. 160–61, 163.

[94] *Ibid.*, pp. 150–51, 155; NA, PROB 11/779, fol. 57.

Works Cited

MANUSCRIPT SOURCES

Bodleian Library, Oxford
Bodley MS 878
Clarendon MSS 39, 47, 59, 126–7, 129
Rawlinson MS, Poet. 16
Tanner MS 52, 57

British Library, London
Add. Ch. 66210
Add. MS 4157
Add. MS 20001
Add. MS 37719
Add. MS 37981
Add. MS 40717
Add. MS 41818
Add. MS 66210
Add. MS 70499
Add. MS 72280
Add. MS 78423
Add. MS 78424
Egerton MS 2535
Harleian MS 5219
Harleian MS 6942
Verney Papers

Connecticut State Library
New Haven Probate Records

Centre for Kentish Studies
U270/T267

Lincoln Cathedral Library
MS 276

The National Archives, Kew
LR 2
PC 2
PROB 11
SP 77, 84

National Library of Wales
MS 5297

Nottingham University Library
Portland MS, Ne D 1662; Ne D 455–6
Portland MS, P1 E 1/1/1, 3, 4
Portland MS, P1 E11/9/1/18
Portland MS, PW 1

Stadsarchief Antwerpen (City Archives, Antwerp)
GF 188/2

Whitney Library, New Haven
MSS 7–8

Yale University, Beinecke Library
Osborn MS b 233

PRIMARY SOURCES

Arnway, John, *The Tablet, or, the Moderation*, 2nd edn, (The Hague, 1649).

Aubrey, John, *Brief Lives*, ed. Andrew Clark, 2 vols (Oxford: Clarendon Press, 1898).

———, *Brief Lives*, ed. Oliver Lawson Dick (London: Secker and Warburg, 1949).

Aylesbury, William, and Sir Charles Cotterell, *History of the Civil Wars of France* (London, 1647).

Bargrave, Robert, *The Travel Diary of Robert Bargrave, Levant Merchant 1647–1656*, ed. Michael G. Brennan (London: Hakluyt Society, 1999).

Basire, Isaac, *Travels through France and Italy (1647–1649)*, ed. Luigi Monga and R. Chris Hassel, Biblioteca del Viaggio in Italia, Testi, xxv (Geneva: Slatkine, 1987).

Bisterfeld, J.H., *De uno deo, patre, Filio ac Spiritu sancto, mysterium pietatis ...* (Leiden, 1639).

Bramhall, John, *The Church of England Defended ...* (London, 1659).

———, *A just vindication of the Church of England, from the unjust aspersion of criminal schism* (The Hague, 1654).

———, *The Works of the most Reverend Father in God, John Bramhall ... With a life of the author, and a collection of his letters*, 5 vols (Oxford: J.H. Parker, 1843–1845).

Calendar of the Proceedings of the Committee for Compounding, ed. Mary A.E. Green (London, 1889–92).

Cary, Elizabeth, the Lady Falkland, *The Tragedy of Mariam, the Fair Queen of Jewry, with the Lady Falkland her Life by One of her Daughters*, ed. Barry

Weller and Margaret W. Ferguson (Berkeley and Los Angeles: University of California Presses, 1994).

Cary, Henry, *Memorials of the Great Civil War in England*, 2 vols (London: Henry Colburn, 1842).

Cary, Lucius, Lord Falkland, *A Speech Made to the House of Commons Concerning Episcopacy* (London, 1641).

Cary, Patrick, *The Poems of Patrick Cary*, ed. Veronica Delany (Oxford: Clarendon Press, 1978).

Cavendish, Margaret, *The Life of William Cavendish, Duke of Newcastle*, ed. C.H. Firth (London: Routledge, 1906).

———, *The Life of the Thrice Noble, High, and Puissant Prince William Cavendishe, Duke, Marquess, and Earl of Newcastle* (London, 1667, 1675).

———, *Nature's Pictures Drawn by Fancies Pencil to the Life* (London, 1656).

———, *Poems and Fancies* (London, 1653).

———, *The Worlds Olio* (London, 1655).

Chillingworth, William, *The Apostolical Institution of Episcopacy Demonstrated* (London, 1644).

———, *The Religion of Protestants A Safe Way to Salvation* (Oxford, 1638).

Coke, Edward, *The Third Part of the Institutes of the Laws of England* (London, 1644).

The Correspondence of Bishop Brian Duppa and Sir Justinian Isham 1650–1660, ed. Gyles Isham (Northampton: Publications of the Northamptonshire Record Society, 17, 1951).

Cowley, Abraham, *The Collected Works of Abraham Cowley*, ed. Thomas O. Calhoun et al., 6 vols (Newark, London, and Toronto: University of Delaware Press, 1989).

———, *Poems*, ed. Alfred R. Waller (Cambridge: Cambridge University Press, 1905).

———, *Poems* (London, 1656)

Crellius, Johannes, and Johannes Völkel, *De Vera Religione ...* (Rakow [Amsterdam], 1642).

Cressy, Hugh, *Exomologesis; or a Faithful Narrative of the Occasion and Motives of the Conversion unto Catholique Unity of Hugh Paulin de Cressy* (Paris, 1647).

Davenant, William, *Sir William Davenant's 'Gondibert'*, ed. David F. Gladish (Oxford: Clarendon Press, 1971).

de la Milletière, Theodore Brachet, *The Victory of Truth for the Peace of the Church to the King of Great Britain to Invite him to Embrace the Roman-Catholick Faith by Monsieur de la Militiere, ... with an Answer thereunto, Written by the Right Reverend John Bramhall, D.D.* (The Hague, 1653).

Denham, John, *The Poetical Works of Sir John Denham*, ed. Theodore H. Banks, 2nd edn (Hamden: Archon Books, 1969).

De Vera Religione (Rakow [Amsterdam], 1642).

De Viau, Theophile, *Oeuvres poétiques*, ed. Guido Saba (Paris: Classiques Garnier, 1990).

Dryden, John, *The Works of John Dryden*, ed. Niles Hooker and H.T. Swendenberg, Jr, 20 vols (Berkeley: University of California Press, 1956–2006).

Evelyn, John, *Diary and Correspondence of John Evelyn*, ed. William Bray (London: Routledge, n.d.).

———, *The Diary of John Evelyn*, ed. E.S. de Beer, 6 vols (Oxford: Clarendon Press, 1955).

Ferne, Henry, *Of the Division between the English and Romish Church upon the Reformation by Way of Answer to the Seeming Plausible Pretences of the Romish party* (London, 1652).

Gryphius, Andreas, *Ermordete Majestät oder Carolus Stuardus König von Gross Brittannien* (Trauerspiel, 1657, rev. 1663).

Hammond, Henry, *Considerations of Present Use Concerning the Danger Resulting from the Change of Our Church Government* (London, 1645).

———, *Dissertationes Quatuor, quibus Episcopatus Jura ex S. Scripturis et Primaeva Antiquitate adstruuntur, contra Sententiam D. Blondelli et aliorum* (London, 1651).

———, *A Letter of Resolution to Six Quaeres of Present Use in the Church of England* (London, 1653).

———, *Of the Power of the Keyes, or Of Binding and Loosing* (London, 1647)

———, *Of the Reasonableness of the Christian Religion* (London, 1650).

———, *Of Schisme* (London, 1654).

———, *A View of Some Exceptions which Have Beene Made by a Romanist to the Lord Viscount Falkland's Discourse Of the Infallibilitie of the Church of Rome* (London, 1646).

Herbert, Edward, *The Life of Edward, Lord Herbert of Cherbury*, ed. James M. Shuttleworth (Oxford: Oxford University Press, 1976).

Herrick, Robert, *The Poetical Works of Robert Herrick*, ed. L.C. Martin (Oxford: Clarendon Press, 1956).

Hobbes, Thomas, *Correspondence*, ed. Noel Malcolm, 2 vols (Oxford, 1994).

———, *Critique du 'De mundo' de Thomas White*, ed. Jean Jacquot and Harold W. Jones (Paris: Librarie philosophique J. Vrin, 1973).

———, 'A Dialogue Between a Philosopher and a Student, of the Common Laws of England', in *Writings on Common Law and Hereditary Right*, ed. Alan Cromartie and Quentin Skinner (Oxford: Clarendon Press, 2005).

———, *Human Nature and De Corpore Politico – The Elements of Law Natural and Politic*, ed. J.C.A. Gaskin (Oxford and New York: Oxford University Press, 1994).

———, *Leviathan*, ed. Richard Tuck (Cambridge: Cambridge University Press, 1991).

———, *Leviathan* (London, 1651).

———, *Mr Hobbes Considered in his Loyalty, Religion, Reputation, and Manners, by Way of Letter to Dr Wallis* (London, 1662).

———, *Thomas Hobbes malmesburiensis opera philosophica quae latine scripsit omnia*, ed. William Molesworth, 5 vols (London: Bohn, 1839–45).

Holles, Gervase, *Memorials of the Holles Family, 1493–1665*, ed. A.C. Wood (London: Royal Historical Society, 1937)

Howell, James, *Instructions for Forreine Travell*, ed. Edward Arber (London, 1869).

Hutchinson, Thomas, *The History of Massachusetts*, 3rd edn, 2 vols (Boston, 1795).

Hyde, Edward, first Earl of Clarendon, *A Brief View and Survey of the Dangerous and Pernicious Errors to Church and State, In Mr. Hobbes's Book, Entitled Leviathan* (Oxford, 1676).

———, *Miscellanous Works of the Right Honourable Edward, Earl of Clarendon*, 2nd edn (London, 1751).

———, *The History of the Rebellion and Civil Wars in England*, ed. W. Dunn Macray, 6 vols (Oxford: Clarendon Press, 1888).

———, *The Life of Edward, Earl of Clarendon*, 3 vols (Oxford, 1827).

———, *State Papers Collected by Edward, Earl of Clarendon*, ed. Richard Scrope and Thomas Monkhouse (Oxford, 1767–86).

———, *Two Dialogues: 'Of the Want of Respect Due to Age' and 'Concerning Education'*, ed. Martine W. Brownley, Augustan Reprint Society, 227–8 (Los Angeles: William Andrews Clark Memorial Library, University of California, 1984).

Jenkyn, Pathericke, *Amorea. The Lost Lover. Or, The Idea of Love and Misfortune. Being Poems, Sonets* [sic]*, Songs, Odes, Pastoral, Elegies, Lyrick Poems, and Epigrams. Never before Printed* (London, 1661).

Journals of the House of Commons.

Journals of the House of Lords.

Ludlow, Edmund, *The Memoirs of Edmund Ludlow*, ed. Charles Firth, 2 vols (Oxford: Clarendon Press, 1894).

The Memoirs of Anne, Lady Halkett and Ann, Lady Fanshawe, ed. John Loftis (Oxford: Clarendon Press, 1979).

Mercurius Politicus, no. 39, 637 (5 March 1651).

Mersenne, Marin, *Correspondance du P. Marin Mersenne*, ed. Paul Tannery and Cornelis De Waard, 17 vols (Paris: Éditions du Centre national de la recherche scientifique, 1932–1988).

Micanzio, Fulgenzio, *Lettere a William Cavendish (1615–1628)*, trans. Thomas. Hobbes, Scrinium Historicale, XV (Rome: Istuto storico O.S.M., 1987).

Nedham, Marchamont, *The Case of the Commonwealth of England, Stated*, ed. Philip Knachel (Charlottesville: University Press of Virginia, 1969).

The Nicholas Papers: Correspondence of Sir Edward Nicholas, Secretary of State, ed. G.F. Warner, 4 vols (London: Camden Society, 1886–1920).

Owen, John, *Review of the Annotations of Hugo Grotius* (London, 1656).

The Oxinden and Peyton Letters 1642–1670, ed. Dorothy Gardiner (London: Sheldon Press, 1937).

Petavius, *Dionysius, Dogmata theologica* (Paris, 1644).

Quarles, John, *Regale Lectum Miserae, or, a Kingly Bed of Miserie* (s.l. 1649).

————, *Fons lachrymarum, or, A fountain of teares* (London, 1648).

Reresby, John, *Memoirs and Travels of Sir John Reresby*, ed. Albert Ivatt (London, 1904).

Schleder, *Johann Georg, Theatrum Europaeum* (Frankfurt am Main, 1663).

Statutes of the Realm, 2nd edn, 12 vols (London, 1963).

Taylor, Jeremy, *A sermon preached in Christs-Church, Dublin, July 16, 1663, at the funeral of the most Reverend Father in God John, late Lord Archbishop of Armagh and primate of all Ireland with a succint narrative of his whole life* (London, 1663).

Van den Bosch, Jan, *Kort Beworp vande dry Teghenwoordighe aenmerckens-weerdighe Wonderheden des Wereldts* (Cologne, 1656).

Vaughan, Henry, *Silex Scintillans: Sacred Poems and private Ejaculations*, 2nd edn (London, 1655).

Vondel, Joost van den, *Faeton of Reuckeloze Stoutheit (Phaeton, or Reckless Audacity)*, (1663).

————, *Mary Stuart or Tortured Majesty*, trans. with Introduction and Notes by Kristiann P. Aercke (Ottawa: Dovehouse Editions, 1996).

Waller, Edmund, *The Poems of Edmund Waller*, ed. G. Thorn Drury, 2 vols (London, 1901).

Walton, Izaak, *The Compleate Angler, or, The Contemplative man's recreation* (London, 1653).

SECONDARY SOURCES

Agamben, Giorgio, *Homo Sacer: Sovereign Power and Bare Life* (Stanford: Stanford University Press, 1998).

————, *Means Without Ends: Notes on Politics* (Minneapolis: University of Minnesota Press, 2000).

Akkerman, Nadine N.W., and Paul R. Sellin, 'A Stuart Masque in Holland: *Ballet de La Carmesse de La Haye* (1655)', *Ben Jonson Journal*, 11 (2004), 207–58, 12 (2005), 141–64.

Alexander, R.J., 'A Possible Historical Source for the Figure of Poleh in Andreas Gryphius' *Carolus Stuardus*', *Daphnis*, 3.2 (1974), 203–7.

Anderson, Virginia, *New England's Generation: The Great Migration and the formation of society and culture in the seventeenth century* (Cambridge: Cambridge University Press, 1991).

Anselment, Raymond, 'The Countess of Carlisle and Caroline Praise: Convention and Reality', *Studies in Philology*, 82 (1985), 212–33.

Arendt, Hannah, *The Origins of Totalitarianism*, 2nd edn (London: Allen and Unwin, 1958).

Arnold, E.B., 'A Sussex Family during the Commonwealth', *Sussex County Magazine*, x (1936), 740–43.

Ashcraft, Richard, *Revolutionary Politics and Locke's Two Treatises of Government* (Princeton: Princeton University Press, 1986).

Ashley, Maurice, *John Wildman: Plotter and Postmaster* (London: Jonathan Cape, 1947).

Auden, W.H., *Collected Poems*, ed. Edward Mendelson (New York: Random House, 1976).

Balfour, Ian, and Eduardo Cadava (eds), 'And Justice For All? The Claims of Human Rights', *South Atlantic Quarterly*, 103, 2/3 (2004), 277–96.

Battigelli, Anna, *Margaret Cavendish and the Exiles of the Mind* (Lexington: University of Kentucky Press, 1998).

Bennett, Alexandra G., '"Now let my language speake": The Authorship, Rewriting, and Audience(s) of Jane Cavendish and Elizabeth Brackley', *Early Modern Literary Studies*, 11.2 (September, 2005), 3.1–13.

Bentley, Gerald E. (ed.), *The Jacobean and Caroline Stage*, 7 vols (Oxford: Clarendon Press, 1941–68).

Berghaus, Günther, *Die Quellen zu Andreas Gryphius' Trauerspiel 'Carolus Stuardus'. Studien zur Entstehung eines Historisch-Politischen Martyrerdramas der Barockzeit* (Türbingen: Niemeyer, 1984).

Bjurström, Per, *Giacomo Torelli and Baroque Stage Design*, Acta Universitatis Upsaliensis. Figura. n.s. ii (Stockholm: Nationalmuseum, 1972).

Bobbio, Norberto, *Thomas Hobbes and the Natural Law Tradition* (Chicago: University of Chicago Press, 1993).

Bosher, Robert S., *The Making of the Restoration Settlement: The Influence of the Laudians 1649–1662* (London: Dacre Press, 1951).

Bots, Hans, and Pierre Leroy, 'Hugo Grotius et la Reunion des Chrétiens: Entre le Savoir et l'Inquietude', *XVIIe Siècle*, 35 (1983), 451–69.

Boym, Svetlana, *The Future of Nostalgia* (New York: Basic Books, 2001).

Bremer, Francis J., *Congregational Communion: Clerical Friendship in the Anglo-American Puritan Community* (Boston: Northeastern University Press, 1994).

———, 'Increase Mather's Friends: The Transatlantic Congregational Network of the Seventeenth Century', *Proceedings of the American Antiquarian Society*, 94 (1984), 59–96.

Brennan, Michael G. (ed.), *English Civil War Travellers and the Origins of the Western European Grand Tour* (London, 2002).

———, *The Origins of the Grand Tour: The Travels of Robert Montagu, Lord Mandeville (1649–1654), William Hammond (1655–1658), Banaster Maynard (1660–1663)* (London: Hakluyt Society, 2004).

Brenner, Robert, *Merchants and Revolution: Commercial Change, Political Conflict, and London's Overseas Traders, 1550–1653* (London: Verso, 1993).

Brett, Annabel, *Liberty, Right and Nature: Individual Rights in Later Scholastic Thought* (Cambridge: Cambridge University Press, 1997).

Britland, Karen, '"All emulation cease, and jars": Political Possibilities in *Chloridia*, Queen Henrietta Maria's Masque of 1631', *Ben Jonson Journal*, 9 (2002), 87–108.

————, *Drama at the Courts of Queen Henrietta Maria* (Cambridge: Cambridge University Press, 2006).

————, '*Florimène*: The Author and Occasion', *Review of English Studies*, n.s. 53 (2002), 475–83.

Burgess, Glenn (ed.), 'Contexts for the Writing and Publication of Hobbes's *Leviathan*', *History of Political Thought*, 11 (1990), 675–702.

————, *The New British History: Founding a Modern State 1603–1715* (London and New York: I.B. Tauris, 1999).

————, 'Usurpation, Obligation and Obedience in the Thought of the Engagement Controversy', *Historical Journal*, 29 (1986), 515–36.

Buruma, Ian, 'The Romance of Exile', *The New Republic* (February 12, 2001), 33–8.

Campbell, Gordon, and Thomas N. Corns, *John Milton: Life, Work, and Thought* (Oxford: Oxford University Press, 2008).

Campbell, L.B., *Scenes and Machines on the English Stage During the Renaissance: A Classical Revival* (Cambridge: Cambridge University Press, 1923).

Canova-Green, Marie-Claude, *La Politique-spectacle au grand siècle: les rapports franco-anglais* (Paris, Seattle and Tübingen: Biblio 17, 1993).

Canterbury Marriage Licences ... 1619–60, ed. Joseph M. Cowper (Canterbury: Cross & Jackman, 1894).

Carter, Alice C., *The English Reformed Church in Amsterdam* (Amsterdam: Scheltema, & Holkema, 1964).

Catterall, Ralph C.H., 'Sir George Downing and the Regicides', *American Historical Review*, 17 (1911–12), 268–89.

Chalmers, Hero, *Royalist Women Writers 1650–1689* (Oxford: Clarendon Press, 2004).

Chaney, Edward, *The Evolution of the Grand Tour* (London and Portland: Frank Cass, 2000).

————, *The Grand Tour and the Great Rebellion: Richard Lassels and 'The Voyage of Italy' in the Seventeenth Century* (Geneva: Slatkine, 1985).

Christie, William D., *A Life of Anthony Ashley Cooper, 1st Earl of Shaftesbury*, 2 vols (London: MacMillan & Co., 1871).

Claassen, Jo-Marie, *Displaced Persons: The Literature of Exile from Cicero to Boethius* (Madison: The University of Wisconsin Press, 1999).

Clancy, Thomas H., 'The Jesuits and the Independents', *Archivum historicum Societatis Iesu*, 40 (1971), 67–90.

Clucas, Stephen, 'The Atomism of the Cavendish Circle: A Reappraisal', *Seventeenth Century*, 9 (1994), 247–73.

Colie, Rosalie L., '*Some Thankfulnesse to Constantine*': A Study of the English Influence upon the Early Works of Constantijn Huygens* (The Hague: Nijhoff, 1956).

Collins, Jeffrey, *The Allegiance of Thomas Hobbes* (Oxford: Oxford University Press, 2005).

————, 'The Restoration Bishops and the Royal Supremacy', *Church History*, 68 (1999), 549–80.

————, 'Thomas Hobbes and the Blackloist Conspiracy of 1649', *Historical Journal*, 42 (2002), 305–31.

Condren, Conal, *Argument and Authority in Early Modern England: The Presupposition of Oaths and Offices* (Cambridge: Cambridge University Press, 2006).

————, 'Casuistry to Newcastle: *The Prince* in the World of the Book', in *Political Discourse in Early Modern Britain*, ed. Nicholas Phillipson and Quentin Skinner (Cambridge: Cambridge University Press, 1993), pp. 164–86.

Conforti, Joseph A., *Explorations of Personal Identity from the Pilgrims to Mid-Twentieth Century* (Chapel Hill and London; University of North Carolina Press, 2001).

————, *Saints and Strangers: New England in British North America* (Baltimore: John Hopkins University Press, 2006).

Corns, Thomas N., *Uncloistered Virtue: English Political Literature, 1640–1660* (Oxford: Oxford University Press, 1992).

Corp, Edward, *A Court in Exile: The Stuarts in France, 1689–1718* (Cambridge: Cambridge University Press, 2004).

————, *The Stuart Court in Rome: The Legacy of Exile* (London: Ashgate, 2003).

Cowan, Brian, *The Social Life of Coffee: The Emergence of the British Coffeehouse* (London and New Haven: Yale University Press, 2005).

Cressy, David, *Coming Over: Migration and Communication between England and New England in the Seventeenth Century* (Cambridge: Cambridge University Press, 1987).

D'Addario, Christopher, *Exile and Journey in Seventeenth-Century Literature* (Cambridge: Cambridge University Press, 2007).

Daemen-de Gelder, Katrien, and J.P. Vander Motten, 'Thomas Ross's *Second Punick War* (1661 and 1672), Royalist Panegyric and Artistic Collaboration in the Southern Netherlands', *Quaerendo*, 38 (2008), 32–48.

Darley, Gillian, *John Evelyn: Living for Ingenuity* (New Haven and London: Yale University Press, 2006).

Davies, Randall, 'An Inventory of the Duke of Buckingham's Pictures, etc. at York House in 1635', *The Burlington Magazine for Connoisseurs* 10 (1907), 48: 376–382.

De Beer, E.S, 'An Uncollected Poem by Waller', *Review of English Studies*, 8 (1922), 203–5.

De Bussey, A., 'The English Church at Amsterdam', *Baptist Quarterly*, 12 (1948), 423–8.

De Groot, Jerome, 'John Denham and Lucy Hutchinson's Commonplace Book', *Studies in English Literature*, 48 (2008), 147–63.

————, *Royalist Identities* (Basingstoke: Palgrave, 2004).

De Krey, Gary S., *London and the Restoration, 1659–83* (Cambridge: Cambridge University Press, 2005).

———, 'London Radicals and Revolutionary Politics, 1675–1683', in *The Politics of Religion in Restoration England*, ed. Tim Harris et al. (Oxford: Blackwell, 1990).

De la Bédoyère, Guy, 'John Evelyn's Library Catalogue', *The Book Collector*, 43 (1994), 529–48.

Delbanco, Andrew, 'Looking Homeward, Going Home: The Lure of England for the Founders of New England', *New England Quarterly*, 59 (1986), 358–86.

Dentz, Fred, *History of the English Church at the Hague, 1586–1929* (Delft: W.D. Meinema, 1929).

Dexter, Franklin B., 'Dixwell Papers', *Papers of the New Haven Colony Historical Society*, 6 (1900), 341–74.

———, *New Haven Town Records I, 1649–1662* (New Haven Historical Society, 1917).

———, *New Haven Town Records II, 1662–1684* (New Haven Historical Society, 1919).

Dowlin, Cornell M., *Sir William Davenant's 'Gondibert', its Preface, and Hobbes's Answer: A Study in English Neo-Classicism* (Philadelphia: Pennsylvania University Press, 1934).

Downing, Taylor, and Maggie Millman, *Civil War* (London: Collins & Brown, 1991).

Doyle, A.I., 'John Cosin (1595–1672) as a Library Maker', *The Book Collector*, 40 (1991), 335–57.

Dubois, E., 'La bibliothèque de l'évêque Cosin à Durham et sa collection des livres français de théologie et de spiritualité protestantes des XVIe et XVIIe siècles', *Bulletin de la Société de l'Histoire du Protestantisme Français*, 128 (1982), 173–88.

Duncan-Jones, Elsie E., 'English Exiles in Paris in the 1640s' (unpublished dissertation, University of Cambridge, 1930–31).

Durston, Christopher, *Cromwell's Major Generals: Godly Government during the English Revolution* (Manchester: Manchester University Press, 2001).

Duverger, Erik (ed.), *Antwerpse Kunstinventarissen uit de Zeventiende Eeuw*, 13 vols (Brussels: Koninklijke Academie voor Wetenschappen, Letteren en Schone Kunsten van België, 1984–2006).

Edmond, Mary, *Rare Sir William Davenant* (Manchester: Manchester University Press, 1987).

Ellis, Markman, *Eighteenth-Century Coffee-House Culture* (London: Pickering & Chatto, 2006).

Engberg, Jens, 'Royalist Finances during the English Civil War, 1642–1646', *Scandinavian Economic History Review*, 14 (1966), 73–96.

'The English Benedictine Nuns of the Convent of Our Blessed Lady of Good Hope in Paris', *Miscellanea*, VII (Publications of the Catholic Record Society, IX, 1911), 341–2.

Eyre, George E.B., and Charles R. Rivington (eds), *A Transcript of the Registers of the the Worshipful Company of Stationers from 1640–1708 A.D.*, 3 vols (London, 1913–14).

Ezell, Margaret J.M., '"To be your daughter in your pen": The Social Function of Literature in the Writings of Lady Elizabeth Brackley and Lady Jane Cavendish', reprinted in *Readings in Renaissance Women's Drama: Criticism, History, and Performance, 1594-1998*, ed. S.P. Cesarano and Marion Wynne-Davies (London and New York: Routledge, 1998).

Firth, C.H., 'The Royalists under the Protectorate', *English Historical Review*, 52 (1937), 634–48.

Fitzmaurice, James, 'Front Matter and the Physical Make-up of *Natures Pictures*', *Women's Writing*, 4:3 (1997), 353–6.

Fletcher, Angus, *Allegory: The Theory of a Symbolic Mode* (Ithaca: Cornell University Press, 1964).

Fletcher, Anthony, 'The Religious Motivation of Cromwell's Major-Generals', in *Religious Motivation: Biographical and Sociological Problems for the Church Historian*, ed. Derek Baker (Oxford: Basil Blackwell, 1978), pp. 259–66.

Fletcher, J.B., 'Précieuses at the Court of Charles I', *Journal of Comparative Literature*, 1 (1903), 120–53.

Foot, Mirjam, 'John Evelyn's Bookbindings', in *John Evelyn and his Milieu*, ed. Francis Harris and Michael Hunter (London: British Library, 2003), pp. 61–70.

Ford, Alan, *James Ussher: Theology, History, and Politics in Early-Modern Ireland and England* (Oxford: Oxford University Press, 2007).

Foucault, Michel, *Society Must be Defended*, ed. Mauro Bertani and Alessandro Fontana (London: Penguin, 2004).

Galter, P., 'Petau et la preface de son "de trinitate"', *Recherches de science religieuse*, 21 (1931), 462–76.

Games, Alison, *The Web of Empire: English Cosmopolitans in an Age of Expansion, 1560–1660* (New York: Oxford University Press, 2008).

Gardiner, S.R. (ed.), *The Constitutional Documents of the Puritan Revolution, 1625–1660*, 3rd edn (Oxford: Clarendon Press, 1906).

———, *History of England, from the Accession of James I to the Outbreak of the Civil War, 1603–1642*, 10 vols (London: Longman Green & Co., 1883–84).

Gardner, Ginny, *The Scottish Exile Community in the Netherlands, 1660–1690* (East Linton: Tuckwell, 2004).

Gaukroger, Stephen, *Descartes: An Intellectual Biography* (Oxford: Clarendon Press, 1995).

Glad, John (ed.), *Literature in Exile* (Durham and London: Duke University Press, 1990).

Goldsmith, M.M., 'Hobbes on Liberty', *Hobbes Studies*, 2 (1989), 23–39.

Gough, Melinda, 'A Newly Discovered Performance by Henrietta Maria', *Huntington Library Quarterly*, 65 (2002), 435–47.

———, '"Not as Myself": The Queen's Voice in *Tempe Restored*', *Modern Philology*, 101 (2003), 48–67.

Greaves, Richard, *Deliver Us from Evil* (New York: Oxford University Press, 1986).

———, *Secrets of the Kingdom* (Stanford: Stanford University Press, 1992).

Green, Mary Elizabeth, 'The Poet in Solomon's House: Abraham Cowley as Baconian Apostle', *Restoration*, 2 (1986), 68–75.

Greenspan, Nicole, 'Public Scandal, Political Controversy, and Familial Conflict in the Stuart Courts in Exile: The Struggle to Convert the Duke of Gloucester in 1654', in *Albion*, 35 (3) Autumn (2003), 398–427.

Grimes, Charles, *The Early Story of the English Church at Utrecht* (Chambéry: Imprimeries Réunies, 1930).

Guibbory, Achsah, 'Imitation and Originality: Cowley and Bacon's Vision of Progress', *Studies in English Literaure*, 29 (1989), 99–120.

Habersetzer, Karl-Heinz, *Politische Typologie und Dramatisches Exemplum* (Stuttgart: Metzler, 1985).

Haley, Kenneth, *The First Earl of Shaftesbury* (Oxford: Clarendon Press, 1968).

Hardacre, Paul H., *The Royalists During the Puritan Revolution* (The Hague: Nijhoff, 1956).

———, 'The Royalists in Exile During the Puritan Revolution, 1642–1660', *Huntington Library Quarterly*, 16 (1952–53), 353–70.

Hehir, Brendan O., *Harmony from Discords: A Life of Sir John Denham* (Berkeley and Los Angeles: University of California Press, 1968).

Henning, Basil D., *The History of Parliament: The House of Commons, 1660–1690*, 3 vols (London: Secker & Warburg, 1983).

Hillyer, Richard, *Hobbes and his Poetic Contemporaries: Cultural Transmission in Early Modern England* (Basingstoke and New York: Palgrave, 2007).

Hinman, Robert, *Abraham Cowley's World of Order* (Cambridge: Harvard University Press, 1960).

Hoadly, Charles J., *Records of the Colony or Jurisdiction of New Haven ... 1653–65* (Hartford: Case, Lockwood & Co., 1858).

Hoekstra, Kinch, 'The *de facto* Turn in Hobbes's Political Philosophy', in *Leviathan After 350 Years*, ed. Tom Sorell and Luc Foisneau (Oxford: Oxford University Press, 2004).

Hoftijzer, P.G., 'Between Mercury and Minerva: Dutch Printing Offices and Bookshops as Intermediaries in Scholarly Seventeenth-century Communication', in *Commercium litterarium 1600–1750: la communication dans la république des lettres: forms of communication in the republic of letters*, ed. Hans Bots and Françoise Waquet (Amsterdam: APA-Holland University Press, 1994), pp. 119–29.

Holberton, Edward, *Poetry and the Cromwellian Protectorate: Culture, Politics, and Institutions* (Oxford: Oxford University Press, 2008).

Hughes, Ann, and Julie Sanders, 'The Hague Courts of Elizabeth of Bohemia and Mary Stuart: Theatrical and Ceremonial Cultures', *Early Modern Literary Studies*, Special Issue 15 (August 2007), 3.1–23.

Hunter, Michael, 'John Evelyn in the 1650s: A Virtuoso in Quest of a Role', in Hunter, *Science and the Shape of Orthodoxy* (Woodbridge: Boydell, 1995), pp. 66–98.

Israel, Jonathan I., *The Anglo-Dutch Moment: Essays on the Glorious Revolution and its World Impact* (Cambridge: Cambridge University Press, 1991).

———, *The Dutch Republic* (Oxford: Oxford University Press, 1998 paperback).

Israel, Nico, *Outlandish: Writing Between Exile and Diaspora* (Stanford: Stanford University Press, 2000).

Jackson, Nicholas D., *Hobbes, Bramhall and the Politics of Liberty and Necessity: A Quarrel of the Civil Wars and Interregnum* (Cambridge: Cambridge University Press, 2007).

Jacob, James R., and Timothy Raylor, 'Opera and Obedience: Thomas Hobbes and *A Proposition for Advancement of Moralitie*, by Sir William Davenant', *Seventeenth Century*, 6 (1991), 205–50.

Jacquot, Jean, 'Sir Charles Cavendish and his Learned Friends', *Annals of Science*, 3 (1952), 13–27, 175–91.

Jardine, Lisa, *Going Dutch: How England Plundered Holland's Glory* (London: Harper, 2008).

Judd, Sylvester, *History of Hadley* (Springfield: H.R. Hunting and Co., 1905).

Kaminski, Thomas, 'Edmund Waller: English Precieux', *Philological Quarterly*, 79 (2000), 19–43.

Kaplan, Caren, *Questions of Travel: Postmodern Discourse of Displacement* (Durham: Duke University Press, 1996).

Keblusek, Marika, 'The Exile Experience: Royalist and Anglican Book Culture in the Low Countries, 1640–1660', in *The Bookshop of the World: The Role of the Low Countries in the Book Trade, 1473–1941*, ed. Lotte Hellinga et al. (Houten: Hes & De Graaf, 2001), pp. 151–8.

———, 'Introduction. Profiling the Early Modern Agent', in *Your Humble Servant: Agents in Early Modern Europe*, ed. Hans Cools et al. (Hilversum: Verloren, 2006), pp. 9–15.

———, 'Wine for Comfort: Drinking and the Royalist Exile Experience, 1642–1660', in *A Pleasing Sinne: Drink and Conviviality in Seventeenth-Century England*, ed. Adam Smyth (Woodbridge: Boydell, 2004).

Kerrigan, John, *Archipelagic English: Literature, History, and Politics, 1603–1707* (Oxford: Oxford University Press, 2008).

Klein, P.W., 'Little London: British Merchants in Rotterdam during the Seventeenth and Eighteenth Centuries', in *Enterprise and History: Essays in Honour of Charles Wilson*, ed. D.C. Coleman and Peter Mathias (Cambridge: Cambridge University Press, 1984).

Knights, Mark, *Politics and Opinion in Crisis, 1678–81* (Cambridge: Cambridge University Press, 1994).

Knoppers, Laura Lunger, '"The Antichrist, the Babilon, The Great Dragon": Oliver Cromwell, Andrew Marvell, and the Apocalyptic Monstrous', in *Monstrous Bodies? Political Monstrosities in Early Modern Europe*, ed. Laura Lunger Knoppers and Joan B. Landes (Ithaca: Cornell University Press, 2004), pp. 93–123.

Knowles, James R., 'The "Running Masque" Recovered: A Masque for the Marquess of Buckingham (c. 1619–20)', *English Manuscript Studies 1100–1700*, 8 (2000), 79–135.

Knuttel, W.P.C., *Catalogus van de Pamfletten-Verzameling Berustende in de Koninklijke Bibliotheek*, 9 vols in 10 (The Hague, 1889–1920; Utrecht: HES, 1978).

Lacey, Andrew, *The Cult of King Charles the Martyr* (Woodbridge: Boydell, 2003).

Langley, T.R., 'Abraham Cowley's "Brutus": Royalist or Republican?', *Yearbook of English Studies*, 6 (1976), 41–52.

Lentfer, Dirk, *Die Glogauer Landesprivilegen des Andreas Gryphius von 1653* (Frankfurt: P. Lang, 1996).

'Letters and Papers Relating to the Regicides', *Collections of the Massachusetts Historical Society*, 4th Series, 8 (1868), 122–225.

Lough, John, *France Observed in the Seventeenth Century by British Travellers* (Stocksfield: Oriel Press, 1985).

Loxley, James, *Royalism and Poetry in the English Civil Wars: The Drawn Sword* (Basingstoke: Palgrave, 1997).

Lustig, Mary Lou, *The Imperial Executive in America: Sir Edmund Andros, 1637–1714* (Madison: Fairleigh Dickenson University Press, 2002).

Lutz, Cora, 'Ezra Stiles and the Legend of Hadley', *Yale University Library Gazette*, 73 (3–4) (April 1998), 115–23.

Macinnes, Allan I., and Arthur H. Williamson (eds), *Shaping the Stuart World 1603–1714: The Atlantic Connection* (Leiden, Boston: Brill, 2006).

Maddison, R.E.W., *The Life of the Honourable Robert Boyle, F.R.S.* (London: Taylor & Francis, 1969).

Maguire, Nancy Klein, *Regicide and Restoration: English Tragicomedy, 1660–1671* (Cambridge: Cambridge University Press, 1992).

Major, Philip, 'Funerary Rites in the Royalist Exile: George Morley's Ministry in Antwerp, 1650–1653', *Renaissance and Reformation/Renaissance et Réforme*, 31.3 (2009), 35–50.

———, '"Twixt Hope and Fear": John Berkenhead, Henry Lawes, and Banishment from London during the English Revolution', *Review of English Studies*, n.s. 59 (2008), 270–80.

Malcolm, Noel, *Aspects of Hobbes* (Oxford: Oxford University Press, 2002).

———, *De Dominis (1560–1624), Venetian, Anglican, Ecumenist and Relapsed Heretic* (London: Strickland & Scott, 1984).

———, 'Hobbes, The Latin Optical Manuscript, and the Parisian Scribe', *English Manuscript Studies, 1100–1700*, 12 (2005), 210–32.

———, and Jacqueline Stedall, *John Pell (1611–1685) and his Correspondence with Sir Charles Cavendish: The Mental World of an Early Modern Mathematician* (Oxford: Oxford University Press, 2005).

Maltzahn, Nicholas von, *An Andrew Marvell Chronology* (Basingstoke and New York: Palgrave, 2005).

Marciari, John, *Grand Tour Diaries and Other Travel Manuscripts in the James Marshall and Marie-Louise Osborn Collection*, Yale University Library Gazette, Occasional Supplement, ii (New Haven: Yale University Press, 1999).

Martin, Catherine Gimelli, *The Ruins of Allegory: 'Paradise Lost' and the Metamorphosis of Epic Convention* (Durham: Duke University Press, 2001).

Martinich, A.P., *Hobbes: A Biography* (Cambridge: Cambridge University Press, 1999).

The Mather Papers (Massachussetts Historical Society Collections, 4th series, 8, 1868).

Matthews, Arnold G., *Walker Revised: Being a Revision of John Walker's Suffering of the Clergy during the Great Rebellion, 1642–60* (Oxford: Clarendon Press, 1948).

McElligott, Jason, *Roger Morrice and Britain in the Llate 1680s* (Burlington, Aldershot:Ashgate, 2006).

———, *Royalism, Print and Censorship in Revolutionary England* (Woodbridge: Boydell, 2007).

———, and David L. Smith (eds), *Royalists and Royalism during the English Civil Wars* (Cambridge: Cambridge University Press, 2007).

———, *Royalists and Royalism during the Interregnum* (Manchester: Manchester University Press, 2010).

McEvansoneya, Philip, 'A Note on the Duke of Buckingham's Inventory', *The Burlington Magazine*, 128 (1986), 1001: 607.

———, 'The Sequestration and Dispersal of the Buckingham Collection', *Journal of the History of Collections*, 8 (1996) 2: 133–54.

———, 'An Unpublished Inventory of the Hamilton Collection in the 1620s and the Duke of Buckingham's Pictures', *The Burlington Magazine*, 134 (1992), 1073: 524–6.

McKay, Derek, *The Great Elector: Frederick William of Brandenburg-Prussia* (Harlow: Longman, 2001).

McWilliams, John, *New England's Crisis and Cultural Memory: Literature Politics, History and Religion, 1620–1860* (Cambridge: Cambridge University Press, 2004).

Mill, David van, *Liberty, Rationality and Agency in Hobbes's* Leviathan (Albany: State University of New York Press, 2001).

Millar, O., 'An Exile in Paris: The Notebooks of Richard Symonds', in *Studies in Renaissance and Baroque Art Presented to Anthony Blunt*, ed. Michael Kitson and John Shearman (London and NewYork: Phaidon, 1967), pp. 157–64.

Miller, Perry, *The New England Mind: The Seventeenth Century*, 2nd edn (Boston: Bacon Press, 1965).

Millman, Jill S., and Gillian Wright (eds), *Early Modern Women's Manuscript Poetry* (Manchester: Manchester University Press, 2005).

Milton, Anthony, *Laudian and Royalist Polemic in Seventeenth-Century England* (Manchester: Manchester University Press, 2007).

Morrill, John, 'The Church in England 1642–1649' in *The Nature of the English Revolution* (London: Longman, 1993), pp. 158–60.

Murdoch, K.B., *Increase Mather: The Foremost American Puritan* (Cambridge, MA: Harvard University Press, 1925).

Nethercot, Arthur, *Sir William D'Avenant: Poet Laureate and Playwright-Manager* (Chicago: University of Chicago Press, 1938).

Nevo, Ruth, *The Dial of Virtue* (Princeton: Princeton University Press, 1963).

Newton, Caroline, 'Letters of a New England Exile', *Americana*, 14 (1920), 208–26.

Noble, Mark, *Lives of the English Regicides*, 2 vols (London: J. Stockdale, 1878).

———, *Memoirs of the Protectorate House of Cromwell*, 2 vols (Birmingham: Pearson & Rollason, 1784).

Packer, John, *The Transformation of Anglicanism 1643–1660: With Special Reference to Henry Hammond* (Manchester: Manchester University Press, 1969).

Parente, James A., *Religious Drama and the Humanist Tradition: Christian Theater in Germany and in the Netherlands, 1500–1680* (Leiden: Brill, 1987).

Patterson, Annabel, *Censorship and Interpretation: The Conditions of Writing and Reading in Early Modern England* (Madison: University of Wisconsin Press, 1984).

Paul, Robert S., *The Assembly of the Lord: Politics and Religion in the Westminster Assembly and the 'Grand Debate'* (Edinburgh: T & T Clark, 1985).

Peacey, Jason, 'Order and Disorder in Europe: Parliamentary Agents and Royalist Thugs, 1649–1650', *Historical Journal*, 40 (1997), 953–76.

———, 'Thomas Westrowe', *History Today* (October 2003), 62.

Peacock, John, 'The French Element in Inigo Jones's Masque Designs', in *The Court Masque*, ed. David Lindley (Manchester: Manchester University Press, 1984), pp. 149–68.

———, *The Stage Designs of Inigo Jones: The European Context* (Cambridge: Cambridge University Press, 1995).

Peck, Linda Levy, *Consuming Splendor: Society and Culture in Seventeenth Century England* (Cambridge: Cambridge University Press, 2005).

Petersson, Robert T., *Sir Kenelm Digby: The Ornament of England 1603–1665* (London: Jonathan Cape, 1956).

Pettit, Philip, 'Liberty and Leviathan', *Politics, Philosophy and Economics*, 4 (2005), 131–51.

Pickel, Margaret, *Charles I as Patron of Poetry and Drama* (London: Frederick Muller, 1936).

Potter, Lois, *Secret Rites and Secret Writing: Royalist Literature 1641–1660* (Cambridge: Cambridge University Press, 1989).

Powers, Zara J., *New Haven Town Records III, 1684–1769* (New Haven Colony Historical Society, 1962).

Quehen, H. de, 'Politics and Scholarship in the Ignation Controversy', *Seventeenth Century*, 13 (1998), 69–84.

Quilligan, Maureen, *The Language of Allegory: Defining the Genre* (Ithaca: Cornell University Press, 1979).

Ravelhofer, Barbara, 'Burlesque Ballet, a Ballad, and a Banquet in Ben Jonson's The Gypsies Metamorphos'd (1621)', *Dance Research*, 25 (2007), 144–55.

———, *The Early Stuart Masque: Dance, Costume, and Music* (Oxford: Oxford University Press, 2006).

Raylor, Timothy, *Cavaliers, Clubs, and Literary Culture: Sir John Mennes, James Smith, and the Order of the Fancy* (Newark: University of Delaware Press, 1994).

———, 'The Date and Script of Hobbes's Latin Optical Manuscript', *English Manuscript Studies, 1100–1700*, 12 (2005), 201–9.

———, 'The Early Poetic Career of Edmund Waller', *Huntington Library Quarterly*, 69 (2006), 239–65.

———, *The Essex House Masque of 1621: Viscount Doncaster and the Jacobean Masque* (Pittsburgh: Duquesne University Press, 2000).

———, 'Hobbes, Payne, and A Short Tract on First Principles', *Historical Journal*, 44 (2001), 29–58.

———, 'Milton, Hartlib, and the Education of the Aristocracy', in *The Oxford Handbook of Milton*, ed. Nicholas McDowell and Nigel Smith (Oxford: Oxford University Press, 2009), pp. 38–406.

———, 'Thomas Hobbes and "The Mathematical Demonstration of the Sword"', *Seventeenth Century*, 15 (2000), 175–98.

Raymond, Joad, *The Invention of the Newspaper: English Newsbooks 1641–1649* (Oxford: Oxford University Press, 1996).

Reade, Brian, 'William Frizell and the Royal Collection', *The Burlington Magazine for Connoisseurs*, 89 (1949), 528: 70–75.

'Records of the Abbey of our Lady of Consolation at Cambrai, 1620–1793', *Miscellanea*, VIII (Publications of the Catholic Record Society, XIII, 1913), 44–5.

Rees, Emma, *Margaret Cavendish: Gender, Genre, Exile* (Manchester: Manchester University Press, 2003).

Revard, Stella, 'Cowley's "Pindarique Odes" and the Politics of the Inter-regnum', *Criticism*, 35 (1993), 393–410.

Rossi, Mario M., *La Vita, Le Opere, I Tempi di Edoardo Herbert di Chirbury*, 3 vols (Florence, 1947).

Rubin, Davida, *Sir Kenelm Digby F.R.S 1603–1665: A Bibliography Based on the Collection of K. Garth Huston, Sr., M.D.* (San Francisco: Jeremy Norman & Co., 1991).

Sachse, William L., 'The Migration of New Englanders to England, 1640–1660', *American Historical Review*, 55 (1948), 251–78.

Sanders, Julie, 'Caroline Salon Culture and Female Agency: The Countess of Carlisle, Henrietta Maria, and Public Theatre', *Theatre Journal*, 52 (2000), 449–64.

Sargent, M.L., 'Thomas Hutchinson, Ezra Stiles, and the Legend of the Regicides', *William and Mary Quarterly*, 3rd ser., 49 (3) (1992), 431–48.

Schmitt, Carl, *The Concept of the Political* (Chicago: University of Chicago Press, 1996).

———, *Natural Right and History* (Chicago: University of Chicago Press, 1953).

———, *Political Theology: Four Chapters on the Concept of Sovereignty* (Chicago: University of Chicago Press, 2005).

Schofield, Mary-Peale, 'The Three Judges of New Haven', *History Today*, 12 (1962), 346–53.

Schuhmann, Karl, 'Le *Short Tract*: première oeuvre philosophique de Hobbes', *Hobbes Studies*, 8 (1995), 3–96.

Scott, David, *Politics and War in the Three Stuart Kingdoms, 1637–49* (Basingstoke: Palgrave, 2004).

———, 'Rethinking Royalist Politics: Faction and Ideology 1642–49', in *The English Civil War: Conflict and Contexts, 1640–49*, ed. John Adamson (Basingstoke: Palgrave Macmillan, 2009), pp. 36–60.

Scott, Jonathan, *Algernon Sidney and the English Republic, 1623–1677* (Cambridge: Cambridge University Press, 1988).

———, *Algernon Sidney and the Restoration Crisis, 1677–1683* (Cambridge: Cambridge University Press, 1991).

———, *England's Troubles: Seventeenth-Century English Political Instability in a European Context* (Cambridge: Cambridge University Press, 2000).

Sharpe, Kevin, 'Transplanting Revelation, Transferring Meaning: Reading the Apocalypse in Early Modern England, Scotland and New England', in *Shaping the Stuart World 1603–1714: The Atlantic Connection*, ed. Allan I. Macinnes and Arthur H. Williamson (Leiden, Boston: Brill, 2006), pp. 117–46.

Skinner, Quentin, *Hobbes and Republican Liberty* (Cambridge: Cambridge University Press, 2008).

———, *Visions of Politics*, 3 vols (Cambridge: Cambridge University Press, 2002).

Smith, Charles K., 'French Philosophy and English Politics in Interregnum Poetry', in *The Stuart Court and Europe: Essays in Politics and Political Culture*, ed. R. Malcolm Smuts (Cambridge: Cambridge University Press, 1996), pp. 177–209.

Smith, David, *Constitutional Royalism and the Search for Settlement, c. 1640–1649* (Cambridge: Cambridge University Press, 1994).

Smith, Geoffrey, *Cavaliers in Exile* (Basingstoke and New York: Palgrave, 2003).

Smuts, R. Malcolm, *The Stuart Court and Europe: Essays in Politics and Political Culture* (Cambridge: Cambridge University Press, 1996).

Smyth, Adam, '"Rend and teare in peeces": Textual Fragmentation in Seventeenth-Century England', *Seventeenth Century*, 19 (1) (2004), 36–52.

Snapp, Harry F., 'The Impeachment of Roger Maynwaring', *Huntington Library Quarterly*, 30 (1967), 217–32.

Southgate, Beverley, *'Covetous of Truth': The Life and Work of Thomas White, 1593–1676* (Dordrecht, Boston, and London: Kluwer Academic Publications, 1993).

Spingarn, Joel E. (ed.), *Critical Essays of the Seventeenth Century*, 3 vols (Bloomington: Indiana University Press, 1957).

Spurr, John, *The Restoration Church of England, 1646–1689* (New Haven and London: Yale University Press, 1991).

Stackhouse, Janifer Gerl, *The Constructive Art of Gryphius' Historical Tragedies* (Bern: Lang, 1986).

Stiles, Ezra, *A History of Three of the Judges of King Charles I* (Hartford, CT, 1794).

Stout, Harry, 'The Morphology of Re-migration: New England University Men and their return to England, 1640–1660', *Journal of American Studies*, 10 (1976), 151–72.

Stoye, John, *English Travellers Abroad 1604–1667: Their Influence in English Society and Politics* (1952, repr. 1968, revised edn, New Haven and London: Yale University Press, 1989).

Strauss, Emil, *Sir William Petty: Portrait of a Genius* (Glencoe, IL: Free Press, 1954).

Strauss, Leo, *The Political Philosophy of Hobbes* (Chicago: University of Chicago Press, 1952).

Summers, Claude J., and Ted-Larry Pebworth (eds), *The English Civil Wars in the Literary Imagination* (Columbia and London: Missouri Press, 1999).

Sutch, Victor D., *Gilbert Sheldon: Architect of Anglican Survival* (The Hague: Nijhoff, 1973).

Szarota, Elida Maria, *Geschichte, Politik und Gesellschaft im Drama des 17. Jahrhunderts* (Bern: Francke, 1976).

Tatham, G.B., 'The Sale of Episcopal Lands during the Civil Wars and Commonwealth', *English Historical Review*, 23 (1908), 91–108.

Teskey, Gordon, *Allegory and Violence* (Ithaca: Cornell University Press, 1996).

Thomas Hutchinson Papers, 3 vols (London: Print Society, 1865).

Trevor-Roper, Hugh, *Europe's Physician: The Various Life of Sir Theodore de Mayerne* (New Haven and London: Yale University Press, 2006).

———, 'The Great Tew Circle', in *Catholics, Anglicans and Puritans: Seventeenth-Century Essays* (London and Chicago: Secker & Warburg, 1987), pp. 166–230.

Trotter, David, *The Poetry of Abraham Cowley* (Totowa: Rowman and Littlefield, 1979).

Trumbull, J. Hammond, *The Public Records of the Colony of Connecticut*, 3 vols (Hartford, CT, 1850–59).

Tuchin, J., *The Bloody Assizes*, ed. Joseph G. Muddiman (Edinburgh: William Hodge, 1929).

Turnbull, George H., *Hartlib, Dury and Comenius: Gleanings from Hartlib's Papers* (London and Liverpool: Hodder & Stroughton, 1948).

Tyacke, Nicholas (ed.), *The English Revolution, c.1590–1720: Politics, Religion and Communities* (Manchester: Manchester University Press, 2007).

Ugrešić, Dubravka, *Nobody's Home*, trans. Ellen Elias-Bursać (London, San Francisco and Beirut: Telegram, 2007).

Underdown, David, *Royalist Conspiracy in England* (New Haven: Yale University Press, 1960).

van Beneden, Ben, and Nora de Poorter (eds), *Royalist Refugees: William and Margaret Cavendish in the Rubens House 1648–1660* (Antwerp: BAI, Rubenianum, 2006).

van de Schoor, R.J.M., *The Irenic Theology of Théophile Brachet de la Milletière (1588–1665)* (Leiden: Brill, 1995).

Vander Motten, J.P., '"The Saucy Zeal of Layman": The Religious Views of Thomas Killigrew (1612–1683)', *Lias*, 20 (2002), 81–110.

———, 'Thomas Killigrew's "Lost Years", 1655–1660', *Neophilologus*, 82 (1998), 311–34.

———, and Katrien Daemen-de Gelder, 'A "Copy as Immortal, as its Original": Thomas Ross' *Second Punick War* (London, 1661 and 1672)', in *Living in Posterity: Essays in Honour of Bart Westerweel*, ed. Jan Frans van Dijkhuizen et al. (Hilversum: Uitgeverij Verloren, 2004), pp. 185–90.

———, '"Les plus rudes chocs de la fortune": Willem Frederik, Stadholder of Friesland (1613–1664), Thomas Killigrew (1612–1683) and Patronage in Exile', *Anglia: Journal of English Philology*, 127 (2009), 65–90.

———, 'Sir Samuel Tuke (c.1615–1674) at the "Little Court" of Mary Stuart (1631–1660)', *Notes and Queries*, 251 (2006), 168–70.

Veevers, Erica, *Images of Love and Religion: Queen Henrietta Maria and Court Entertainments* (Cambridge: Cambridge University Press, 1989).

Vermeylen, Filip, 'The Art of the Dealer: Marketing Paintings in Early Modern Antwerp', in *Your Humble Servant: Agents in Early Modern Europe*, ed. Hans Cools et al. (Hilversum: Verloren, 2006), pp. 109–19.

Vernon, Elliot, 'A Ministry of the Gospel: The Presbyterians during the English Revolution', in *Religion in Revolutionary England*, ed. Christopher Durston and Judith Maltby (Manchester: Manchester University Press, 2006), pp. 115–36.

Villani, Stefano, 'The English Civil Wars and the Interregnum in Italian Historiography in the 17th century', in *Cromohs Virtual Seminars. Recent Historiographical Trends of the British Studies (17th–18th Centuries)*, ed. M. Caricchio and G. Tarantino (2006–2007), pp. 1–4; http://www.cromohs.unifit.it/seminari/villani_ecv.html.

Vlieghe, Hans, *Flemish Art and Architecture, 1585–1700* (New Haven: Yale University Press, 1998).

Walker, J., 'The English Exiles in Holland during the Reigns of Charles II and James II', *Transactions of the Royal Historical Society*, 4th series, 30 (1948), 111–25.

Wallace, John, *Destiny His Choice: The Loyalism of Andrew Marvell* (Cambridge: Cambridge University Press, 1968).

Weesop, John, *Eyewitness Representation of Execution of Charles I*, Private Collection; Bridgeman Art Library.

Welles, Lemuel, *The Regicides in Connecticut* (New Haven: Yale University Press, 1935).

Whitaker, Katie, *Mad Madge: The Extraordinary Life of Margaret Cavendish, Duchess of Newcastle, the First Woman to Live by Her Pen* (New York: Basic Books, 2002).

————, *Mad Madge: Margaret Cavendish, Duchess of Newcastle, Royalist, Writer and Romantic* (London: Chatto and Windus, 2003).

Wickham, Glynne, *Early English Stages, 1300–1600*, 5 vols (London and New York: Routledge & Kegan Paul, 1972).

Wilcher, Robert, *The Writing of Royalism, 1628–1660* (Cambridge: Cambridge University Press, 2001).

Wilkie, R.W. (ed.), *Historical Atlas of Massachusetts* (Amherst: University of Massachusetts Press, 1991).

Wolfe, Heather, 'The Scribal Hands and Dating of *Lady Falkland: Her Life*', in *Writings by Early Modern Women* (*English Manuscript Studies 1000–1700*, 9, 2000), ed. Peter Beal and Margaret J.M. Ezell, pp. 187–217.

Wormald, Brian, *Clarendon: Politics, History and Religion* (Cambridge: Cambridge University Press, 1951).

Zaslaw, Neal, 'The First Opera in Paris: A Study in the Politics of Art', in *Jean-Baptiste Lully and the Music of the French Baroque: Essays in Honor of James R. Anthony*, ed. John H. Heyer et al. (Cambridge: Cambridge University Press, 1989).

Zwicker, Steven, 'Is There Such a Thing as Restoration Literature?', *Huntington Library Quarterly*, 69 (2006), 425–50.

————, *Lines of Authority: Politics and English Literary Culture 1649–1689* (Ithaca and London: Cornell University Press, 1993).

Index

Printed in Great Britain
by Amazon

23367223R00137